Using the Open Archives Initiative Protocol for Metadata Harvesting

Using the Open Archives Initiative Protocol for Metadata Harvesting

Timothy W. Cole and Muriel Foulonneau

Third Millennium Cataloging
Susan Lazinger and Sheila Intner, Series Editors

LIBRARIES UNLIMITED

A Member of the Greenwood Publishing Group

Westport, Connecticut • London

Library of Congress Cataloging-in-Publication Data

Cole, Timothy W.
   Using the Open Archives Initiative protocol for metadata harvesting / Timothy W. Cole and Muriel
Foulonneau.
       p. cm. — (Third millennium cataloging)
   Includes bibliographical references and index.
   ISBN 978-1-59158-280-9 (alk. paper)
   1. Metadata harvesting. 2. Open Archives Initiative. I. Foulonneau, Muriel. II. Title.
   Z666.7.C65 2007
   025.3—dc22   2007009006

British Library Cataloguing-in-Publication Data is available.

Library of Congress Catalog Card Number: 2007009006
ISBN: 978-1-59158-280-9

First published in 2007

Libraries Unlimited, 88 Post Road West, Westport, CT 06881
A Member of the Greenwood Publishing Group, Inc.
www.lu.com

Printed in the United States of America

The paper used in this book complies with the
Permanent Paper Standard issued by the National
Information Standards Organization (Z39.48–1984).

10 9 8 7 6 5 4 3 2 1

Contents

Illustrations

FIGURES

TABLES

Preface

The Open Archives Initiative Protocol for Metadata Harvesting (OAI-PMH) is a Web-based protocol defining a narrowly focused class of computer-to-computer interactions. It is relatively new, having been publicly introduced only in January of 2001. In the six years since, a sufficient body of experience has emerged to confirm the protocol's viability and value as a building block of digital library systems, even as developers continue to explore and learn the technical nuances of OAI-PMH-based implementations. The discipline of descriptive cataloging, by contrast, has been around much longer. A long tradition of descriptive practices informs the discipline as it evolves to meet the varied and unique requirements of digital libraries.

This book focuses on the intersection of these two domains—one new and still in some flux, one much more established but still evolving. The text is designed to introduce the reader to the technical details of OAI-PMH and how it works. We provide a summary of the architectural model implicit in the protocol and describe the technological antecedents, terminology, features, and rules of the protocol. This book also is intended to give the reader an understanding and appreciation of the ways in which OAI-PMH can be used to facilitate and enhance digital library interoperability and the sharing and effective use of digital information resources—that is, how the protocol furthers the traditional objectives of descriptive cataloging, albeit in new ways. To this end, we provide examples, insights, and advice as to what the protocol can and cannot do and how the protocol impacts the way implementers of it (for example, librarians participating in the development of digital libraries) use OAI-PMH to create, manipulate, and exploit descriptive metadata in order to provide useful digital library services.

The hybrid nature of the book will be apparent to the observant reader in the blending of terminologies and perspectives throughout. While some reader familiarity with the basics of both descriptive cataloging and computing technology is expected, our assumption in writing this book is that many readers will not be experts simultaneously in both metadata and the details of digital library technologies. We strive throughout to avoid unnecessary use of jargon and acronyms, to introduce and fully explain specialized concepts and terms as they are used, and to avoid including information and detail not essential to the objectives of the text. Nonetheless, in these domains terminology can be a potential minefield of confusion for a reader new to a topic. For example, OAI-PMH syntax makes specialized use of several English-language words and concatenations of words. Forms such as "from," "until," "identifier," and "metadataPrefix" have specific and sometimes nonintuitive meanings when used as protocol verbs, arguments, or codes. To help distinguish such usage and facilitate the readability of this book, typographic conventions are used. In instances when the use of a word or term is meant to be restricted to its meaning as a part of OAI-PMH, the word or term will be shown in a special font, for example: `from`, `until`, `identifier`, `metadataPrefix`. XML examples embedded in the text will also be shown in this style. Other terms, acronyms, and concepts of special note and importance for topics treated in this work, but not part of OAI-PMH syntax, are defined when introduced and will be highlighted typographically on first usage in each chapter, for example: *document-like objects*.

In the process of designing and implementing digital library systems we learn a great deal. The observations, lessons, and advice embedded in this text are drawn from our own experiences and those shared with us by colleagues and collaborators. Accordingly, we must acknowledge the support of sponsors, collaborators, and other colleagues who have contributed to our understanding and appreciation of OAI-PMH. Among our sponsors we single out for special thanks the Scholarly Communications Program of the Andrew W. Mellon Foundation, the National Leadership Grant Program of the Institute of Museum and Library Services, the National Science Digital Library Program of the National Science Foundation, and the Committee on Institutional Cooperation. The research grants provided by these sponsors and programs provided us with unique opportunities to use and study OAI-PMH from a variety of perspectives. This book could not have been written without such support; however, we must in all fairness add the disclaimer that the opinions, findings, conclusions, and recommendations expressed in this publication are those of the authors and do not necessarily reflect the views of the Andrew W. Mellon Foundation, the Institute of Museum and Library Services, the National Science Foundation, or the Committee on Institutional Cooperation.

We would like to thank also collaborating colleagues at the University of Illinois at Urbana-Champaign and elsewhere, including especially Sarah Shreeves, Thomas Habing, William Mischo, Jerome McDonough, Jenn Riley, Michael Seadle, Kat Hagedorn, and Charles Blair. Thanks as well to other members of the OAI virtual community, especially members of the OAI Technical Committee and the OAI Steering Committee. There are too many to thank all individually, so in lieu of doing so, we would like to acknowledge by name the OAI Executive, Carl Lagoze, and Herbert Van de Sompel. Without them, OAI-PMH would never have existed, and we would all be the poorer for the lack. Finally, we would like to thank our editors, Susan Laz-inger and Sheila S. Intner, the University of Illinois at Urbana-Champaign Library Research and Publication Committee, and Carolyn Sanford for invaluable assistance and encouragement during the writing of this book.

Timothy W. Cole, Urbana, Illinois, USA
Muriel Foulonneau, Lyon, France

PART I

Introduction and Context

CHAPTER 1

Definition and Origins of OAI-PMH

The Open Archives Initiative Protocol for Metadata Harvesting (OAI-PMH)[1] is designed to enable greater interoperability between digital libraries and to facilitate the more efficient dissemination of information. Specifically, it provides rules and a framework for sharing *descriptive metadata*, both for making metadata available and for acquiring metadata records once they are made available. From a technical perspective, OAI-PMH is relatively simple compared to other protocols with similar or related objectives. It is, for example, much simpler in technical terms than the National Information Standard Organization's Z39.50 Information Retrieval Protocol,[2] a search-and-retrieval protocol ubiquitous across the library community and frequently discussed in concert with OAI-PMH. While there can be both advantages and disadvantages to a lightweight, easy, technical approach, in the case of OAI-PMH the emphasis on technical simplicity is very much by design. The original authors of the protocol and the OAI Technical Committees that oversaw testing and development of OAI-PMH went to significant effort to maintain technical simplicity (Lagoze and Van de Sompel 2003). Results to date confirm that they knew what they were doing. Overall, the simplicity of OAI-PMH has proven an asset and is one of the prime reasons for the protocol's quick and widespread adoption.

Although technically straightforward, OAI-PMH has proven remarkably robust and useful for a broad range of purposes. Even though the technical concepts embodied in the protocol are easy for the non-computer scientist to grasp, the ways in which the protocol is used and the tasks that it facilitates can be complex. In many ways the most interesting aspects of OAI-PMH are not the technical details of the protocol itself, but the impact OAI-PMH is having on descriptive cataloging practice and on our perceptions of how digital libraries should operate and interoperate. While this text covers the essential architectural concepts and basic technical details of OAI-PMH, the protocol is introduced and discussed in the broader context of digital library applications generally. A primary focus of this book is on the implications of OAI-PMH for building digital libraries and creating and using metadata to describe and facilitate the sharing of digital information resources.

SCOPE OF OAI-PMH

OAI-PMH works with structured data, specifically (as described in more detail in chapter 2) with data expressed using *XML* (Extensible Markup Language). Originally, the intended scope of OAI-PMH was metadata—more specifically, descriptive metadata. Advanced users of the protocol are beginning to experiment with ways to extend and expand this scope to include other classes of metadata and even full content, but the developers of OAI-PMH were unabashedly focused on descriptive metadata when they created the protocol. The scope of OAI-PMH also is defined by its implicit focus on metadata that describes discrete, digital, *document-like objects* (DLOs). OAI-PMH can be used for metadata describing other kinds of information resources, but it was created with digital information resources analogous to traditional classes of print-format library documents in mind.

For the objectives of this text, the general-purpose definition of metadata as "data about data" is a good starting point. This definition, however, still encompasses several, sometimes overlapping classes of metadata, for example, technical metadata, structural metadata, preservation metadata, descriptive metadata, administrative metadata, and rights metadata. As a subclass of metadata generally, a collection of descriptive metadata records is to a collection of digital library information resources what the card catalog once was to the shelved collection of library books at your local library. A descriptive metadata record inventories those attributes of a digital information resource that are useful for discovering, locating, classifying, clustering, relating, interpreting, and uniquely identifying that resource. Typical attributes contained in a descriptive metadata record include familiar bibliographic attributes such as the title, the author name(s), the publisher, the publication date, and subject headings (including temporal and geographic coverage headings). The physical description fields of card catalog records are augmented for digital content descriptions with attributes such as digital object format, extent (for example, file size), and resource type. A library call number may be replaced with a URL (Universal Resource Locator, the Web address of the digital resource) or some other similarly appropriate identifier, such as a DOI (Digital Object Identifier).[3] Any attribute of a digital resource that would help a user find a resource and determine whether it might be useful to meet his or her immediate information need could qualify as descriptive metadata. Descriptive metadata considered in the realm of digital libraries is a broad term, but one that is relatively easy for librarians trained in traditional cataloging to understand and appreciate.

The concept of DLO is a bit more amorphous, but still useful for this discussion. DLO is a consensus term that emerged in a library context in the mid-1990s. DLO as a concept is easiest to understand by example. Just as a database of descriptive metadata records is the digital library's analog to the traditional public library card catalog, a DLO can be thought of as an analog to the traditional library book on the shelf—only the analogy is somewhat less precise. DLOs encompass many of the information constructs typical of the

World Wide Web. For instance, HTML Web pages, though often multipart and multimedia in nature, usually have many descriptive and use attributes in common with print publications found in traditional libraries. The Web, however, is more of a melting pot for diverse content than are many traditional libraries. Streaming video lives side by side with textual Portable Document Format (PDF) documents, 3-D computer graphic images of physical artifacts, and digital works of art. So DLOs must be understood very broadly, at least as far as format is concerned. Still, the concept has utility. As Carl Lagoze suggests, "The DLO is useful as a simple metaphor for characterizing the variety of Web resources that form the corpus for so-called cross-domain resource discovery" (Lagoze 2001).

The salient implication for this discussion of OAI-PMH is that while the protocol is designed to work well for descriptive metadata describing a wide range of heterogeneous information resource object formats—that is, OAI-PMH is not limited just to metadata about textual resources—the protocol was created with a certain implicit resource granularity and autonomy in mind. OAI-PMH was created specifically to enable the development of services across distributed repositories of discrete, relatively independent information objects, similar in size, scope, and complexity. This includes information resources such as online journal articles, digitized images, discrete video and audio clips, and individual Web pages.

As a result of this intention and scope, users of OAI-PMH must guard against a tendency to decontextualize metadata records shared using OAI-PMH. This is less a technical issue than a matter of usage and implementation. Metadata records describing larger, complex compound information resources—such as cohesive manuscript archives containing the lifetime output of a famous researcher or complex multipart online learning objects—deal with resources that are of a distinctly different granularity from DLOs. Such metadata typically must include complex technical and structural attributes best expressed using rich content description schemes designed to deal with hierarchies and structures encompassing items of multiple granularities—for example, the Encoded Archival Description format (EAD)[4] or the Sharable Content Object Reference Model (SCORM).[5] A manuscript archive will contain many discrete items—for instance, letters, photos, and drafts of lectures—but these items will be related in complex hierarchies that place each item in temporal and topical context over the course of the researcher's career. A classroom learning object also will have its discrete components, and these too will be related in specific ways, for example, by the sequence in which the student is required to study and assimilate each component of the learning resource. To treat each component of such compound resources as wholly independent and discrete is to ignore important contextual information.

In certain situations, discoverability of even relatively discrete-seeming items, such as digitized photographs from a library's collection, can be compromised if relationships to the collection of photographs as a whole and to other photographs within the collection are not preserved when sharing metadata. Robin Wendler, a Harvard University librarian, details a rather graphic example in connection with a project that created metadata records describing photographs included in a special library collection on the "History of Women in America." As initially generated, none of the metadata records could be retrieved by searching for the term "women." Wendler explains that, "Within Schlesinger, the fact that the photographs were in some way about 'women' was assumed, but when the records were shared outside their institution, the context was lost." (Wendler 2004). The usefulness of the metadata records in other contexts was compromised.

So, while OAI-PMH can be used to transport metadata describing the discrete components of complex, multifaceted resources and collections, it is important when using OAI-PMH for this purpose to preserve critical entity relationships and context. Sometimes, ancillary rules, practices, and specifications external to OAI-PMH must be applied. This facet of the original scope and intent of OAI-PMH has important implications for the practitioner; these are discussed in more detail in later chapters of this book.

PURPOSE OF OAI-PMH

The primary purpose of OAI-PMH is to define a standard way to move metadata from point A to point B within the virtual information space of the World Wide Web. The intent is to facilitate the sharing and aggregation of metadata describing useful information resources. The protocol itself says nothing explicitly about what is to be done with the metadata once they are aggregated, although clearly this is of interest. The process of aggregation is assumed to create an opportunity for benefit. Some examples of OAI-PMH-enabled or OAI-PMH-facilitated value-added services originally envisioned by the protocol's authors were cross-repository searching, current-awareness services, and reference linking between resources.

To accomplish its purpose, OAI-PMH divides the online information universe into *OAI data providers* and *OAI service providers*. OAI-PMH data providers hold collections of primary content (usually) and the metadata describing such content (always). Data providers make descriptive metadata records available in accordance with the rules laid out by the protocol. Service providers harvest metadata records from data providers. In computer network terminology, OAI-PMH is an example of a simple *client-server* architecture implementation.

Because they harvest metadata from data providers, OAI-PMH service providers (in spite of their name) are the clients in OAI-PMH client-server transactions. OAI service providers initiate all OAI-PMH transactions. OAI service providers define, in the requests they make of data providers, which metadata items are wanted and in what metadata format (scheme) they should be delivered. Data providers, as the server half of an OAI-PMH client-server transaction, respond to service provider requests, fulfilling requests if able, or responding with an appropriate error or retry message if the request cannot be fulfilled or cannot be fulfilled immediately. Ultimately, service providers

FIGURE 1-1   OAI-PMH enables integrated searching across metadata aggregated from multiple heterogeneous data providers.

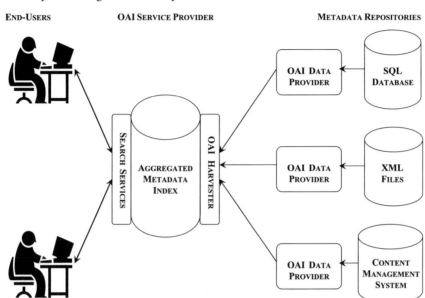

implement appropriate value-added services over aggregations of metadata harvested from multiple data providers, but again, the nature and details of such services are nowhere described or dealt with by the OAI-PMH specification and are not included among the OAI-PMH client-server transactions defined by the protocol.

In the first six years since its introduction, OAI-PMH has been used commonly as a way to aggregate multiple sources of metadata together in a search-and-discovery service providing integrated access to multiple repositories of digital information. Such a service is designed to facilitate a "one-stop shopping" model of information retrieval. In such a model, an OAI-PMH service provider harvests metadata from multiple, often widely distributed and heterogeneous data providers, aggregates harvested metadata records into some sort of data structure or database local to the service provider, and then presents a single, unified search interface to end users. Users come to the service provider's site to search for information resources of interest from any of the several data providers harvested by the service provider, thereby obviating the need to visit each data provider individually. Figure 1-1 illustrates this use of OAI-PMH.

Since the centralized search service in this model has local access only to the harvested metadata, not the described primary information resources themselves, users who identify information resources of interest through their metadata searches are then redirected by the service provider to the URL or another pointer provided by the original data provider to access the individual information resources discovered. This means that in a typical OAI-PMH implementation, data providers retain complete control over access to and presentation of the information resources they hold.

Beyond the "one-stop shopping" advantage, there are additional potential benefits of aggregating metadata together in one place as in the OAI-PMH model. Metadata normalization and augmentation can be done centrally and uniformly across the harvested collections, facilitating and enhancing the effectiveness of end-user searches across heterogeneous content. Pre-coordinated indexing of aggregated metadata can be done to improve performance and the speed with which the metadata aggregation can be searched. Searching across the aggregated metadata is done uniformly by a system designed and optimized for that specific purpose and attuned to the service provider's target audience. Aggregated metadata can be analyzed (prior to searching or dynamically in real time) to discover new relationships between content held by different data providers and to eliminate duplicative metadata records. Results from different data providers can more easily be interleaved and ranked in result sets. Since the metadata are harvested at a time convenient for the purpose, load on data providers and the network can be better managed, and searching can be done even when one or more of the data providers happens to be offline or otherwise unavailable.

Ultimately, OAI-PMH enables collaboration between data providers and service providers. The services offered by an OAI service provider are limited by the quality of the metadata harvested. The practical utility of metadata made available by an OAI data provider is dependent on the quality of the services implemented by an OAI service provider. The collaboration can be overt—that is, service providers and data providers can consult regarding harvesting schedule, metadata enhancements and normalization, and services implemented. Or, the collaborations can be uncoordinated—that is, an OAI service provider is not obligated by the protocol to inform or pre-coordinate metadata harvesting with data providers. However, even in such instances, a de facto, implicit, albeit unspoken, partnership is created.

OAI-PMH ANTECEDENTS

Before delving into more details about the protocol, how it is used, and its implications for catalogers of digital content, it is useful to look back at how OAI-PMH came to be. In July 1999, Paul Ginsparg, Rick Luce, and Herbert Van de Sompel of the Los Alamos National Laboratory (LANL) Library in New Mexico sent out an e-mail call for a meeting of parties interested in advancing work toward achieving "a universal service for author self-archived scholarly literature." The meeting took place on October 21 and 22, 1999, in Santa Fe, New Mexico. In addition to LANL, sponsors included the Council on Library and Information Resources, the Digital Library Federation, and the Scholarly Publishing and Academic Resources Coalition (SPARC).[6]

The call for this meeting noted trends dating from the early 1990s toward alternative digital and network-based models for publishing scholarly research results. Cited in the call were examples of *ePrint archives* such as arXiv,[7] an online Web service then based at Los Alamos (now at Cornell University). ArXiv enables researchers in high-energy physics and selected other scholarly disciplines to deposit with the service digital documents about research-in-progress, thereby effectively self-publishing online preliminary papers and article drafts, the digital equivalents of traditional paper preprints. Nascent ePrint archives in other disciplines, including social science disciplines such as psychology and economics, also were mentioned. Other examples of Web-based self-publishing services mentioned in the call included the Networked Computer Science Technical Reference Library (NCSTRL)[8] and the National Digital Library of Theses and Dissertations (NDLTD).[9] The call for the meeting also mentioned other emerging initiatives to create new models for scholarly publishing, for example, the SPARC initiative for the creation of low-cost, community-based, online-only scholarly research journals. As noted in the call, all of these initiatives had in common the aim to take advantage of emerging Web paradigms to create alternative, more cost-effective ways to publish and disseminate scholarly research. The concern that stimulated the call for a meeting was the observation that the technologies being implemented by each of these initiatives were being developed largely in isolation. The meeting was to explore possible application architectures and frameworks that would enable more seamless interoperability between self-publishing archives and repositories.

The outcome of this meeting was the creation of the Open Archives Initiative (OAI) and the promulgation in early 2000 of a general framework and set of technical agreements known as the Santa Fe Convention (Lagoze and Van de Sompel 2000). A second meeting of the OAI occurred on June 3, 2000, in San Antonio, Texas, engaging additional individuals in the effort and helping to refine the work begun in Santa Fe (Fox 2000). The Santa Fe Convention, somewhat more narrow in scope and not yet as fine-tuned as the OAI-PMH which would later supplant it, was built on earlier work well known to those who attended the meetings in Santa Fe and San Antonio. It sought to leverage this body of prior work and take advantage of lessons learned. In particular, the Santa Fe Convention used technologies and approaches embodied in the Universal Preprint Service (UPS) prototype, developed by Herbert Van de Sompel and several others in the summer 1999 as a proof-of-concept exercise in preparation for the Santa Fe meeting (Van de Sompel et al. 2000). The UPS prototype work in turn took advantage of earlier architectures and technologies, in particular Dienst, an evolving digital library technical architecture that was the underlying foundation for the NCSTRL project. Dienst was created and developed through several iterations by Carl Lagoze and other researchers at Cornell beginning in the mid-1990s (Lagoze and Davis 1995).

Response to the initial call and the success of early experimentation with the UPS prototype and later the Santa Fe Convention confirmed that the time was ripe for the introduction of an updated protocol to facilitate metadata sharing and digital library interoperability. The UPS prototype in particular was successful in demonstrating useful cross-repository search and information-resource linking across several production ePrint repositories. However, the UPS prototype was tightly coupled to ePrint models of online information repositories. In some ways the models embodied in the UPS prototype and the Santa Fe Convention assumed too many specifics about the internal functioning and organization of both data providers and service providers. While the research showed considerable promise for a harvested approach to metadata sharing, the Santa Fe Convention included a number of ePrint repository design dependencies and specializations. The Santa Fe Convention also was tied explicitly and by name to a subset of the Dienst protocol and required the use of a Dienst protocol-specific metadata scheme. As it became clear that interest in the harvesting model of metadata sharing went well beyond the original core group of ePrint data providers who met in Santa Fe in 1999, it also became obvious that the Santa Fe Convention, a good first step, needed to be generalized and refined to meet the broader, more general interest that had developed. OAI also needed a more formal organizational model.

This led to the formation of an OAI Steering Committee in mid-2000, and in turn, the chartering by that Committee of an OAI Executive (Herbert Van de Sompel and Carl Lagoze) to lead the creation and implementation of what was to become the OAI-PMH. An OAI Technical Committee to test, vet, and help refine a replacement for the Santa Fe Convention was also formed at this time. The first meeting of the first OAI Technical Committee was held on September 7 and 8, 2000, at Cornell University. The committee set aside certain details and assumptions about processes upstream and downstream of the actual metadata-harvesting function that previously had been included in the Santa Fe Convention, and the rest of the protocol was generalized and refined. Another meeting of the OAI was held in Europe from September 18 to 20, 2000, in conjunction with the 2000 European Conference on Digital Libraries in Lisbon, Portugal, and the Technical Committee met for a second time on November 25, 2000, at CERN (the European Council for Nuclear Research; the acronym is from the French form of the name) in Geneva, Switzerland.

By early November 2000, an alpha-test version of the new OAI-PMH had been made available by the OAI Technical Committee to an allied group of alpha testers. As compared to the Santa Fe Convention, the alpha version of the new OAI-PMH specification was generalized beyond the ePrint community and focused more exclusively on the process of transporting descriptive metadata from data provider to service provider. Included in the new protocol were XML (Extensible Markup Language) schemas precisely defining the semantics and syntax of valid OAI-PMH transactions. The emphasis on keeping the protocol technically simple, especially for OAI metadata providers, was maintained. Of particular note was the decision to move away from an earlier requirement that data providers support an ePrint-oriented, protocol-specific metadata scheme. Instead, data providers were (and still are) required to disseminate all metadata items in simple *Dublin Core* (DC) metadata format, while at the same time being encouraged to disseminate items in other community-standard metadata formats as well. Although the original metadata-harvesting model of the Santa Fe Convention was largely retained, the

TABLE 1-1 Participants in OAI-PMH alpha-phase testing (November 2000–January 2001).

Consortium for Interchange of Museum Information (CIMI)
Cornell University
Ex Libris Ltd.
Library of Congress
National Aeronautics and Space Administration (NASA)
OCLC Online Computer Library Center, Inc.
Old Dominion University
UKOLN/Resource Discovery Network (UK)
University of Illinois at Urbana-Champaign
University of Pennsylvania
University of Southampton (UK)
University of Tennessee
Virginia Tech (Virginia Polytechnic Institute and State University)

explicit references in the Santa Fe Convention to Dienst-specific metadata semantics, syntax, and transaction structures were dropped. To maintain simplicity and keep the protocol narrowly focused, OAI-PMH was designed from the start to exploit existing, ubiquitous Web technologies managed by the World Wide Web Consortium (W3C),[10] in particular HTTP (Hypertext Transfer Protocol), XML, and the W3C's XML Schema Language.

The continued requirement for DC as a "lingua franca," or lowest common denominator metadata format, remains an issue of some controversy to this day. While the OAI Executive, Steering Committee, and Technical Committee agreed that requiring DC, a more generic and more widely known metadata format, was better than requiring a Dienst- or ePrint-specific metadata format, some members of these groups as well as other would-be implementers of the protocol noted that not all resources of potential interest could be well described using simple DC. The continued requirement for DC reflects the early roots of OAI-PMH in the ePrints and library communities and the desire of the original authors of OAI-PMH to maximize its utility within these groups, even if doing so might make it less optimized for potential implementers from other fields.

Rigorous alpha testing of OAI-PMH was conducted during November and December of 2000. The November 1, 2000, release of the protocol was updated several times during this test period to resolve issues that arose. Alpha testers were recruited from among the OAI Technical Committee membership, the membership of the Digital Library Federation, and other sources. Alpha testers were drawn primarily from within the United States, but included two institutions from the United Kingdom. An effort was made to ensure diversity of institution types and heterogeneity of content and content-format types. A complete list of alpha testers is given in Table 1-1. By the end of the alpha-test period in mid January 2001, the OAI-PMH specification was deemed stable enough to post publicly as a "beta" release.

OAI OPEN DAYS AND PROTOCOL REVISION HISTORY

As suggested by the venues of the OAI and OAI Technical Committee meetings in 2000, the development of OAI-PMH was intended from the start to be international in scope. Even with alpha testing still in progress, plans for public presentation of a beta version of OAI-PMH in both the United States and Europe were under way. The formal public introduction of OAI-PMH took place on January 23, 2001, in Washington, D.C., at what was dubbed OAI Open Day for the United States. An OAI Open Day for Europe was held on February 26, 2001, in Berlin, Germany. Both events featured an in-depth introduction of version 1.0 of the protocol specification (termed a beta release, alpha releases had been numbered 0.xx) and presentations by alpha-phase testers. Also laid out at that time was a schedule for further protocol development and testing, with a stated objective of releasing a 2.0 version of the protocol, targeted as the first production release, by mid-2002. The audiences attending the events in Washington and Berlin were urged to begin testing the protocol immediately and to report any issues that arose. Crucial to the success of beta testing were several spring 2001 grants awarded by the Andrew W. Mellon Foundation supporting the creation of OAI service providers (Waters 2001).

The OAI Technical Committee was reconstituted with some membership changes and additions in the spring of 2001 and was charged with sorting through feedback from beta-phase adopters and identifying changes needed to make the protocol more robust and stable enough for building large-scale production applications. Overall, OAI-PMH version 1.0 proved surprisingly stable and needed little adjustment during the beta phase. On July 2, 2001, a minor revision of the protocol, release version 1.1, was posted to keep the protocol in synchronization with changes made in the W3C XML Schema Language specification. Otherwise, there were no other intermediate 1.x releases of the protocol.

Throughout 2001, the OAI Technical Committee accumulated and refined a list of issues raised by beta-phase implementers. Most of these issues had to do with clarifications and with matters of scope. Throughout this period, the OAI Technical Committee conducted its business entirely via conference calls and e-mails. There were no in-person meetings of the Committee as a whole in either 2001 or 2002. Related issues were combined, and as of early 2002 the OAI Technical Committee had compiled a summary list of eighteen key technical issues that warranted review or further consideration. These are listed in Table 1-2. Subgroups of two or three Committee members were assigned to write a brief white paper for each of these issues, describing concerns and articulating possible resolutions. These white papers were then circulated to the entire Committee, which, in turn, discussed the issues and recommended specific resolutions during Committee conference calls. An effort was made to respond fully to all substantive issues and concerns raised by beta-phase implementers. Generally, the OAI Technical Committee (guided by the OAI Executive) resisted the temptation to broaden or expand the scope and functionality of the OAI-PMH. The emphasis on technical simplicity was

TABLE 1-2 Reviews undertaken and options considered by OAI Technical Committee during beta-phase testing of OAI-PMH (January 2001–June 2002).

Review stringency and completeness of error handling requirements
Add support for optional use of SOAP (non-REST Web services)
Add support for selective harvesting at granularity greater than calendar day
Review requirement to make all metadata items available in simple DC
Enhance set semantics and collection description guidance
Add options to allow use of more than just W3C XML Schema Language
Review flow-control mechanisms, result-set cardinality, and response-level containers
Add mechanisms to facilitate discovery of OAI data providers
Add support for result-set filtering (for example, support for rudimentary search
    functionality)
Add support for return of multiple metadata and/or "best" metadata formats in single
    response
Add support for machine-readable rights information
Modify set definitions to require that sets be orthogonal
Add support for a GetRecords verb (gets less than all but more than one)
Add requirements to facilitate de-duping of harvested metadata records
Resolve idempotency of baseURLs
Add support for an XML format for smaller, more static archives
Add support for response compression
Review protocol requirements regarding deleted records

maintained. The success of the OAI Technical Committee in avoiding feature creep—that is, the natural inclination to overload the protocol with additional features in response to demands from implementers, a process which can tend to bloat a protocol and make it less useful for its original purpose—has had a lot to do with the ongoing success of OAI-PMH.

On June 14, 2002, version 2.0 of OAI-PMH was released. This is considered the official production release of OAI-PMH—that is, it is deemed stable enough that implementers can build conformant applications to use in production environments. As of this writing, in late 2006, version 2.0 remains the current release. Throughout the rest of this book, when mentioning OAI-PMH, we are referring specifically to the 2.0 version of the protocol.

The changes made to version 1.1 of the protocol to create version 2.0 reflect an effort to clarify specification details, correct minor errors, and add a few small items of enhanced functionality. Since the release of version 2.0 of the protocol, the OAI has released several detailed and helpful implementation guideline documents. In addition to providing helpful hints for implementers, a few of these guideline documents also suggest ancillary rules and specifications for special-purpose uses of OAI-PMH. The 2.0 version of the protocol did not include any major shifts in architecture or basic design, but neither was it fully backward compatible. Implementers were asked to migrate to the new version of the protocol within six months. More than four years later, a few data providers still have not migrated. As a result, some OAI service providers retain the capacity to harvest version 1.1 compliant data providers.

OAI-PMH—WHAT IT IS NOT

There remain several common misconceptions about what OAI-PMH is and what it is used for. These are engendered in part by its name and in part by its close association with some of the technologies it exploits. One way to help clear up some of these misconceptions is to define OAI-PMH by stating explicitly what it is not.

To begin with, although it is an outgrowth of a community effort to enhance the utility of self-archived scholarly publishing, OAI-PMH is not inherently an *open access* application. Chapter 3 provides additional context for OAI-PMH by describing the relationship of the protocol to ePrint archives, *institutional repositories*, and open access journals. For now, the reader should keep in mind that just as the protocol is useful for sharing metadata describing a wide range of content in a wide range of formats, OAI-PMH can be and has been used to share and aggregate metadata describing both open access and restricted access and for-fee content, such as commercially published journal article literature. Recognizing the broad usage of OAI-PMH, in late 2003 the OAI chartered a separate new OAI Rights Committee to develop guidelines advising OAI-PMH implementers on how best to associate intellectual property rights with metadata records disseminated by OAI-PMH data providers. As of 2006, this remains an active area of interest for operational and potential OAI-PMH implementers.

Also despite its name, OAI-PMH is not a standard or a specification for archival practice in the scholarly sense. "Archives" as used in the OAI-PMH name should be understood in the context of its generic English-language definition, not in the more restrictive sense assumed when discussing archival functions of university, government, and other cultural heritage institutions. Though there was and remains some confusion in the digital library community (Hirtle 2001), OAI-PMH is entirely distinct and separate from the *Reference Model for an Open Archival Information System* (OAIS),[11] which truly is a fulsome model of best practices for building digital versions of traditional archives. OAI-PMH is not specifically about formal archival records at all. Instead, the use of the word archives in the name OAI-PMH stems from the ePrint community's practice of referring to repositories of ePrints as online archives.

OAI-PMH also is not synonymous with the simple DC metadata format or the Dublin Core Metadata Initiative (DCMI)[12]. Though OAI-PMH references the simple DC metadata format and requires adopters of the protocol to use this format, DC is not part of the protocol, nor is OAI-PMH part of the DCMI. Other metadata formats can be used with OAI-PMH. The text of the protocol actually encourages implementers to use other metadata formats. The protocol is written so that changes in the simple DC format specification made by the DCMI generally do not require changes to OAI-PMH (and vice versa). As far as OAI-PMH is concerned, the metadata records exported and harvested using the protocol are validated using specifications wholly external to OAI-PMH. Mainly, OAI-PMH requires only that metadata records be

FIGURE 1-2   Broadcast searching relies on the simultaneous broadcast of an end-user's search to multiple search services.

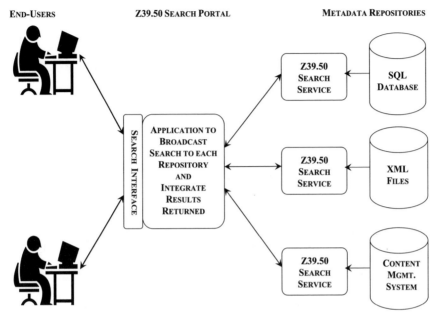

defined as having a specific metadata format that can be validated using externally and explicitly referenced XML Schema Language documents.

Finally, though OAI-PMH is often used to help enable cross-repository searching of information resources, it is not itself a protocol for searching. Unlike Z39.50 and the related SRU (Search/Retrieve via URL) protocol,[13] OAI-PMH is not designed to support arbitrary and dynamic real-time searching. (OAI-PMH does support a very limited concept of *selective harvesting*, which will be detailed later, but this does not translate as a real search capacity.) Nor is OAI-PMH synonymous with *spidering* technologies used by Web search engines such as Google. Rather than rely on and exploit descriptive metadata, spidering technologies rely on embedded links to navigate from Web page to Web page, gathering full-text content objects for later indexing as they go. This approach fails to take advantage of the extra information often intrinsic in descriptive metadata and can miss content not freely accessible or not explicitly and individually linked from Web pages, for example, resources maintained in a database and normally discoverable only through search interaction with that database. This is the so-called "hidden" Web. (Interestingly, Google recently began accepting OAI data provider URLs in lieu of conventional Web site maps.)[14]

The distinction between Z39.50/SRU and OAI-PMH highlights some fundamental differences for search services built using the two approaches. Figure 1-2 depicts a Z39.50-style *broadcast search* interaction. Contrast with Figure 1-1.

TABLE 1-3   Summary of differences between harvested (OAI-PMH) and broadcast (Z39.50/SRU) search approaches.

	OAI-PMH	Z39.50/SRU
Location of full content	Distributed (data provider)	Distributed (data provider)
Control over full content	Distributed (data provider)	Distributed (data provider)
Location of metadata searched	Centralized (service provider)	Distributed (data provider)
Searched performed	Against central metadata index	By each data provider
Search semantics interpreted and applied	Once, by central service provider	Multiple times, by each data provider
Search performance limited	By size of central metadata index and by capacity of central service provider	By slowest individual data provider, but computing load is distributed
Maximum staleness of metadata is a function of	Oldest harvest	No staleness
Pre-search normalization (by service provider)	Possible	Not possible
Integration of search results (sort and merge)	Possible	Not feasible in practice

While both Z39.50 and the OAI-PMH-based model are concerned primarily with descriptive metadata describing DLOs, and both assume that primary source digital information resources remain under the control and management of widely distributed data providers, the implications for how an end user discovers resources differ in significant ways. In Z39.50 or SRU, the end user's search query is simultaneously broadcast by the search portal to multiple data providers of interest. Each search is done in parallel against the most current and up-to-date metadata that each data provider has available. This means that the computational task associated with the search function itself is distributed among all of the data providers rather than being the sole responsibility of a central service. The Z39.50 or SRU portal is responsible only for transforming and broadcasting the user's search in a standard query language and for integrating the search results returned by the participating data providers.

On the other hand, because the search must be done by each participating data provider in real time, any disruption or delay at any data provider, or in network communications with any data provider site, results in an incomplete or delayed return to the end user. Each data provider must implement the technically more challenging and demanding Z39.50 or SRU protocol. Each data provider also is given considerable flexibility in how to implement the search features described in the Z39.50 or SRU standard, meaning that search methods across data providers may be inconsistent. Centralized pre-coordinated normalization or augmentation of metadata for enhanced discovery cannot be done. Ranked interleaving (for example, ordering an integrated list of all results returned by best match) and de-duplication of search results in real time is computationally demanding for the service provider and does not scale well. Table 1-3 summarizes the ways in which harvested and broadcast search models differ.

All of these factors represent trade-offs that must be considered by both data providers and service providers. The reader should keep in mind, however, that broadcast (Z39.50, SRU) and harvested (OAI-PMH) approaches to cross-repository resource discovery, though different, are not irreconcilable. It is perfectly feasible and valid to create a hybrid cross-repository search service that searches a local collection of aggregated metadata harvested from one set of data providers and at the same time broadcasts search queries to a second set of data providers. Done correctly, this can realize the benefits of both approaches (Sanderson et al. 2005).

HOW THE REST OF THIS BOOK IS ORGANIZED

This chapter has summarized the genesis of OAI-PMH and introduced a few of the basic concepts underlying the protocol. Remaining chapters will explore specific aspects of OAI-PMH and the protocol's relationship to digital library services and to metadata authoring and use. The three primary objectives of this text are:

1. to introduce the reader to OAI-PMH and provide context helpful in appreciating the role and function of OAI-PMH as an element of digital library infrastructure;
2. to give an overview of the technical details of the protocol, informing the reader about the technical competencies and organizational prerequisites for implementing OAI-PMH; and
3. to help the reader gain a better appreciation of the intellectual and descriptive practice issues and concerns that arise when sharing and aggregating descriptive metadata using a metadata harvesting protocol such as OAI-PMH.

Accordingly, this book is organized into three major sections, addressing in order each of these objectives. Chapter 2 explores in detail the key protocols, technologies, and best practices that comprise the foundation for OAI-PMH. While a complete discourse about innovative and evolving scholarly communication models is beyond the scope of this book, chapter 3 provides an overview of the relationship and overlaps between OAI-PMH and selected other digital library and open access initiatives. Together these two chapters plus the current chapter address the first objective of this book and are intended to give sufficient background, context, and motivation for the more in-depth discussions of OAI-PMH that follow.

Chapters 4 and 5 provide basic details of how the protocol functions and what it takes to implement an OAI data provider service. An effort has been made to limit the depth and extent of technical details discussed in these two chapters. Readers are assumed to have a general appreciation of how HTTP underlies the client-server architecture of the Web and a basic grasp of the usefulness of XML for encoding structured data. However, detailed practical experience with these protocols and technologies is not essential. No formal background in computer programming is required. More important for the reader than achieving a comprehensive understanding of protocol technical details will be that he or she gains an appreciation of the implications that the technical requirements of OAI-PMH have in terms of essential competencies and organizational workflows and operations.

Given that this book is aimed primarily at library catalogers and cataloging students, the most emphasis is given to the third section, composed of chapters 6, 7, and 8. These chapters discuss the implications of metadata sharing via OAI-PMH for metadata-authoring practices, metadata aggregation procedures, and digital library service design. Chapter 6 examines Dublin Core and other descriptive metadata schemes and their relation to OAI-PMH, and looks at best practices for metadata authoring that are driven by metadata-sharing considerations. Chapter 7 explores related issues for would-be aggregators of metadata, describing approaches to post-harvest metadata normalization and augmentation that are being explored and tested in OAI-PMH-based digital library implementations. Chapter 8 describes and provides illustrations of the kinds of digital library services that can be built over the top of OAI-PMH. Each from a different perspective, these three chapters demonstrate that requirements for enhanced digital library interoperability have implications for the way librarians perform descriptive cataloging and use metadata.

Finally, chapter 9 offers concluding thoughts and a look at emerging trends relating to OAI-PMH. Although no new version of the protocol has been released in some time, there has been considerable evolution in the way that OAI-PMH is used. A body of experience has simultaneously proved the worth of OAI-PMH and suggested additional avenues for further development. Looking forward from the end of 2006, the near future promises continued evolution in the ways OAI-PMH is used and exploited, and even some potential for new complementary protocols from the Open Archives Initiative.

QUESTIONS AND TOPICS FOR DISCUSSION

1. What are some of the major differences between harvesting and broadcast search? What are some scenarios that would favor one approach or the other?
2. What are the characteristics of document-like objects and what are the implications of the implicit optimization of OAI-PMH for DLOs?
3. What are the defining characteristics of descriptive metadata? Can you give some examples of descriptive metadata?
4. OAI-PMH originated in the ePrints community. How has that impacted the digital library functionalities it supports or does not support?
5. What kinds of digital library services might OAI-PMH facilitate or enable? What kinds of digital library services would OAI-PMH not be as useful for?

NOTES

1. http://www.openarchives.org/OAI/openarchivesprotocol.html.
2. http://www.loc.gov/z3950/agency/.
3. http://www.doi.org/.
4. http://www.loc.gov/ead/.
5. http://www.adlnet.gov/Scorm/index.cfm.

6. http://www.arl.org/sparc/.
7. http://www.arxiv.org/.
8. http://www.ncstrl.org/.
9. http://www.ndltd.org/.
10. http://www.w3.org/.
11. http://nost.gsfc.nasa.gov/isoas/ref_model.html.
12. http://www.dublincore.org/.
13. http://www.loc.gov/standards/sru/.
14. Google Webmaster Help Center, Managing My Google Sitemaps Files, Creating Google Sitemaps Files. http://www.google.com/support/webmasters/bin/answer.py?answer=34654.

REFERENCES

Fox, E. 2000. Open Archives Initiative [In Brief]. *D-Lib Magazine* 6 (6), doi: 10.1045/june2000-inbrief, http://www.dlib.org/dlib/june00/06inbrief.html#FOX.

Hirtle, Peter. 2001. OAI and OAIS: What's in a Name? *D-Lib Magazine* 7 (4), doi: 10.1045/april2001-editorial, http://www.dlib.org/dlib/april01/04editorial.html.

Lagoze, Carl. 2001. Keeping Dublin Core Simple: Cross-Domain Discovery or Resource Description? *D-Lib Magazine* 7 (1), doi: 10.1045/january2001-lagoze, http://www.dlib.org/dlib/january01/lagoze/01lagoze.html.

Lagoze, Carl, and J. R. Davis. 1995. Dienst—An Architecture for Distributed Document Libraries. *Communications of the ACM* 38 (4): 47.

Lagoze, Carl, and Herbert Van de Sompel. 2000. The Santa Fe Convention of the Open Archives Initiative. *D-Lib Magazine* 6 (2), doi: 10.1045/february2000-vandesompel-oai, http://www.dlib.org/dlib/february00/vandesompel-oai/02vandesompel-oai.html.

Lagoze, Carl, and Herbert Van de Sompel. 2003. The Making of the Open Archives Initiative Protocol for Metadata Harvesting. *Library Hi Tech* 21 (2): 118–128.

Sanderson, Robert, Jeffrey Young, and Ralph LeVan. 2005. SRW/U with OAI: Expected and Unexpected Synergies. *D-Lib Magazine* 11 (2), doi: 10.1045/february2005-sanderson, http://www.dlib.org/dlib/february05/sanderson/02sanderson.html.

Van de Sompel, Herbert, Thomas Krichel, Michael L. Nelson, Patrick Hochstenbach, Victor M. Lyapunov, Kurt Maly, Mohammad Zubair, Mohamed Kholief, Xiaoming Liu, and Heath O'Connell. 2000. The UPS Prototype: An Experimental End-User Service Across E-Print Archives. *D-Lib Magazine* 6 (2), doi: 10.1045/february2000-vandesompel-ups, http://www.dlib.org/dlib/february00/vandesompel-ups/02vandesompel-ups.html.

Waters, Donald J. 2001. The Metadata Harvesting Initiative of the Mellon Foundation. *ARL Bimonthly Report 217* (August), 10–11, http://www.arl.org/newsltr/217/waters.html

Wendler, Robin. 2004. The Eye of the Beholder. *Metadata in Practice*, 51–69. Chicago, IL: American Library Association.

CHAPTER 2

Underlying Technologies and the Technical Development of OAI-PMH

OAI-PMH articulates a specific model and framework for moving structured data, most often descriptive metadata, from OAI data provider to OAI service provider. It is built on a simple, two-tiered *client-server* network architecture model, as opposed to more complex peer-to-peer models (for example, such as used by several popular file sharing applications) or a multi-tier model (for example, an application that interposes a middleware layer between the ultimate client and a database server). OAI-PMH is a technical prescription for how to share metadata, and it defines specific requirements that data providers and service providers must satisfy to be compliant. The protocol has an explicit bias toward lowering the technical barriers for data providers and minimizing the amount of time and effort they in particular must invest to implement the protocol. To facilitate adoption, OAI-PMH exploits existing, widely implemented technologies. In technical terms, OAI-PMH is a straightforward protocol of focused scope, well-defined functionality, and great utility.

OAI-PMH has become ubiquitous in a relatively short amount of time. Martha Brogan writes, "Given the relative youth of OAI-PMH—first introduced in January 2001—the number, variety, and scope of data providers, and to a lesser degree, service providers, is remarkable" (Brogan 2003, p. 74; see also the follow-up study, Brogan 2006). Five years after its introduction in 2001, there were more than 1,000 OAI data provider services in operation.[1] According to statistics maintained by the University of Michigan's OAIster, the largest OAI service provider,[2] the number of available OAI data providers has grown linearly since the protocol's introduction and shows no signs of slowing down. The number of metadata records harvested from these data providers and aggregated by OAIster has increased at a greater-than-linear rate. By the end of 2006, the aggregation of harvested metadata records indexed by OAIster had grown to more than 10 million items. OAI data providers disseminate metadata describing collections that vary in size from a handful of resources to hundreds of thousands of resources. Experimental OAI data providers containing millions of records have been demonstrated successfully. While some communities have embraced OAI-PMH more broadly than others, there is great diversity among the communities using OAI-PMH. A wide range of institutions have implemented the protocol, from large academic and governmental research libraries to small museums and archives, from commercial publishers to individual collectors and curators of highly specialized content.

There are two main reasons for the rapid spread of OAI-PMH. First, the protocol was written to take maximum advantage of existing technologies already in widespread use. This encouraged implementation, kept the protocol focused exclusively on the technical details of metadata sharing, and avoided the tendency to "reinvent the wheel," a common problem when developing new protocols. Second, the authors of OAI-PMH engaged community interest and participation in development of the protocol while still keeping OAI-PMH technically simple. As a result, OAI-PMH was developed to be responsive to community needs. OAI-PMH provides a general-purpose means by which data providers share metadata with service providers. This obviates the need for each project to create its own idiosyncratic way to share metadata. The same protocol can serve for multiple projects. However, while responsive to community input, protocol developers retained the narrow focus of OAI-PMH. By holding the line against a wide range of suggestions for added features, developers avoided the tendency toward protocol feature bloat, which has plagued a number of past community-based protocol development efforts.

The end result is a technically lightweight yet robust protocol. There were of course trade-offs. The decisions made during OAI-PMH's development impacted the functionality the protocol can support. Both the technical strengths and technical limitations of OAI-PMH must be understood when considering its appropriateness for a specific task. This chapter discusses in more detail the protocol's technical foundation, the factors and considerations that influenced its development, and some of the reasons for its success to date. Trade-offs made to maintain technical quality and keep the protocol simple and tightly focused on the task of metadata sharing are examined. As part of this discussion some broader implications of the decisions made during protocol development are addressed.

OAI-PMH RELIANCE ON EXISTING STANDARDS

The authors of OAI-PMH decided early to take maximum advantage of existing technologies and ubiquitous technical infrastructure. To exchange request and response messages, OAI-PMH relies on the Hypertext Transfer Protocol (HTTP), the same client-server, request-response communication protocol that underlies the Web. For almost all of its transaction syntax OAI-PMH relies on XML. The reliance on existing technical standards for syntax and for low-level conventions governing communication between the service provider (metadata harvester) and the data provider allows OAI-PMH to focus on the substance of the interaction between the service provider and the data provider rather than on the details of how to manage communication and define syntax. The approach enables OAI-PMH implementers to leverage existing infrastructure already available at some institutions (for example, Web servers that can process *HTTP request messages* and generate *HTTP response messages*). An increasing number of libraries also are well along in integrating XML into their workflow. The reliance of OAI-PMH on HTTP and XML is generally viewed as a positive that has spurred its speedy adoption.

More controversial, and arguably more misunderstood, is OAI-PMH's reliance on the Dublin Core (DC) scheme for expressing metadata. While the reliance on DC may have initially helped speed OAI-PMH's adoption, some people now consider OAI-PMH synonymous with DC. Some digital library researchers assume that OAI-PMH has inherited DC's limitations, which is not true. OAI-PMH relies on DC as a lingua franca, or lowest common denominator, for *descriptive metadata*. But the protocol encourages implementers to go beyond DC and use the most expressive scheme available for their specific application. The following sections review the relationship of OAI-PMH to HTTP, XML, and DC, and the implications of these relationships for implementers of the protocol.

Reliance on HTTP

The advent of the World Wide Web has changed the way online information interchange is handled. Before the Web, protocols like telnet, Z39.50 (a pre-Web protocol for broadcast searching—see discussion in chapter 1), and Gopher (a less functional precursor to HTTP) each included their own idiosyncratic ways to structure and manage client-server communications. The advent of the Web in the early 1990s was a watershed. The Web ushered in HTTP, a discreet, stand-alone protocol that defined a new, robust, and flexible way to manage transactions between client applications and servers on the Internet.

HTTP is the underlying protocol used by the Web. When your Web browser communicates with a Web server, it is doing so using HTTP. HTTP is largely independent of the content being exchanged between client and server computers. It is equally useful for transferring *Hypertext Markup Language (HTML)* Web pages, XML documents, Portable Document Format (PDF) files, digital images, and just about any other digital content file type. Since its introduction, newer client-server applications have come to rely on HTTP to manage transactions and information exchange. As mentioned in chapter 1, OAI-PMH is no exception to this trend. By virtue of its reliance on HTTP, OAI-PMH is an example (to first approximation at least) of what has become known as a Representational State Transfer (REST) Web Service (Fielding 2000). One beneficial side effect of OAI-PMH's reliance on HTTP is that OAI data provider implementations can be viewed and debugged using conventional Web browsers.

HTTP is a useful, albeit rather simplistic, model for communication between two computers. The protocol defines a client-server session as comprising exactly one matched pair of messages. In HTTP, the client application initiates a transaction by submitting an HTTP request message to the server. The server responds with an HTTP response message. The session is then deemed complete. From the perspective of HTTP, any subsequent pair of messages exchanged is a new transaction, that is, a new, independent client-server session. This makes HTTP a *stateless* communication protocol.

(By contrast, a *stateful* protocol, such as Z39.50, allows for an extended session between two computers that is comprised of sequences of multiple, related messages exchanged back and forth over a period of time. The session semantics and management rules of such protocols are much more complex. In some scenarios, say for a complex search that involves several intermediate results sets, a stateful approach can be much more efficient overall, but significantly greater overhead is required to manage stateful sessions and transactions. As a result, stateful protocols tend to be more technically difficult to implement. By relying on HTTP, OAI-PMH avoids these complexities. Only a minimal set of pseudo-stateful workarounds had to be included in OAI-PMH to ensure proper functioning and compensate for the state limitations of HTTP. These are detailed in chapter 4.)

To appreciate how OAI-PMH works, it is necessary to understand the basics of HTTP. An *HTTP request message* (see Figure 2-1) is generated by the client application (for example, a Web browser). Each request message consists of up to three major parts. The first part, the *HTTP request line*, is always required and is used to specify what HTTP method is being employed by the client application, the identifier (that is, the name) of the resource desired by the client application, and the HTTP protocol version being used by the client application. The resource requested by an HTTP request message may be a static resource (for example, an HTML Web page) or it may be the name of a script that will generate output from the server dynamically in response to details and specific information provided as part of the HTTP request message (as, for instance, when you submit information across the Web using an HTML form).

The second part of the HTTP request message is a set of *HTTP request header* lines. The number of request header lines included is variable. Typically, HTTP request header lines provide information to the Web server about the request and about what and who is making the request. Each line provides one kernel of information. For example, HTTP request headers might detail the specific Web browser being used (for example, Microsoft Internet Explorer or Mozilla Firefox), the Web IP (Internet Protocol) address of the client, and a range of content types that the Web server application can use to fulfill the request. Standard Web user authentication credentials also are transmitted in HTTP request message header lines when required.

The third part of the HTTP request message, optional and often omitted, is the *HTTP request body*. The request body provides any special or supplemental information not included in the HTTP request line and HTTP request header lines. The HTTP request body is used to include information that might be needed to fulfill the request. For instance, the information you fill in on an HTML form is transmitted in the HTTP request body when using the *HTTP POST method*. (By contrast, when using the *HTTP GET*

FIGURE 2-1   The three parts of an HTTP request message.

```
POST /oai.asp HTTP/1.1                                              ⎫ Request-Line

Accept: text/xml,application/xml,application/xhtml+xml,text/html   ⎫
Accept-Charset: ISO-8859-1,utf-8;q=0.7,*;q=0.7                     ⎪
Accept-Encoding: gzip,deflate                                      ⎪
Accept-Language: en-us,en;q=0.5                                    ⎬ Request Headers
Content-Type: application/x-www-form-urlencoded                    ⎪
Content-Length: 25                                                 ⎪
Host: aerialphotos.grainger.uiuc.edu                               ⎪
User-Agent: Mozilla/5.0 (Windows) Gecko/20060508 Firefox/1.5.0.6   ⎭

verb=ListMetadataFormats                                           ⎫ Request Message Body
```

Method, information entered in an HTML form is added on to the URL and is included in the HTTP request line.) Figure 2-1 illustrates a complete HTTP request message; component parts are labeled.

If the server receiving the HTTP request message has a Web service running, it will respond with an HTTP response message (see Figures 2-2 and 2-3). An HTTP response message also is comprised of three parts. The first part, the HTTP response status line, contains a numeric status code describing whether the Web server was able to fulfill the HTTP request, and if not, why not. For example, a status code of 200 means the HTTP request was fulfilled successfully. A status code of 500, on the other hand, means the HTTP request could not be fulfilled because of an internal error on the server.

The second part of an HTTP response message is a set of one or more HTTP response header lines. HTTP response header lines serve similar purposes as the Header lines of an HTTP request message. Here you find information such as the kind of Web server being used and information about the response body, such as its content type and how many bytes of information are included in the response body.

The third part of an HTTP response message is the HTTP response body. This is where the HTML of a requested Web page resides. The information in the HTTP response status line and in the HTTP response reader lines is interpreted and used by the client application (for example, Web browser), but generally not passed on to the end user. Figure 2-2 illustrates a complete HTTP response message; component parts are labeled. Figure 2-3 shows what this HTTP response message looks like when displayed in a Web browser. The end user sees only the response message body, which happens in this instance to be *valid XML* (the meaning of valid in this context is described below).

OAI-PMH makes use of HTTP in specific ways and is parallel in transactional design to HTTP. OAI-PMH defines a valid transaction as an OAI-PMH request message and a matching OAI-PMH response message. Each matched pair of OAI-PMH request messages and OAI-PMH response messages represents a transaction in OAI-PMH terms. As mentioned, OAI-PMH extends this transactional model slightly beyond standard HTTP to allow a limited range of pseudo-stateful transactions and transactional flow-control functions. But in most respects, OAI-PMH is stateless. Although not as powerful or flexible as a fully stateful transaction model, the pseudo-stateful

FIGURE 2-2   The three parts of an HTTP response message.

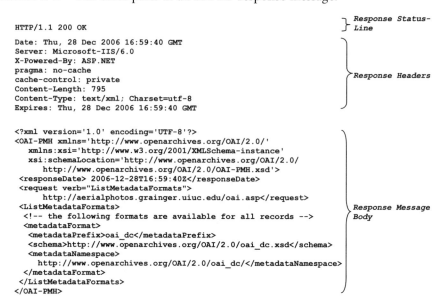

FIGURE 2-3   The HTTP response message of Figure 2-2 as displayed by the Microsoft Internet Explorer Web browser.

techniques used by OAI-PMH are sufficient to accomplish the objectives of OAI-PMH and to do so with less technical complexity than would be required to implement a fully stateful solution.

The OAI-PMH specification defines strictly how HTTP is to be used to convey OAI-PMH transactions. For instance, OAI-PMH allows the use of exactly two HTTP request methods—GET and POST. OAI-PMH data providers must be able to answer OAI-PMH requests using either of these methods. The resource identifier of an OAI-PMH request must always be the identifier (URL) of the script or application on the OAI data provider Web server that responds to and processes OAI-PMH request messages. Except as a way to request that the OAI data provider use HTTP data compression (a method that saves network bandwidth by reducing the size of HTTP response messages), the protocol makes no specific use of HTTP request header lines. OAI applications ignore all HTTP request header lines not pertaining to data compression. However, the Web server on which the OAI data provider application runs may rely on the HTTP request header lines for purposes of its own. For example, the Web server may use the HTTP request header lines to check authentication credentials, in order to determine whether the OAI harvester (client application) submitting the OAI-PMH request is authorized to access the OAI data provider application. This obviates the need for OAI-PMH itself to specify authentication and authorization mechanisms.

An OAI-PMH XML response message is transported as the response body of an HTTP response message. OAI-PMH response messages must be valid XML. Optionally, OAI-PMH data provider applications also may make special use of the HTTP response message status line and HTTP response message header lines. When used for OAI-PMH purposes, these convey added information about how the OAI-PMH request was handled by the data provider application. For example, if its repository data storage is temporarily offline, an OAI data provider may respond to an OAI-PMH request with an HTTP status code of 502 (Service Unavailable). The provider additionally may include an HTTP response header giving a "retry-after" value indicating when the data store is expected to be back online.

Reliance on XML

The Extensible Markup Language, XML, became an official recommendation of the World Wide Web Consortium (W3C) in February of 1998.[3] Only minor, incremental updates of the core specification have been required since the original release. As of mid-2006, XML version 1.1 was the latest version available as a W3C Recommendation,[4] although the latest edition of version 1.0 is still widely used. The reliance of OAI-PMH on XML has several ramifications.

For those already acquainted with HTML, XML will seem familiar. Like HTML, XML consists of markup and content. Markup is contained within angle brackets (that is, <and>). Content is everything else. Markup is used to delineate elements (also called nodes) of the document's structure, Element boundaries are defined by explicit start and end point markup called tags. Elements in turn may contain content and/or other elements. The structure of XML is hierarchical; that is, content is contained within an XML element that may then itself be wholly contained within other, "parent" elements, and so on. However, an element may not start within one parent element and end within a different parent element. Like HTML elements, XML elements may include attributes—that is, name-value pairs that are used to refine or modify the meaning of a base XML element. XML attributes reside within the angle brackets that define the starting point of the XML element they modify or refine. (XML and HTML attributes can also be used as an alternative way to associate content with an element either directly or by

FIGURE 2-4   A simple, well-formed XML document instance.

```
<?xml version="1.0" encoding="UTF-8"?>
<myBook>
   <title>The Wonders of XML</title>
   <author precedence="auth1">
      <familyName>Cole</familyName>
      <givenName>Timothy</givenName>
   </author>
   <author precedence="auth2">
      <familyName>Foulonneau</familyName>
      <givenName>Muriel</givenName>
   </author>
   <publicationDate>January 24, 2007</publicationDate>
   <fileType>PDF</fileType>
   <pages>235</pages>
</myBook>
```

reference, for example, using an attribute to hold a URL pointing to an image, as with the HTML <img> element.) The highest-level element of an *XML document instance*—that is, the element that contains the entirety of the document's markup and content—is called the root element of the document instance. (An XML document instance is a single document or file encoded in XML, as distinguished from a group or class of related XML document instances all sharing the same element and attribute naming conventions or scheme.) Taken together, these syntactical rules mean that an XML document instance may be treated as an ordered hierarchy of non-overlapping content objects.

Figure 2-4 illustrates a very simple, *well-formed XML* document instance (discussed below) giving the title and authors of a fictitious book. The XML elements of this document are: <myBook>, <title>, <author>, <familyName>, and <givenName>. The <author>, <familyName>, and <givenName> elements are repeated. <familyName> and <given-Name> are child elements of <author>, which is a child of <myBook>, the root element of the document instance. <title> also is a child of <myBook>. Each <author> element includes an XML attribute, precedence. For the first <author>, the value of the attribute is ''auth1''; for the second it is ''auth2''.

The primary differences from HTML are that XML has more rigorous requirements and, as the name implies, XML is extensible. Some of the ways the rigor of XML manifests are in the following requirements, all of which are stricter than for HTML.

- All XML elements must be explicitly closed, even empty elements having no content.
- All XML element attributes must have a value, and all attribute values must be enclosed in quotes (either single quotes or double quotes may be used).
- XML element and attribute names must be consistent in their character case.
- Correct Unicode character encoding, UTF-8 (8-bit Unicode Transformation Format) by default, must be maintained throughout an XML document instance.

XML is derived from Standard Generalized Markup Language (SGML), a widely used text-processing standard that became an international standard in 1986. Like XML, SGML treats texts as ordered hierarchies of content objects

(DeRose et al. 1990). SGML predates the Web. Early efforts to use SGML on the Web found that some of SGML's features were difficult and costly to execute in a Web environment. As a result, attempts to implement SGML widely on the Web during the Web's infancy, although showing some promise (Cole and Kazmer 1995), met with only limited success. XML preserves the most useful, most Web-compatible features of SGML while eliminating those SGML features not well suited to the Web. XML also introduced three new features tailored for Web use. These are listed here and discussed in detail below:

- well-formed document instances (as distinguished from valid document instances);
- *XML schemas,* as an alternative to old-style *SGML Document Type Definitions* (DTDs); and
- *XML namespaces.*

The concept of well-formed XML document instances was introduced in the original XML specification and is integral to XML. To understand it you must first understand how extensibility is implemented in XML.

Unlike HTML, the semantics of XML (and also SGML before it) are not fixed. Thus, XML authors can and in fact must choose their own element and attribute names. This gives XML its defining extensibility characteristic. For instance, in HTML the <title> element is the only kind of markup explicitly included to hold title information. In practice, this element is used to contain the title of the HTML page. There is, however, no easy way to differentiate in HTML markup the main title of a Web page from its subtitle, nor is there any HTML standard way to mark up subsection titles interior to a Web page. There is also no standard way in HTML to identify alternative forms of any of these kinds of titles (for example, in another language). On the other hand, in an XML document, the document author, if he or she desires, can define a markup scheme that includes multiple elements that distinguish one kind of title from another. Each element may be given a distinctive name and a specific meaning. So you could create a markup scheme for your class of XML document instances that allowed all of the following elements: <pageTitle>, <alternatePageTitle>, <subTitleForPage>, and <sectionTitle>.

To exploit extensibility features fully, client applications that process your documents must be informed of the semantic scheme in use. In SGML, it is a requirement that markup schemes be formally described as regards element and attribute names and how they may be used in relation to one another. This is done in SGML using a specially formatted file called a DTD (Document Type Definition). SGML applications will not process an SGML document instance without availability of the associated DTD to define all element names and attribute names used in creating the document instance.

In XML, markup schemes are documented using either an XML version of a DTD or an XML schema file (a new alternative to DTDs introduced as part of XML). However, in XML, formal documentation of markup schemes is not required. In the absence of an XML DTD or schema, some XML applications will still process your XML document instances as long as they are well formed (that is, meet XML well-formedness requirements). Some applications, notably most Web browsers, will ignore a DTD or XML schema associated with an XML document instance even when available. In practical terms, well-formedness means that an XML document instance must conform to proper XML syntax as defined in the XML specification (for example, no overlapping elements, all elements properly closed, all attribute values enclosed in quotes, correct character encoding, etc.). By contrast, an XML document instance is considered valid if it is both well formed and conforms semantically to an available XML, DTD, or XML schema.

Allowing for well-formed XML document instances facilitated and encouraged the early use and adoption of XML on the Web. Making a DTD or schema optional simplified the use of XML in situations where the rigor of validation is not essential, such as for displaying XML in a Web browser. But as technologies for the Web and XML have matured, the importance of the well-formedness feature of XML has waned somewhat. For some newer XML applications, schemas and DTDs have proven desirable or even essential as a standard way to ensure that the XML document instances being processed do conform structurally to intended semantics.

The authors of OAI-PMH deemed that this is the case for OAI-PMH applications. In particular they felt it was important that an OAI service provider (the metadata harvester) have a standard way to verify the semantic structure of all OAI-PMH responses, including the semantics of an OAI data provider's metadata records. For this reason, OAI-PMH requires that all OAI responses be valid XML rather than just well-formed XML. These days, with increasing numbers of XML schemas for standard metadata formats and the general availability of standard, off-the-shelf validating XML parser software to verify the correctness of XML document instances, both syntactically and semantically, this requirement has proven manageable, albeit with some added cost and increased complexity for OAI data providers. The consensus is, however, that the added cost and complexity for data providers is small compared to the extra work OAI service providers would have to do if only well-formed XML were required for OAI-PMH.

As mentioned, there are two approaches available in XML for defining the semantics of a class of XML document instances, DTDs and XML schemas. The W3C XML Schema Language, which is managed as a distinct activity within the W3C, was well in progress when OAI-PMH was being developed. The W3C XML Schema Language became a formal W3C recommendation in May 2001. The W3C XML Schema specification is published in three parts.[5] As of mid-2006, the last release of W3C XML Schema specification was dated October 28, 2004. (Work is under way on an update, with its release expected in late 2006 or in 2007.)

While DTDs have a long history of usage with SGML, they have disadvantages. XML DTDs are not themselves well-formed XML document instances. (SGML DTDs are not proper SGML document instances, either.)

FIGURE 2-5 XML schema for the XML document instance shown in Figure 2-4.

```
<?xml version="1.0" encoding="UTF-8"?>
<schema xmlns="http://www.w3.org/2001/XMLSchema">
  <element name="myBook">
    <complexType>
      <sequence>
      <element name="title" type="string" />
      <element name="author" maxOccurs="unbounded">
        <complexType>
          <sequence>
            <element name="familyName" type="string" />
            <element name="givenName" type="string" />
          </sequence>
          <attribute name="precedence" type ="string"/>
        </complexType>
      </element>
      <element name="publicationDate" type="string" />
      <element name="fileType" type="string" />
      <element name="pages" type="string" />
    </sequence>
    </complexType>
  </element>
</schema>
```

XML DTDs use a different syntax than do XML document instances. This means that you need a different application to parse DTDs than to parse XML document instances. The defining characteristic of XML schemas of all types is that they are valid XML document instances. As compared to DTDs, XML schemas also allow authors to be more prescriptive in specifying allowable document instance content models and data types. Confounding these advantages somewhat is the presence of multiple different and generally incompatible schema languages for creating XML schemas.

The authors of OAI-PMH considered several trade-offs in how to implement the requirement for valid XML. The first trade-off, between DTDs and XML schemas, was resolved in favor of XML schemas. This decision maintained focus on clarity and simplicity. Obviating the need for OAI-PMH applications to parse DTDs was an obvious way to keep protocol overhead low. In addition, the OAI Executive and the OAI Technical Committee anticipated that XML schemas would become far more ubiquitous than XML DTDs. This anticipation was proven correct. Though not as obvious, the timing also was right to go with the W3C XML Schema Language. The W3C XML Schema Language has emerged as favored for most general-purpose applications. Validating XML parsers for the W3C XML Schema Language are ubiquitous and easy to acquire. To facilitate use of W3C-style XML schemas with OAI-PMH, the OAI maintains canonical copies of XML schemas formally documenting all semantics specific to OAI-PMH. The decision to rely only on the W3C XML Schema Language for XML document instance validation in the context of OAI-PMH has proven satisfactory.

Namespaces are another innovation of XML. XML namespaces are a way to delineate the origin of semantics (element and attribute names) used within an XML document. XML namespaces allow the reuse in a new application of XML semantics already defined and codified in an XML schema created for another, earlier application. In the context of OAI-PMH, the use of XML namespaces is enabling. Although introduced as a concept almost concurrent with the release of the first XML specification in 1998, the XML namespace specification did not become a W3C Recommendation until early 1999. As of late 2006, the *W3C Recommendation for Namespaces in XML* version 1.1 is the current release.[6]

In somewhat simplified terms, XML namespaces work as follows. Semantics for an original class of XML document instances are developed by John Smith. The rules for the element names and attribute names and how they fit together are codified in an XML schema. This XML schema is assigned an XML namespace—that is, is associated with a unique namespace URI (Uniform Resource Identifier). At a later point in time, another person, Jane Doe, then wants to define semantics for another class of XML document instances she plans to create. The semantics for the new class of XML document instances overlap with the semantics for the earlier class. Rather than describe the overlapping semantics all over again, Jane Doe can write her new XML schema to allow the reuse of the semantics (all or selected) from the earlier XML schema created by John Smith. The unique namespace URI that John Smith assigned to his XML schema provides the essential referential link. In each of the document instances created by Jane Doe, namespace prefixes are defined, and those prefixes followed by a colon are pre-appended to element and attribute names to distinguish which semantics belong to John Smith's original XML schema and which belong to Jane Doe's XML schema. This avoids element and attribute name collisions. (A default namespace can be defined to which all elements and attributes lacking a namespace prefix are assumed to belong.) By using XML namespaces, it is thus possible to include and validate XML document instances containing semantics taken from multiple different XML schemas.

The implications for OAI-PMH are profound. XML namespaces allow the protocol to prescribe only the semantics necessary for the proper functioning of OAI-PMH. These semantics have been defined in XML schemas and associated with XML namespace URIs owned and managed by the Initiative. The details of metadata record semantics are left to be defined in other XML schemas associated with other XML namespaces. Thus, XML schemas associated with OAI-PMH namespaces are designed to define only the essential transactional semantics and enveloping for metadata record payloads. The semantics of the metadata record to be carried within an OAI-PMH envelope are left to be defined elsewhere by specific communities of use. This decouples the protocol from changes in and evolution of metadata record semantics (and vice versa). Technical details of metadata harvesting are encapsulated and kept separate from descriptive and cataloging practice details.

The primary XML schema for OAI-PMH[7] does not declare the semantics for labeling the title of a resource being described by a metadata record. The metadata record embedded in an OAI-PMH response must express this descriptive attribute using its own semantics for labeling the resource title. The semantics used for metadata records embedded in an OAI-PMH response must be defined in XML schemas associated with non-OAI XML namespaces. This translates to a requirement that the semantics of any metadata record format used with OAI-PMH must be defined in an XML schema written in the W3C XML Schema Language. With this one restriction, the reliance on W3C XML Schema Language and on XML namespaces facilitates the use of OAI-PMH to disseminate metadata in different metadata formats, including metadata formats yet to be developed. As a result, OAI-PMH does not need to change to support new metadata formats. This is one of the most powerful features of OAI-PMH.

Reliance on Dublin Core

The Dublin Core Metadata Initiative (DCMI) grew out of a series of discussions in the mid-1990s among librarians, computer scientists involved in the development of the Web, and researchers involved in text-encoding initiatives. The DCMI takes its name from an initial workshop convened in March 1995 in Dublin, Ohio, the home of OCLC Online Computer Library Center (Weibel et al. 1995). This first workshop was convened by OCLC, the University of Illinois National Center for Supercomputing Applications, and SoftQuad, Inc., creators of SGML and later XML editing and rendering software.

One of the objectives of the initial workshop was to reach a consensus on a core set of easy-to-use metadata elements for describing networked resources. After several additional meetings, version 1.0 of the Dublin Core Metadata Element Set (DCMES) was formally released in September 1998 (Weibel et al. 1998; also).[8] This release was comprised of the fifteen core elements listed in Table 2-1. These fifteen elements are usually referred to as *simple DC* or *unqualified DC*. The focus was (and remains) on descriptive metadata elements, especially those useful for Web resource discovery and use. As of late 2006, the current version of unqualified DC is version 1.1,[9] initially released in July 1999. Since the 1.1 release of the DCMES, DCMI has added the following: several new top-level elements; a set of refinements and encoding schemes, each mapped to one of the top-level elements; multiple application profiles for specialized use of DC; and a number of guidelines and recommendations for how to encode DC semantics in a number of syntaxes, including XML. Collectively, the fifteen elements of unqualified DC and the new top-level elements, refinements, and encoding schemes added since the initial release of DCMES version 1.1 are known as *qualified DC*. Figure 2-6 shows a

TABLE 2-1 The fifteen elements of unqualified (simple) Dublin Core.

Contributor	Format	Rights
Coverage	Identifier	Source
Creator	Language	Subject
Date	Publisher	Title
Description	Relation	Type

FIGURE 2-6 An example of unqualified Dublin Core metadata expressed as an XML document instance.

```
<?xml version="1.0" encoding="UTF-8"?>
<myMetadata
    xmlns="http://example.org/myBook/"
    xmlns:dc="http://purl.org/dc/elements/1.1/"
    xsi:schemaLocation="http://example.org/myBook/
        http://example.org/mySchema.xsd">
 <dc:title>The Wonders of XML</dc:title>
 <dc:creator>Cole, Timothy W.</dc:creator>
 <dc:creator>Foulonneau, Muriel</dc:creator>
 <dc:date>2007-01-24</dc:date>
 <dc:type>Text</dc:type>
 <dc:format>application/pdf</dc:format>
 <dc:format>235 pages</dc:format>
</myMetadata>
```

minimal unqualified DC record in XML. (Compare to Figure 2-4. Note the use of XML namespaces.)

As mentioned in chapter 1, OAI-PMH stemmed from an initial desire to explore new architectural designs and frameworks that might enable more seamless interoperability between and among self-publishing archives and repositories. Given this original context, a priority for the protocol authors was ensuring that OAI service providers could harvest metadata records disseminated by any and all OAI data providers. To implement this, OAI-PMH mandates the use (as a minimum requirement) of unqualified DC and embeds an XML schema in the protocol that defines a root container element for simple DC metadata and references (imports) an XML schema for unqualified DC maintained by the DCMI. The decision of OAI-PMH authors to require that all metadata items in an OAI data provider repository be made available for dissemination in at least unqualified DC is a trade-off between uniformity and flexibility. The decision has proven to be the most controversial requirement of the protocol.

Clearly, DC is not optimized for use with all kinds of content. As a generic, core set of semantics with a broad scope, it is not well suited to more specialized types of resources meant to be used in specialized ways. A number of communities have found it necessary to augment DC with additional semantics. For instance, the life sciences research community has developed significantly different and extended metadata semantics, such as the Darwin Core,[10] which is a metadata scheme specifically designed for describing collections of specimens collected and photographed in the field. Librarians and researchers who work with visual resources (photographs, artwork, etc.) have developed the VRA Core,[11] a standard maintained by the Visual Resources Association Data Standards Committee,[12] as a descriptive metadata scheme for better describing resources in this domain.

Unqualified DC is also a relatively shallow metadata set. Contrast it to the MARC (MAchine-Readable Cataloging) format standard used widely in the library community. As discussed in later chapters, unqualified DC is limited in terms of the digital library services it can support. For instance, no semantics are included in simple DC to explicitly express the different parts of a creator or contributor name, to differentiate between personal and corporate names, or to describe the specific role a creator or contributor had in developing the described resource. Such information can be essential to developing name-browsing interfaces, supporting searches by author affiliation, or enabling fine-grained discovery according to who created different parts of a complex resource. Similar drawbacks apply to several other unqualified DC elements.

What unqualified DC does offer is a simple, lowest-common-denominator metadata format for sharing descriptive metadata about document-like online information resources. The prescriptive requirement in OAI-PMH mandating the use of DC is intended only as a starting point. Especially early in the development and deployment of OAI-PMH, its reliance on DC, like its reliance on HTTP and XML, made it easier for would-be OAI-PMH implementers already familiar with DC. It also gave would-be OAI service providers a needed and reliable first target on which to build their initial OAI service provider implementations. OAI-PMH's use of unqualified DC for these purposes is not intended as an all-encompassing endorsement of unqualified DC. OAI-PMH explicitly encourages the use of OAI-PMH with other, more expressive metadata formats. By design, the built-in flexibility to use other metadata record formats is a strength of the protocol. As is discussed in later chapters, many OAI data providers and service providers are moving beyond unqualified DC to use other metadata formats with OAI-PMH. This is exactly what was intended and envisioned by the authors of OAI-PMH.

KEEPING IT TECHNICALLY SIMPLE

As noted above, exploiting existing standards such as HTTP, XML, and DC has helped to maintain the simplicity of the OAI-PMH specification and to keep the protocol uncluttered with ancillary details tangential to its main intent and purpose. That alone, however, was not enough to ensure that OAI-PMH would develop as a useful, technically low-barrier, relatively easy-to-implement protocol. Several other attributes of the process of creating and developing OAI-PMH were determinant as well. In their article on the making of OAI-PMH, Carl Lagoze and Herbert Van de Sompel (2003) credit several factors as contributing to the success that OAI-PMH has enjoyed. Dominant among these were:

- the definition of an effective organizational model that blended decisive leadership with community participation;
- a sharp and steady focus on a well-scoped problem;
- a proactive effort to build community; and
- a consistent effort to make sound technical decisions throughout the process.

Their success in keeping OAI-PMH appropriately focused and technically low barrier has had a lot to do with the relatively rapid adoption of the protocol.

Organization of the OAI

The organizational model that evolved during the early development of the OAI-PMH specification proved especially well suited to its purpose. During the critical period of development, the OAI organizationally consisted of an OAI Executive (Lagoze and Van de Sompel), an OAI Steering Committee composed of respected and expert leaders from across the spectrum of activities relating to digital libraries, and an OAI Technical Committee composed of selected technical experts actively involved in testing and implementing the protocol. While the OAI Steering Committee itself brought considerable credibility and quality leadership to the protocol from the outset, arguably the decision by the OAI Steering Committee to form and charge the two-person OAI Executive proved just as important.

As members of the OAI Steering Committee, co-chairs of the OAI Technical Committee, and vested with the day-to-day decision making authority, the OAI Executive of Lagoze and Van de Sompel served as a counterbalance to any tendency on the part of the OAI Technical Committees to obfuscate technical and process questions. This is a common problem with committee-based standards and protocol-writing bodies. The Executive especially kept the Technical Committee on task and on schedule, effectively bringing closure and finality to technical issues in a timely manner. They also kept work focused unwaveringly on the original scope and objectives. Having two rather than just a single individual serving as OAI Executive also added to the legitimacy of decisions made and engendered an additional measure of credibility. With the help especially of Michael Nelson, Simeon Warner, and a few others, the OAI Executive took the lead in writing specification drafts and collecting and organizing feedback and input from the larger community. The model for the development of the OAI-PMH relied on a variety of individuals and groups. The common attribute of the OAI organizational model was to have sufficient numbers and involvement to accomplish each task efficiently and achieve community buy-in, while not involving more in any task or decision-making process than was absolutely necessary.

Avoiding Feature Bloat

Avoiding featurism creep and feature bloat is a common challenge in the development of technical standards and protocols. Too often protocols tend to include features and details not essential to their main purpose. This especially became an issue for OAI-PMH during the interval between the public release of the beta versions of the protocol (versions 1.0 and 1.1) and the release of the production version of the protocol (version 2.0). During that time, testers and early adopters of the protocol suggested numerous ways that OAI-PMH could be improved. (See the summary of issues listed in Table 1-2.) Much of this feedback was useful, but much of it also suggested additions to the protocol outside its primary scope.

It became the responsibility of the OAI Executive and the OAI Technical Committee to identify which proposals and suggestions were germane and essential to the core protocol focus and which were not. This partitioning process was made easier by recognizing that some suggestions were implementation-specific and could best be handled in implementation guidelines and recommendations issued separately from the core protocol. Other suggestions, although proposing interesting and useful functionality, belonged wholly in the domain of either service providers or data providers individually rather than in the intersection of those domains, which was the only area within the purview of the protocol itself. Ultimately, the other factor which precluded feature creep was the willingness of the OAI Executive to step in when clear consensus could not be reached and say, "we will do this" or "we will not do that" based on their own assessment of whether the issue was within or outside the desired scope of the protocol. This authority was used sparingly, but decisively.

Building Community

There was a conscious effort by all involved in the early development of OAI-PMH to engage the digital library community broadly defined and to build a cohesive community of use around OAI-PMH itself. This also contributed to the relatively rapid uptake of the protocol by members of the digital library community. From the outset, the OAI has maintained online (e-mail) discussion lists to which implementers and others interested in the protocol can subscribe. These lists have engendered full and wide-ranging discussions of protocol issues and implementation details and have proven invaluable in identifying protocol details in need of revision or improvement. Efforts of early adopters to promote the protocol through informal sharing of results, preparation of protocol tutorials, and presentations at meetings and journal articles describing ways it is being used have been crucial to the rapid promulgation of OAI-PMH as well.

Additionally, the building and sharing of tools built by OAI-PMH implementers, even at the level of sharing source code, has been key in the development and promulgation of the protocol. The collaboration among early adopters is difficult to overstate. A case in point is the OAI Repository Explorer service developed by Hussein Suleman (2001) while he was a doctoral student at Virginia Tech University. (Both Suleman and the Repository Explorer service[13] have since moved to the University of Cape Town.) This utility, which became available late in the alpha test phase of protocol development, allows interactive testing of OAI data provider sites and has greatly facilitated data provider development and validation.

Maintaining Technical Quality and Scope

Ultimately, however, the technical quality of the protocol and its success in practice has had the most to do with the rapid spread of OAI-PMH. This is the result of careful and correct decisions about the technical details of the protocol. (The devil is most certainly in the details, and it is no coincidence that OAI-PMH has the technical details right.)

From the outset, OAI-PMH has been informed by extensive experimentation and testing. As noted in chapter 1, even before the original meeting in Santa Fe that led to the formation of the OAI, experimentation was under way in the form of the Universal Preprint Service prototype. Alpha testing in late 2000 and the year-and-a-half time period between release of OAI-PMH version 1.0 (beta) and OAI-PMH version 2.0 (production) also provided invaluable technical insights to help make the protocol technically better and more sound.

The technical validity of the protocol is manifest in several ways. Fundamentally, the division between data provider and service provider has proved useful and surprisingly flexible, and is an example of the clean and consistent architectural model that underlies the protocol. Similarly, the definitions provided in the protocol—for example, the distinction between metadata items and metadata records, paralleling as it does the distinction between metadata items stored in a repository or archive and metadata records disseminated for harvest—are clear, concise, and pragmatic. OAI-PMH also benefits in technical quality from conscious efforts to accommodate a wide range of use models. The embedded use of XML namespaces to allow use of arbitrary metadata record formats and the inclusion of an optional <about> container node to accommodate provenance and statements regarding metadata rights and other attributes show the insight and ability to plan for the future that are the hallmarks of technically high-quality protocols.

Balancing these technical decisions were the choices of what not to include. For example, there was early interest in expanding the scope of OAI-PMH to allow dynamically defined sets and selective dissemination of records from repositories based on arbitrary Boolean search criteria. This would have positioned OAI-PMH to compete directly with Z39.50. While such functionality may in some instances be desirable, the OAI Executive and Technical Committee correctly recognized that adding such complexities would dilute the main purpose and adversely impact the technically low-barrier objectives at the core of the protocol. Also resisted was the temptation to release OAI-PMH as a fully stateful Web service application (for example, as a SOAP-based protocol instead of as an HTTP-based REST-style service protocol). Again, given the resources and timeline for developing OAI-PMH, this would have jeopardized the technical quality of the protocol while not furthering its core mission.

QUESTIONS AND TOPICS FOR DISCUSSION

1. What are some of the differences between stateful and stateless Web communication protocols? How do those differences impact on the utility of one protocol or another as regards digital library system design and interoperability?
2. What is the difference between valid and well-formed XML and under what circumstances would you prefer one or the other?
3. What are the advantages and disadvantages of OAI-PMH's requirement for Dublin Core? Enumerate a few arguments in favor of or against the requirement. (Consider these questions again after having read the entire book.)
4. How did the organization and operational approach of the Open Archives Initiative facilitate its development and broad adoption?
5. What features or functionalities do you feel OAI-PMH should have included that aren't included? Why?

SUGGESTIONS FOR EXERCISES

1. Create well-formed XML document instances containing descriptive metadata for a few of your favorite books or CDs. You can use DC element names as given in Table 2-1 or you can make up your own metadata element names. View these files in your Web browser.
2. The University of Illinois maintains a registry of OAI data providers.[14] Because OAI-PMH uses HTTP, you can use your Web browser to link from registry listings directly to live OAI data providers. Explore several OAI data providers using your Web browser. Visit the OAI Repository Explorer hosted at the University of Cape Town[15] and try the same thing.
3. Create an XML document instance that is intentionally not well formed. Exchange with another student so he or she can find the well-formedness error in your document instance while you look for the error in his or her document instance.

NOTES

1. According to the most comprehensive index of OAI-PMH data providers, the University of Illinois OAI-PMH Data Provider Registry, http://oai.grainger.uiuc.edu/registry.
2. http://oaister.umdl.umich.edu/o/oaister/charts.xls.
3. http://www.w3.org/TR/1998/REC-xml-19980210.
4. http://www.w3.org/TR/2004/REC-xml11-20040204/.
5. http://www.w3.org/TR/xmlschema-0/, http://www.w3.org/TR/xmlschema-1/, and http://www.w3.org/TR/xmlschema-2/.
6. http://www.w3.org/TR/xml-names11/.
7. http://www.openarchives.org/OAI/2.0/OAI-PMH.xsd.
8. http://dublincore.org/documents/1998/09/dces/.
9. http://dublincore.org/documents/dces/.
10. http://darwincore.calacademy.org/.
11. http://www.vraweb.org/datastandards/VRA_Core4_Intro.pdf.
12. http://www.vraweb.org/datastandard2.html.
13. http://re.cs.uct.ac.za/.
14. According to the most comprehensive index of OAI-PMH data providers, the University of Illinois OAI-PMH Data Provider Registry, http://oai.grainger.uiuc.edu/registry.
15. http://re.cs.uct.ac.za/.

REFERENCES

Brogan, Martha L. 2003. *A Survey of Digital Library Aggregation Services*. Washington, D.C.: Digital Library Federation, Council on Library and Information Resources, http://purl.org/dlf/pubs/dlf101/.

Brogan, Martha L. 2006. *Contexts and Contributions: Building the Distributed Library*. Washington, D.C.: Digital Library Federation, http://purl.org/dlf/pubs/dlf106/.

Cole, Timothy W., and Michelle M. Kazmer. 1995. SGML as a Component of the Digital Library. *Library Hi Tech* 13 (4): 75–90.

DeRose, Steven J., David G. Durand, Elli Mylonas, and Allen H. Renear. 1990. What is Text, Really? *Journal of Computing in Higher Education* 1/2 (1990): 3–26.

Fielding, R. T. 2000. Architectural Styles and the Design of Network-Based Software Architectures. PhD dissertation, University of California, Irvine.

Lagoze, Carl, and Herbert Van de Sompel. 2003. The Making of the Open Archives Initiative Protocol for Metadata Harvesting. *Library Hi Tech* 21 (2): 118–128.

Suleman, Hussein. 2001. Enforcing Interoperability with the Open Archives Initiative Repository Explorer. *Proceedings of the First ACM/IEEE-CS Joint Conference on Digital Libraries, June 24–28, 2001, Roanoke, VA*, 63–64. New York: The Association for Computing Machinery (ACM).

Weibel, Stuart, Jean Godby, Eric Miller, and Ron Daniel. 1995. *Dublin Core Metadata Initiative—OCLC/NCSA Metadata Workshop Report*. Dublin, Ohio: Dublin Core Metadata Initiative, http://dublincore.org/workshops/dc1/report.shtml.

Weibel, Stuart, J. Kunze, Carl Lagoze, and M. Wolf. 1998. *Dublin Core Metadata for Resource Discovery, IETF #2413*. The Internet Society, http://www.ietf.org/rfc/rfc2413.txt.

CHAPTER 3

Context for OAI-PMH: ePrints, Institutional Repositories, and Open Access

OAI-PMH grew out of a desire to facilitate scholarly communications on the Web. Access to, management of, and preservation of scholarly research and literature all fall within the realm of scholarly communications. The advent of the Web has raised new issues and opened up new possibilities in this domain and has led to the emergence of new paradigms for scholarly discourse. As a technical framework for metadata sharing and interoperability, OAI-PMH plays a pivotal role in a number of these emerging new models.

To provide essential context for the study of OAI-PMH, this chapter examines new models of scholarly communications as exemplified by *ePrint archives*, *institutional repositories*, and *open access* journals. Discussion of these new models is prefaced by a review of the main elements of the traditional scholarly communications process. The chapter closes with a brief summary of the technological approaches and specific solutions in this domain. There is one caveat: the scholarly communication models which dominate the discussion in this chapter and which led to OAI-PMH itself assume open access to managed content; however, as a technical protocol, OAI-PMH has utility across a wide range of scholarly publishing solutions and should not be thought of as having applicability only in systems which implement open-access models.

THE TRADITIONAL SCHOLARLY COMMUNICATIONS PROCESS

Researchers publish their most important scholarly work and results in peer-reviewed publications. In academia especially, the quality of a researcher's work is evaluated in large measure according to the number of peer-reviewed publications he or she has in prestigious outlets and the number and significance of citations to his or her articles that appear in other publications of similar quality. These criteria are very important to obtain funding for further research, to gain esteem among peers, and to further the researcher's academic career.

In preparing to submit an article to a specific journal for pre-publication peer review, researchers in some disciplines generate a *preprint*, or first, preliminary version of the article. A preprint documents the essential explanations and demonstrations of the innovative results he or she has obtained. The researcher circulates the preprint to colleagues and gets feedback before submitting a final draft to the journal or other outlet where he or she would like the paper to be published. Journals typically have a scholarly committee composed of peer experts in the domain who evaluate the quality of the submitted article and recommend acceptance, rejection, or further modification of the article before publication (hence the term "peer review"). Peer review is common for both print publications and increasingly for online-only publications.

If the expert reviewers reject an article, the researcher can still send it to another journal for review. If the expert reviewers request modifications to the article, the author either: makes the requested modifications, working closely with the journal editor while doing so; submits the article elsewhere; or withdraws the article from consideration. If deemed of sufficient quality and significance, the article will be published in the journal. The actual publication of the article means that its scholarly content has been vetted or validated by the journal's editorial review board. The quality and value of the research described in the article are thereby recommended to the journal's readers. The prestige of the journal and its reputation for rigorous peer review bring a proportional guarantee of the work's quality and importance.

The process before publication of the article frequently takes several months, up to even a year or more. If the article has been rejected by one journal, it might be submitted successively to other journals. In such cases, the delay in its publication is increased proportionally. This tempers the newness of results reported in peer-reviewed journals.

The publication of an article has a number of consequences regarding both the text and the published research results, as compared to content that has not yet been exposed in a formal publication. Frequently, by the time an article is published, the author(s) have transferred to the publisher (in whole or in part) the rights to republish the article in another publication or in another language or format (including digitally). If the researcher's institution wants to make a copy of a published article available to its students and other faculty, it must buy it back from the publisher by subscribing to the journal in which the article appeared. According to the laws of the country in which research is published and the international agreements to which the country is a party, the timing and circumstances of the first public release of research results also can impact the potential to patent the results of the research.

Any version of an article shared with colleagues before peer review and publication is considered a preprint. Its content is likely more current than it will be by the time of formal publication, but the content has not yet been validated by a peer-review process. Once published, any version successive to the published version becomes a *post-print*. The advent of the World Wide Web (in combination with protocols like OAI-PMH) has greatly facilitated the ease with which preprints and post-prints may be shared. ePrint is a term commonly applied to both preprints and post-prints published on the Web. Author(s) typically retain all rights on preprint versions of an article. However, wide availability and circulation of a preprint draft of an article may be considered by some publishers as a disqualification when considering an article for publication. Alternatively, a journal publisher may require that access to a preprint version be restricted (taken off the Web) before an article is published. Some publishers also restrict when and even whether post-prints may be posted on the Web. At a minimum, publishers at least require acknowledgement of prior publication in their journal when making post-prints available.

ePRINT ARCHIVES

ePrint archives and repositories can be thought of as databases containing articles—mostly preprint or post-print articles. ePrint archives are fed by researcher contributions. Typically, researchers are allowed to upload their own ePrints, providing the descriptive metadata necessary to enable users to find and retrieve the items.

In 1991, Paul Ginsparg, then at the Los Alamos National Laboratory in New Mexico, created the first major ePrint archive, called arXiv. ArXiv[1] initially gathered together articles about high-energy physics, a discipline with a strong and robust history of preprints in print format. arXiv has since expanded to cover multiple domains, including mathematics, computer science, and biology, and has moved (with Ginsparg) to Cornell University, with continued support from the National Science Foundation. The aim of arXiv is to collect researchers' contributions on a voluntary basis and to archive and make them accessible on the Web. Following Paul Ginsparg's initiative, other research institutions began to implement similar ePrint archives in a wide range of disciplines. (A community-based ePrint archive in library and information science was established in 2003.[2]) The need for sharing and interoperability quickly became apparent, and this led to the creation of the OAI-PMH as described in chapter 1.

The concept of ePrints has more recently been expanded to include content whether or not it is aimed at eventual peer-review publication. Contributing to an ePrint archive has become known as *self-archiving*, since it typically relies on researchers voluntarily archiving their scholarly papers. However, it remains distinct from publication in a peer-reviewed journal. ePrint services aim to disseminate, and increasingly to preserve content—not necessarily to publish it in competition with traditional publication outlets. Publishing involves specific formatting according to an editorial policy and the validation of content through peer review. The formally published journal in which an article appears provides additional context and authority for the work. This is not the primary goal of most ePrint archives, although it may be a secondary consideration for some.

ePrints Software and Services

The development of ePrint archives has been facilitated by the creation of standard open source software for self-archiving. In order to facilitate self-archiving of scholarly literature, tools have to be user friendly for everyone, including researchers not well-versed in traditions of descriptive cataloging. The de facto standard ePrints software[3] was developed at the University of Southampton in the United Kingdom to support the Budapest Open Access Initiative's action plan. (The Budapest Open Access Initiative is discussed below.) The Southampton software is known simply as the ePrints software package. It is an open-source software package available under the GNU open source license. (GNU is not an acronym in the usual sense. The computer hacker community, early advocates of open source in all its forms, defines GNU as a "recursive acronym" standing for "GNU's not Unix.")

The ePrints software application is adapted for the quick and easy creation of ePrint archives. It supports OAI-PMH and the larger set of Santa Fe Convention standards mentioned in chapter 1. The software allows experts to manage articles and scientific contributions and to define metadata for each contribution. The ePrints software is accompanied by an ePrints handbook[4] which describes organizational and technical issues related to an ePrint archive.

An ePrint archive aggregates documents from multiple researchers. The collection must be cognizant of and implement internal rules related to any relevant intellectual property rights in force—for example, explicit prior agreements entered into by an author on the use of materials to be archived must be respected. Policies regarding the use of aggregated content and the ways authors can make repository contributions and deletions (if allowed) also must be defined and implemented. The content scope and policies of an ePrint archive can be described through a standard metadata format.[5] The collection-development policy for an ePrint archive typically articulates proactive behaviors to encourage as many author contributions as possible.

To use OAI-PMH in the context of an ePrint repository requires the presence of descriptive metadata for each item in the repository. In the ePrints self-archiving model, authors typically provide such metadata themselves. This largely precludes the adoption of controlled vocabularies or other advanced descriptive catalog techniques. However, each domain-specific scientific community can define for that community how to use ePrint metadata, what information is necessary to include in metadata records, and ways to improve metadata workflow efficiency. Ultimately, since most ePrint archives aim at facilitating resource discovery, the primary quality indicator of metadata records maintained by an ePrint archive is their accuracy and utility for resource discovery.

ePrint services can be characterized by hosting organizations and by submission policies and practices. In some cases, domain-specific research facilities host ePrint servers. In other cases, libraries do. ePrint services typically include documents from more than one institution. They are typically domain specific in scope. Most often authors submit their own contributions, along with at least some metadata. Additional metadata may be automatically generated. The archive administrator or other staff may then create additional metadata and/or review the document and metadata appropriateness relative to the archive's scope. Documents in more than one format may be (and are likely to be) included in a single ePrint archive.

ePrints and OAI-PMH

OAI-PMH is ubiquitous in the ePrints community. As of 2006, all major software applications used for building ePrint archives in the academic community worldwide implemented OAI-PMH. The use of OAI-PMH-compliant software helps to ensure interoperability of ePrint archives, enhance the visibility of ePrint archives and their contents, and further the utility of ePrints archives as a component of the scholarly communications infrastructure (Warner 2003).

There are several good examples of communities using OAI-PMH in concert with ePrint archiving applications. The Open Language Archives Community (OLAC) has built an efficient network of content sharing on the foundation of the ePrints model and OAI-PMH. In particular, OLAC has defined the special attributes that characterize its content and set up domain-specific rules that supplement and refine the more generic rules of OAI-PMH (Simons and Bird 2003).

In the private sector, the scientific publisher Elsevier relies on a mix of technologies to gather and harvest content and metadata to feed its Scirus portal,[6] providing access (as of mid-2006) to 250 million scientific digital resources, ranging from Web pages, to journal-published literature, to ePrints. Focused crawling (spidering) is used to gather relevant Web page content. Partnerships with selected publishers (for example, BioMed Central) and abstracting and indexing services (such as Medline) are used to gather additional content for indexing. OAI-PMH is used to harvest metadata from ePrints sources (for example, arXiv and Cogprints) and from additional publishers and journal aggregators (such as Project Euclid).

Other types of services (that is, beyond simple search-and-discovery services) take advantage of ePrint archives. *CiteBase*[7] at the University of Southampton, for example, relies on OAI-PMH to identify ePrints that can then be parsed for citations to scientific articles. The European project *Cyclades*,[8] relying on OAI-PMH, provides tools and services that include advanced browsing, filtering, and recommender features as well as mechanisms that allow users to structure the ePrint and open-access information space dynamically into meaningful (from the perspective of a particular community) virtual collections.

However, archive reliability and quality issues exist with regard to ePrint repositories. This can impact the quality and scope of services. Through experimentation, OAI service providers have discovered that not all ePrint repositories meet their requirements. ePrint self-archiving involves a range of practices. As a result, internal consistency of archives can be quite variable. Even when authors have common backgrounds and submit their contributions in similar ways, author-submitted metadata typically are poorly harmonized. Online availability of some ePrint archives can be sporadic.

Nonetheless, the ePrints model of scholarly communication offers the potential of a new, "intermediate" way to publish scientific research. The DINI in Germany (DINI stands for the German Initiative for Information Networks, Deutsche Initiative für Netzwerkinformation) has set up a certification system for ePrint archives. The system takes into account functions such as author support, authenticity and data integrity, logs and statistics, and the service's stability. The gradual development of more formal standards for ePrints should make it possible to fulfill the promise that the ePrints model offers.

FROM ePRINTS TO INSTITUTIONAL REPOSITORIES

A newer impulse for scholarly communications is the movement to create institutional repositories. Institutional repositories aim at collecting, archiving, and providing access to the intellectual production of a single research institution. Whereas ePrint archives are usually built around one or more specific subject disciplines, institutional repositories address the same need at the level of individual research institutions. Indeed, the institutional repository is seen as a way to guarantee the collection, dissemination, and preservation of the institution's intellectual assets. Again, support for OAI-PMH is a common attribute of most institutional repository implementations.

Objectives of Institutional Repositories

While there is some overlap, a typical institutional repository has a different scope than does an ePrint archive in a number of ways, and also has a larger scope. It not only hosts the formats commonly found in ePrint archives (for example, journal article style document files), but often also hosts a variety of additional resource types and formats, including internal reports, thesis and dissertations, classroom lecture slides, student and faculty works-in-progress, student Web sites, research data sets, and any other kind of information resource which can be considered an intellectual asset of the institution. Between a new research initiative and a published article, there are many stages and expressions of work and innovation in progress that may warrant preservation and/or dissemination separate from the final result. Institutional repositories must take into account these varied forms of content.

Institutional repositories offer yet another economic model for open access. While the ePrints model places the burden for disseminating and preserving research literature at the domain level, and (as discussed below) open access journal projects frequently seek to push publication costs back on those who pay for or generate the research itself, the institutional repository model assumes that research institutions have the central role in the preservation and dissemination of their intellectual assets. Cliff Lynch, executive director of the Coalition for Networked Information (CNI), articulated this obligation in a 2003 article published in the *Bimonthly Report* of the Association of Research Libraries (ARL).

At the most basic and fundamental level, an institutional repository is a recognition that the intellectual life and scholarship of our universities will increasingly be represented, documented, and shared in digital form, and that a primary responsibility of our universities is to exercise stewardship over these riches: both to make them available and to preserve them. An institutional repository is the means by which our universities will address this responsibility both to the members of their communities and to the public. It is a new channel for structuring the university's contribution to the broader world, and as such invites policy and cultural reassessment of this relationship (Lynch 2003).

Viewed in this light, institutional repositories represent a new framework for institutional knowledge management as well as a new approach to scholarly communication.

In January 2004, a study (Ware 2004) was published by the Publisher and Library/Learning Solutions (PALS) group, a UK collaborative initiative between commercial UK publishers and the publicly funded *Joint Information Systems Committee* (JISC). In this work, Mark Ware reviewed forty-five institutional repositories. He found that their objectives were diverse: scholarly communication, education, digital publishing, collection management, long-term preservation, enhanced institutional prestige, knowledge management, and assessment of research work. Whether institutional repositories are well positioned to fulfill all of these mandates is still unclear, but the reasons given for setting up an institutional repository demonstrate the importance being placed on aggregating and managing information from all parts of universities and other research institutions.

The evolution of institutional repositories is being driven by a variety of agents and agencies, each with varying agendas. The DARE project (*Digital Academic Repositories*)[9] in the Netherlands encourages the creation of interoperable institutional repositories nationwide. High-level coordination at the national level of such an effort is evidence of the belief that education and the public good can be furthered through the proactive sharing of scholarly research results. Interoperability in this context—for example, by using OAI-PMH—is recognized as having a key role in supporting the creation of a national network of active and reliable stakeholders.

In the UK, the FAIR Program (Focus on Access to Institutional Resources) was launched in 2002 to investigate issues related to deposit and disclosure of institutional material, whether in cultural or in scientific institutions. The RoMEO Project (Rights MEtadata for Open archiving), initiated under the FAIR Program and now allied with the SHERPA Project (Securing a Hybrid Environment for Research Preservation and Access), was particularly focused on resolving the intellectual property rights issues, which have proven a major obstacle to the development of both institutional repositories and ePrint archives. By simultaneously lobbying publishers and making known the constraints specific publishers place on the deposit of preprints and post-prints in institutional repositories, Project RoMEO has encouraged publishers in

TABLE 3-1 Project RoMEO publisher color-coded categories.

Project RoMEO color code	Publisher policy on preprints and post-prints
Green	Author may deposit in institutional repository both pre- and post-print
Blue	Author may deposit in institutional repository post-print only
Yellow	Author may deposit in institutional repository preprint only
White	Archiving of publication in institutional repository not supported

Source: http://www.sherpa.ac.uk/romeoinfo.html#colours.

almost all disciplines to be more accepting of institutional repositories. A searchable database, known as the SHERPA/RoMEO database, detailing publisher policies pertaining to self-archiving, is available online.[10] The simple color-coded system this database uses for categorizing publisher policies regarding preprints and post-prints is shown in Table 3-1.

The SPARC Project (Scholarly Publishing and Academic Resources Coalition)[11] was initiated in 1998 by the ARL. Focused in particular on finding ways to slow the growth in prices paid by libraries for scholarly journals, SPARC is international in scope and (among other things) has taken a leadership role in encouraging the creation of institutional repositories (Crow 2002). Similarly, the Open Society Institute (2004), founded by George Soros and also international in scope, includes among its publications a technical guide for implementing institutional repositories (now in its third edition).

Accordingly, given the range of players involved and the mix of motivations, the objectives of institutional repository projects vary but in each instance should be clearly stated and must follow from the priorities defined by the institutions involved. Three major objectives should always be present in any institutional repository:

- archiving: preserving content;
- disseminating: ensuring better discoverability, allowing metadata sharing with other services, and supporting the efficient indexing of material; and
- stewardship: representing institutional assets and orienting users to institutional collections.

Implementation Details

Institutional repositories offer another way to support the implementation of new types of applications and tools that manage research activities, preserve research output, and facilitate the assessment and measurement of research results and worth. Since the institutional repositories movement has built upon the ePrint archives movement, the interoperability issue is typically dealt with in a similar way—thus Ware identified institutional repositories as simply another subgroup of OAI-compliant repositories. The technical framework is typically the same as for ePrint archives, and frequently the same software applications are used. Similarities are tempered by the differences in the motivation for institutional repositories and the organizations involved in promoting their evolution.

The types of content which are to be included in an institutional repository should be of major concern from the outset. From the earliest stages of a project, it is important to define a collection-development policy by setting the scope of the project and the conditions under which material will be included, considering quality, provenance, qualifications as an institutional intellectual asset, copyright, publishing stage, etc. Particularly important are policies for dealing with traditionally published items for which intellectual property rights have been assigned to someone other than the author. Some institutional repositories allow deposit of an item with restricted access for purposes of preservation only (that is, they provide a deposit option that precludes, temporarily or permanently, access to the item by end users via the institutional repository search interface). Technical aspects of content to be included—size range, file formats, and structural arrangement—must also be considered in setting a collection policy.

Once a collection policy is set, the technical infrastructure and anticipated workflows to feed the institutional repository can be considered. The technical infrastructure is chosen according to priorities and strategic requirements, considering who is going to contribute, their location (on or off campus), the types of material supported, accessibility constraints (client platforms, disabled users), interoperability requirements, data curation needs, preservation and archiving requirements, processing and indexing requirements, etc. Not all institutional repositories are expected to perform all possible functions. Most institutional repository models (although still not all) have grown to encompass the role of centralized preservation and long-term archiving.

With workflow and infrastructure determined, software application options then can be characterized and evaluated according to the features they offer and the functionality they support. Institutional repository applications most often differ in the type of content they support, their preservation features, the interoperability options supported (for example, whether both OAI-PMH and Z39.50 are included), the number of documents they have been tested with (scalability), their interfaces to upload and access documents, their collaborative work features, and functions included to manage intellectual property and access rights.

The success of an institutional repository and its ability to guarantee the preservation and dissemination of institutional intellectual assets are highly dependent on the amount and quality of contributions. Awareness among the institution's administrative and decision-making authorities, faculty, researchers, and students is a major concern for this type of project. Participation can be achieved through general solicitations, by presentations, and by contacting potential contributors directly or by contacting aggregators of institutional documents, such as the library, the university archives, or those in charge of maintaining an ePrint repository or other unofficial initiatives to preserve research results within a given department. Submission to an institutional repository can also be made a matter of policy. A few institutions have made deposits to the institutional repository mandatory for certain kinds of material. Librarians may be asked to serve as selectors and/or mediators of content submissions for their institution's repository.

Once implemented, an institutional repository system has to be maintained on an ongoing basis to ensure the quality of metadata, the transformability of content formats, and support for publication, access, collection, and validation of documents. The system also must be maintained to ensure the preservation of digital content, data integrity, migration/emulation processes, and the maintenance of adequate contextual information to ensure that content meaning is adequately preserved. The maintenance of the system should be accompanied by plans to build services that exploit collections, ensure usability and stewardship of content, and promote reuse of content in additional products and venues, such as in teaching.

OPEN ACCESS JOURNALS

Open access is understood to mean free access granted by authors to their research as published or otherwise made available on the Web. In practice, the open access movement has tended to promote both an alternative model of traditional scholarly journal publishing and new models of self-archiving individual papers directly to the Web (as typified by ePrint archives and institutional repositories). Open access journals are the more complete alternative to traditional journal publishing. Open access journals attempt to preserve the essential nature of traditional scholarly journal publishing, for example, by incorporating peer review, by colocating related articles under the umbrella of individual journal titles, and by giving papers published in high-quality open access journals some of the same prestige and validation publication in an established print journal gives.

The Advent of Open Access Journals

University libraries subscribe to a large number of journals in order to offer their researchers and students up-to-date information about domains of interest. They subscribe to journals in multiple formats, including both printed and online. In some disciplines, a relatively small number of publishers publish most scholarly journals and control the subscription prices for large pools of journals. While some publishers are not-for-profit, for example, learned societies, a few commercial publishers control the largest number of journals, particularly in the life and physical sciences. In 2006, for reasons of cost, it is impossible for even major university libraries to subscribe to all available journals of interest, especially in the scientific fields, where traditional journal subscription prices tend to be highest. In recent years, commercial publishers also have increased their numbers of scholarly journals by starting new titles and by buying journals published by other publishers and/or research institutions.

Each subscription can cost of thousands dollars annually. Increasingly, subscription costs depend on the institution size, making journals most expensive for the largest institutions, even though these are the same institutions contributing the largest share of the research being published. For large academic research libraries, journal subscriptions are the greatest component of library acquisition budgets. Conversely, university libraries are increasingly the major if not the only subscribers to some scholarly journals, which tends also to drive up per-subscription costs. At the same time, library budgets are growing little if at all in real dollars, and in some cases budgets are decreasing. As a consequence, institutions are increasingly squeezed financially. This is particularly the case in developing countries, where the impact from lost access to the latest research publications can have grave consequences. Access to academic and scientific information is an essential part of successful research.

A movement for open access journals has emerged in reaction to these difficulties. The open access journal movement begins from a premise that as research institutions fund researchers to perform the work published in scholarly journals, research institutions should be paying less, not more, for access to the published results of the research they have collectively funded. In the digital era, as self-publishing is becoming relatively easier to do, universities, research institutions, and funding agencies should be able to find a better economic model for publishing which allows greater access to research results for the same or lesser expenditure. Some institutions also denounce the market trend to increase inequality between rich and poor nations' access to science and research results, which tends to hamper the growth of vital research sectors in developing countries. While the cost of publishing peer-reviewed content is not insignificant, proponents of open access believe it can be done adequately online for much less than it has been done historically in print. They also suspect that academic universities in recent years have been victimized by pricing policies set by commercial publishers too focused on profits.

Scholarly journals aim at certifying the quality of research through the peer-review process and the broad dissemination of research results. The movement toward open access journals seeks to retain this function even while changing the economic model that supports it. As measured by the number of open access journal titles, the movement is having an impact. The Lund University Library in Sweden maintains an online directory of open access journals.[12] This directory listed 2,331 open access journal titles as of mid-2006. Several large initiatives have been launched to create open access journals as credible alternatives to existing journals, including BioMed Central, which publishes more than 100 journals in the area of biomedical research, and the Public Library of Science (PLoS), which launched *PLoS Biology* in October 2003 and *PLoS Medicine* in October 2004. (More recently the success of BioMed Central has led to the launch of PhysMath Central and Chemistry Central, hoping to do for domains of physics, mathematics, and chemistry what BioMed Central has done for biomedicine.) The impact in other ways is more difficult to quantify; however, early indications as measured by such metrics as cross-citations (impact factors) are that open access journals can have at least as much impact as traditional journals (Testa and McVeigh 2004).

In order to offer genuine alternatives to traditional journals, open access journals must implement proper peer-review processes and guarantee a similar level of credibility in terms of content quality. They also must ensure a comparable or higher level of dissemination. Finally, they must commit to a model for preserving the articles published. In the print realm, this is a role undertaken not by publishers but by libraries. However, this model has broken down with digital content, which publishers typically prefer to retain on their Web sites. Various replacement approaches are being tried. For several years, Elsevier has allowed the Royal Library of the Netherlands to archive a copy of its content. Other approaches, including some in which libraries retain a role in the preservation model, are being investigated (for example, the LOCKSS, or Lots of Copies Keep Stuff Safe Initiative[13]). With paper format journals, multiple subscriptions by major libraries have ensured availability of copies for posterity, but an equivalent safety net for digital material is not yet in place. Some open access journals grant authors the right to self-archive the final versions of their articles as a way to shift the preservation role to ePrint archives and/or institutional repositories. PLoS is recognizing the need to plan for a trusted repository in the future.

Ultimately, the open access journal movement seeks to reverse the state of the market by proposing that research institutions, funding agencies, and authors rather than subscribers pay directly for the peer-review process and the publication of articles, either by taking on the publishing role directly or by soliciting per-article fees paid by authors or authors' institutions at the time of submission and/or publication. (Even when collected from authors, the assumption is that research institutions and/or grant-funding agencies ultimately would pay article submission and publication fees.) By paying all costs up front, the journal's content can be made freely accessible on the Web when published. This enables developing countries to access research results and eliminates or reduces the intermediary role of traditional, subscription-based publishers in the publication of results from scholarly research.

Key Initiatives and Milestones

Some of those most involved in the implementation of open access journals have direct or indirect ties to the ePrints and/or institutional repository communities. This demonstrates the degree of overlap in interests and objectives of the ePrints, institutional repository, and open access journal communities. All three are trying to come to grips with new, more economical modes of scholarly communication, and to this point at least, there has been significant cooperation among and between the parties involved.

The primary intent of the SPARC initiative, for example, a higher priority than its encouragement of institutional repositories as mentioned above, is to advocate for and partner in the creation and promulgation of open access and low-cost alternative scholarly journals. Originated in the United States by the

ARL, SPARC quickly became international in scope, joining in 2001 with the Ligue des Bibliothèques Européennes de Recherche (LIBER, an association of the major research libraries of Europe)[14] to announce the creation of SPARC-Europe, a companion initiative based in Oxford, England, to pursue SPARC objectives in Europe. By 2006, the combined membership of SPARC and SPARC-Europe had topped more than 300 institutions worldwide. Together, SPARC and SPARC-Europe aim to find a way around the continuing increase in prices of scientific journals by encouraging publications with zero or moderate subscription costs and by encouraging the creation of information aggregations and portals serving specific communities.

In late 2001, stakeholders in the open access movement met in Budapest to coordinate their efforts. From this meeting, the Budapest Open Access Initiative (BOAI) was launched to develop free access to scientific literature through a two-pronged strategy, focusing first on the creation of a digital framework to disseminate research results, and second on the creation of new open access journals. With regard to the first objective, the BOAI framework blends features of ePrints and open access journal initiatives by encouraging both self-archiving and open access journal publishing. The BOAI framework also explicitly encourages the development of tools which both enable researchers to easily contribute to ePrint archives and also to comply with the OAI-PMH and related recommended implementation guidelines. To fulfill the second objective, the BOAI has enlisted support for the creation of open access journals from the Open Society Institute, a network of foundations funded by the billionaire George Soros which act in the fields of government, education, health, etc., in more than fifty countries. Early in 2002, a defining declaration was published on the Web by the BOAI. By the end of 2006, there were more than 4,600 signatories to the declaration.[15] The BOAI declaration includes an argument that open access follows logically from the tradition and mission of academia.

> An old tradition and a new technology have converged to make possible an unprecedented public good. The old tradition is the willingness of scientists and scholars to publish the fruits of their research in scholarly journals without payment, for the sake of inquiry and knowledge. The new technology is the Internet. The public good they make possible is the worldwide electronic distribution of the peer-reviewed journal literature and completely free and unrestricted access to it by all scientists, scholars, teachers, students, and other curious minds. Removing access barriers to this literature will accelerate research, enrich education, share the learning of the rich with the poor and the poor with the rich, make this literature as useful as it can be, and lay the foundation for uniting humanity in a common intellectual conversation and quest for knowledge.[16]

The BOAI seeks to modify the scholarly publishing model in the long term. By including ePrint repositories as a part of its strategy for revamping scholarly communication, it is moving the role of ePrints repositories from self-archiving to "self-publishing." This model seeks to leverage the Web as a new medium for publishing scholarly literature and assumes a place in the scholarly publishing model for article-by-article publication without peer-review.

In order to promote the alternative economic model promised by open access journals for scholarly literature, the BOAI has published the *Open Access Journal Business Guides*.[17] Separately, PALS[18] has published a study on "charging mechanisms" to assess impacts to publishers when they switch to an alternative model based on authors or funding agencies paying for the publication of research articles.

The Bethesda Statement[19] was issued in June 2003 following a meeting held in Bethesda, Maryland, in April of that year on the subject of open access in the domain of biomedical research. Participants came from research institutions, funding agencies, libraries, publishers, and scientific societies. The Bethesda Statement was published on the Web in the hope of stimulating the biomedical research community to embrace open access sooner and more widely. The Statement proposes actionable principles for practitioners to adopt and defines relevant terms. It also includes a functional definition of open access publications.

> An Open Access Publication is one that meets the following two conditions:
>
> The author(s) and copyright holder(s) grant(s) to all users a free, irrevocable, worldwide, perpetual right of access to, and a license to copy, use, distribute, transmit, and display the work publicly and to make and distribute derivative works, in any digital medium, for any responsible purpose, subject to proper attribution of authorship, as well as the right to make small numbers of printed copies for their personal use.
>
> A complete version of the work and all supplemental materials, including a copy of the permission as stated above, in a suitable standard electronic format, is deposited immediately upon initial publication in at least one online repository that is supported by an academic institution, scholarly society, government agency, or other well-established organization that seeks to enable open access, unrestricted distribution, interoperability, and long-term archiving (for the biomedical sciences, PubMed Central is such a repository).[20]

While a range of funding agencies and political entities have committed to the development of open access journals, it has been more difficult to convince the best and most influential authors in major academic domains to contribute to open access journals (thereby ensuring recognition of open access journals as a quality alternative model for dissemination of research results). To help encourage their faculties and staffs in this direction, a large number of major research institutes in Europe signed the Berlin Declaration[21] in October 2003. This document stipulates that signatories have defined a common understanding of open access publishing by establishing that "the author(s) and right holder(s) of such contributions grant(s) to all users a free, irrevocable, worldwide, right of access to, and a license to copy, use, distribute, transmit, and display the work publicly and to make and distribute derivative works, in any digital medium for any responsible purpose, subject to proper attribution of authorship [...]." Signatories also commit to encourage their researchers to publish in open access journals and contribute to ePrint and institutional repositories and to take those contributions into account in their assessments of researchers and research results. Finally, signatories commit to contribute to the development of the technical tools (for example, OAI-PMH) supporting open access initiatives. The Berlin Declaration has been signed by institutes from Germany, France, Italy, Hungary, Norway, Spain, Belgium, Austria, Greece, Estonia, China, India, and Egypt, as well as European and international organizations such as SPARC and the Open Society Institute.

Open access has also stimulated interest at the governmental level. In the United States, Minnesota Congressman Martin Sabo offered a bill in 2003 calling for the furtherance of open access to scientific literature and underlining the necessity to make available to the public the results of publicly funded research. On January 30, 2004, in Paris, the "Declaration on access to research data from public funding"[22] was adopted by the Organization for Economic Co-operation and Development (OECD) ministers to promote open access for publicly funded research. This was followed in December 2006 by a favorable statement on open access issued by the European Research Council and in January 2007 by a communication on the importance of access to scientific information in the digital age issued by the European Commission. While these initiatives have had limited success to date, open access proponents are encouraged that the issues are gaining the attention of legislators and ministers in the public sector.

THE STATE OF OPEN ACCESS AT THE END OF 2006

ePrint archives, institutional repositories, and open access journals are intended to facilitate faster, broader, and, according to some, better dissemination of scholarly research results. Early experience with open access journals suggests that in some disciplines, their impact can be at least as great as traditional, subscriber-supported journals (Testa and McVeigh 2004). ePrint archives and institutional repositories also have been seen to affect positively the use of research in at least some disciplines (for example, Schwarz and Kennicutt 2004). Certainly the sheer number of open access resources has grown rapidly. The E-Print Network, by no means comprehensive, claims to track more than 14,000 Web sites containing ePrints and to index in aggregate more than one million ePrint documents.[23] ROAR (the Registry of Open Access Repositories)[24] provides brief descriptions and record counts for more than 700 open access repositories, the vast majority of which are OAI-PMH compliant.

Institutional repositories, and to a lesser extent ePrint archives, by dealing with broader ranges of material than traditional publishers (for example, theses, preprints, learning materials, data sets, student work, research project planning and progress reports, and other forms of gray literature), facilitate dissemination of more up-to-date research and research still in progress. This provides an opportunity not just to supplant traditional scholarly publishing (an objective of open access journals), but also to modify the model of what is disseminated and when. This could affect the way research is conducted and ultimately impact the results of scholarly research.

Publishers meanwhile are seeking to find their place in this environment. Under pressure from initiatives like Project RoMEO, a number of publishers now offer authors at least some preprint and/or post-print options. In May 2004, one of the largest, Elsevier, announced a modification in its policy to allow authors to self-archive their final papers (thus peer-reviewed) on their institutional repository and to post it on their personal Web site. Some traditional publishers are actively transitioning to hybrid or "sponsored-article" models that enable authors to pay individually to make a specific article open access from within an otherwise closed journal issue.

However, obstacles remain. For instance, the greatest difficulties encountered in setting up institutional repositories relate to the necessity to ensure contributions from teachers, researchers, students, and sometimes administrative staff. A representative range of researchers' concerns was identified in a breakout session chaired by David Prossner (of SPARC Europe) during OAI3: CERN Workshop on Innovations in Scholarly Communication (February 2004).

- Researchers are not willing to take on additional work.
- Copyright issues are not clearly identified and explained.
- Papers freely available before publication can be plagiarized.
- Researchers can publish their articles on their own Web sites. They do not perceive any additional discoverability by being included in an ePrint or institutional repository compared to any classic search engine.
- Papers freely available before publication might not be published commercially.
- Open access journals and ePrint repositories might hinder learned societies.
- A perceived lack of quality control exists for ePrint repositories, open access journals, and institutional repositories.

OAI-PMH IS NOT JUST FOR OPEN ACCESS

Open access journals, ePrint archives, and institutional repositories offer alternative models for access to and dissemination of scientific information, transferring the cost to different hands. Central to these alternative economic models is the predicate that open access can translate directly into broader access. Interoperability thus becomes not an afterthought for open access repositories, but rather an essential prerequisite. OAI-PMH, as a means to achieve greater interoperability and thereby greater visibility for repository contents, becomes an enabling protocol.

However, while OAI-PMH has played a major role in all parts of the open access movement, OAI-PMH as a protocol is itself neutral with regard to open access. OAI-PMH must be seen as a tool, not as an embodiment of policy. As a tool, OAI-PMH helps to transform archiving, scholarly communication, and publishing models in the digital world, but does not itself force scholarly communications one way or another regarding open access.

OAI-PMH is designed to create an interoperability framework for repositories and to change how content is archived and published on the Web. The use of OAI-PMH has expanded from initial use with open access scholarly literature to use with other types of resources, including even subscriber-based, commercially published journal literature. It is a technical framework and is maintained independently from the political and economic issues dealt with in the context of open access and self- and institutional-archiving movements.

OPEN ACCESS TECHNICAL IMPLEMENTATIONS

Functionalities of content-management systems designed for scholarly communication and archiving are still being investigated. However, most software available in this domain as of 2006 can be classified as follows:

- ePrint servers are facilities for self-archiving submission process, metadata creation, indexing, search/retrieval functionalities, subject classification, OAI data provider services, and sometimes long-term archiving.
- Open access journal publication applications add facilities for online peer review and organizing of articles within virtual online journal titles.
- Institutional repositories have the same applications as for ePrint servers, plus additional disclosure and access-rights facilities, more flexible deposit options and formats, workflow management, overall broader material handling, and additional use and deposit statistics.
- Aggregation services gather items from multiple institutional repositories or ePrint archives, provide integrated services, and sometimes build new constructs, such as learning modules or composite e-books. They represent a major challenge in terms of rights.

Open source software applications have been developed to support open access implementations, essentially content-management systems with features that make them particularly convenient and adapted to the management of research output. Most include some or all of the following features:

- Archiving features, including support for preservation processes, for example, preservation metadata, data integrity checking, and format migration.
- Versioning features. (Versioning issues are particularly important for digital content since the documents may be modified over time. The whole issue of how to reliably cite a particular version of a paper contained in an ePrint or institutional repository is a major concern.)
- Support for vetting and/or reviewing processes. (Not only peer review, but just vetting of appropriateness of documents deposited and completeness/correctness of the metadata provided.)

- Authentication features. (For institutional repositories particularly, some of the documents might not be available to everyone. Applications must handle contributor, editor, and end-user authentication, authorization, and access control.)
- Search-and-discovery functionalities.
- Usability features (for contributors, editors, and, ultimately, consumers).
- Support for a range of metadata and metadata formats (not only descriptive metadata, but also structural, administrative, and preservation metadata).
- Support for a range of content object formats supported. (With institutional repositories, the potential number of document types to include in repositories has grown. Support for Unicode is also a major discriminator.)

Generally, the difference between applications lies in the validation workflow, long-term preservation functionalities, the maintenance granted to creators, and the orientation toward either self-archiving, dissemination, or collection management and preservation. The following is a list of selected major open access software applications:

- **ePrints**: The ePrints application was created by the University of Southampton in 2000. It is written in Perl. It is very widespread (its usage is tracked by ROAR). The ePrint software[25] is OAI-PMH compliant and comes with extensive documentation on how to implement an archive, not only in technical terms, but also referring to political and content-related issues.
- **DSpace**: DSpace[26] was released in 2002 as a joint initiative of Hewlett Packard and the Massachusetts Institute of Technology. It is written in Java and is OAI-PMH compliant. As with ePrints application, there are a large number of installations, especially in institutional repository market segments. DSpace handles document versioning and includes an identification system based on the Corporation for National Research Initiatives' Handles System®, a general purpose distributed information system that supports the creation, maintenance, and resolution of persistent identifiers for digital resources; DOIs rely on Handles. Though used heavily for institutional repositories, it is not itself a full and complete long-term preservation solution.
- **Greenstone**: Greenstone[27] was created by the University of Waikato in New Zealand with some funding from UNESCO. It is available in five languages: English, French, Spanish, Russian, and Kazakh. It is written in Perl and C++. Newest versions support OAI-PMH. Project Gutenberg, a global effort to digitize and distribute digital editions of literature, uses Greenstone.
- **CDS Invenio**: CDS Invenio,[28] previously known as CDSware, was created by the CERN and is related also to CERN's Indico application. CDS Invenio handles MARC 21 metadata, is written in PHP and Perl, and is OAI compliant. CERN uses it to handle 620,000 bibliographic records and 250,000 full-text documents. It was conceived for large-scale repositories of heterogeneous content, including multimedia and images.
- **FEDORA**: FEDORA (Flexible Extensible Digital Object and Repository Architecture)[29] was created by the University of Virginia and Cornell University and is a digital object repository management system which aims at handling all types of documents. It must be customized for specific use, such as to be an ePrint server. It deals with document versioning and includes code for handling OAI-PMH. Most recent versions include performance enhancements to support larger repositories.

- **ARNO**: ARNO (Academic Research in the Netherlands Online)[30] was created in 2003 by the University of Amsterdam, the University of Tilburg, and the University of Twente. ARNO is written in Perl. It handles peer-reviewing processes. It is made for the centralized creation of content and for end-user submission.
- **I-Tor**: I-Tor[31] was created in 2002 by the Netherlands Institute for Scientific Information services. It is written in Java and is oriented toward collection management for static documents. It can be used to publish documents from a wide variety of databases and file systems. It can harvest data directly from a researcher's personal Web site.
- **PKP**: PKP (Public Knowledge Project)[32] is a suite of software applications stemming from a project begun in 1998 by John Willinsky at the University of British Columbia in Canada. PKP includes an open-access journal application (OJS), an open-access conference application (OCS), and, most recently, an OAI-PMH-compliant harvesting application. Both OJS and OCS support an extensive range of online review and editing features and are OAI-PMH compliant. OJS even supports a subscription model that allows content to be embargoed from non-subscribers for a fixed period of time.

These systems have diverse goals. All encourage wide access to scholarly literature and more generally to intellectual content created in the scope of publicly funded research.

QUESTIONS AND TOPICS FOR DISCUSSION

1. Why would a researcher choose to publish in an open access journal? Why might he or she not want to do so? Ask the same questions regarding the deposit of research outputs in an ePrint archive or institutional repository.
2. What are the three economic models for scholarly communications inherent in the various forms of open access discussed in this chapter? Argue in favor of one economic model over the other two.
3. In what ways does OAI-PMH help further the objectives of the open access scholarly communication models discussed in this chapter?
4. What software application features are more important for an institutional repository than for an ePrints archive and vice versa?

SUGGESTIONS FOR EXERCISES

1. Find an article of interest related to digital libraries which is available in either an ePrints archive or institutional repository. Is it (or a version) available also in a subscriber-based, for-fee publication? If so, would it have been easier to find the free or the for-fee copy?
2. Select two of the open access software applications described above and visit their Web sites to learn more about each. Rank the applications as to their suitability for an ePrint archive. Rank them as to their suitability for an open access journal implementation.
3. Visit at least two institutional repository sites and two scientific or cultural heritage ePrint archives. Discuss the differences in policy, interface design, and the metadata used.

NOTES

1. http://www.arxiv.org/.
2. E-LIS: E-prints in Library and Information Science (home page), http://eprints.rclis.org/.
3. http://www.eprints.org/software.
4. http://software.eprints.org/handbook/.
5. Implementation Guidelines for the Open Archives Initiative Protocol for Metadata Harvesting: XML Schema to describe content and policies of repositories in the e-print community. Document Version 2003/11/21T19:15:00Z, http://www.openarchives.org/OAI/2.0/guidelines-eprints.htm.
6. http://www.scirus.com/srsapp/.
7. http://www.citebase.org/.
8. http://www.ercim.org/cyclades/.
9. http://www.darenet.nl/en/toon.
10. http://www.sherpa.ac.uk/romeo.php.
11. http://www.arl.org/sparc/home/index.asp?page=0.
12. http://www.doaj.org.
13. http://www.lockss.org/lockss/Home.
14. http://www2.kb.dk/liber/.
15. http://www.soros.org/openaccess/read.shtml.
16. Ibid.
17. http://www.soros.org/openaccess/oajguides/index.shtml.
18. http://www.palsgroup.org.uk/.
19. http://www.earlham.edu/~peters/fos/bethesda.htm.
20. Ibid.
21. http://www.zim.mpg.de/openaccess-berlin/berlindeclaration.html.
22. http://www.oecd.org/document/0,2340,en_2649_34487_25998799_1_1_1_1,00.html.
23. http://eprints.osti.gov/about.html.
24. http://archives.eprints.org/.
25. http://www.eprints.org/software.
26. http://www.dspace.org/.
27. http://www.greenstone.org/.
28. http://cdsware.cern.ch/.
29. http://www.fedora.info/.
30. http://www.uba.uva.nl/arno.
31. http://www.i-tor.org/en/.
32. http://www.pkp.ubc.ca/.

REFERENCES

Crow, Raym. 2002. *SPARC Institutional Repository Checklist and Resource Guide*. Scholarly Publishing and Academic Resources Coalition, Association of Research Libraries, http://www.arl.org/sparc/IR/IR_Guide.html.

Lynch, Clifford. 2003. Institutional Repositories: Essential Infrastructure for Scholarship in the Digital Age. *ARL Bimonthly Report* 226 (February), 1–7, http://www.arl.org/newsltr/226/ir.html.

Open Society Institute. 2004. *A Guide to Institutional Repository Software*, 3rd edition. Budapest Open Access Initiative, http://www.soros.org/openaccess/software/.

Schwarz, G. J., and R. C. Kennicutt. 2004. Demographic and Citation Trends in Astrophysical Journal Papers and Preprints. *Bulletin of the American Astronomical Society* 36 (5): 1,654–1,663, http://arxiv.org/abs/astro-ph/0411275.

Simons, Gary, and Steven Bird. 2003. Building an Open Languages Archive Community on the OAI Foundation. *Library Hi Tech* 21 (3): 210–218.

Testa, J., and M. E. McVeigh. 2004. *The Impact of Open Access Journals: A Citation Study from Thomson ISI*. Philadelphia, PA: The Thomson Corporation, http://www.isinet.com/media/presentrep/acropdf/impact-oa-journals.pdf.

Ware, Mark. 2004. *Pathfinder Research on Web-based Repositories*. Publisher and Library/Learning Solutions (PALS), http://www.palsgroup.org.uk/.

Warner, Simeon. 2003. E-Prints and the Open Archives Initiative. *Library Hi Tech* 21 (3): 151–158.

PART II

Protocol Implementation

CHAPTER 4

Technical Details of the Protocol

OAI-PMH expresses the technical obligations of both parties involved in a metadata-harvesting transaction. OAI-PMH describes explicitly and in detail the requests that an OAI service provider, the harvesting agent, may make of an OAI data provider, the supplier of metadata being harvested. The protocol also prescribes the acceptable responses that a conforming OAI data provider is allowed to make or must make in response to both valid and invalid OAI-PMH requests. It is important to appreciate that the protocol itself is concerned only with the technical and syntactical details of the interaction between the service provider and the data provider. With only one exception—the mandate to use at least Dublin Core (DC) alone or in addition to other metadata formats—OAI-PMH does not address the underlying metadata semantics and values being disseminated by the data provider, nor does it address what the service provider might do with harvested metadata.

These latter issues are important to consider when planning an OAI-PMH implementation, and will be discussed more extensively in chapters 6 through 8. First, however, this chapter examines the technical rules and regulations of the harvesting process itself, defining the key concepts and terms used in the OAI-PMH 2.0 specification,[1] summarizing protocol semantics and syntax, and exploring how OAI-PMH approaches error management and the management of transaction states and flow control. The implications of protocol technical requirements for would-be data providers and the range of technical competencies required to implement an OAI data provider correctly are addressed in chapter 5.

KEY CONCEPTS, TERMS, AND DEFINITIONS

There are several underlying concepts that are helpful in understanding how OAI-PMH works. To begin with, the protocol distinguishes between the descriptive metadata, that with which OAI-PMH is primarily concerned, and the resource being described. As defined by the protocol (paraphrasing), a resource is the object or "stuff" that a metadata item contained in an OAI data provider repository describes. Where the resources are stored, who maintains and controls access to them, how and whether they may be downloaded, and how they are to be presented to users are all outside the scope of the protocol, although all or some of this information may be expressed in metadata records shared using OAI-PMH.

OAI-PMH also carefully defines the roles of the entities involved in a metadata harvest transaction. In OAI-PMH terms, a conforming data provider repository holds metadata items, is accessible over the Internet, and responds to OAI-PMH requests as defined in the protocol and as issued by a conforming metadata harvester implementation. In OAI-PMH, a metadata harvester is defined as any client application (that is, computer program) that issues correct and valid OAI-PMH requests as defined in the protocol. As envisioned by OAI-PMH, metadata harvesters are operated by OAI service providers in order to collect metadata from OAI data providers.

OAI-PMH also distinguishes between the metadata items held in an OAI data provider repository and the metadata records disseminated by that data provider. OAI metadata items are entities that contain metadata describing an object. OAI-PMH defines a metadata item as containing the full set of metadata available to a data provider describing a specific resource. Each data provider has flexibility in defining the metadata properties needed to describe its resources and in deciding the format and structure of metadata items within an OAI data provider repository. Metadata items comprise the contents of an OAI data provider repository. Metadata records are metadata items which have been transformed for dissemination as structured XML records conforming to predefined metadata formats. Metadata records may contain the entirety of the information contained in the original metadata item, or may contain only a subset of that information, depending on the scope and capacity of the metadata format chosen for expressing the metadata record.

An OAI data provider must select simple DC as one of its metadata formats. The data provider must disseminate all metadata items in a repository in at least simple DC. It may optionally also disseminate all or selected metadata items in additional metadata formats. These may be community-standard metadata formats; for example, U.S. MARC 21, qualified DC, MODS (Metadata Object Description Schema),[2] CDWA-Lite (based on the Categories for the Description of Works of Art),[3] or an OAI data provider may make up its own metadata formats. Each metadata format used by a data provider must have a name or label, known in the terminology of the protocol as the `metadataPrefix`. The `metadataPrefix` for simple DC is predefined by the protocol as `oai_dc`. Other `metadataPrefixes` are defined by each OAI data provider and need only be unique and meaningful in the context of the defining data provider repository. Each metadata format must conform with and be explicitly linked to a publicly available XML schema. OAI-PMH includes the XML schema for the `oai_dc` metadata format. This schema imports schema elements from the Dublin Core Metadata Initiative (as described in chapter 2).

Each metadata item in an OAI-PMH repository has a unique and persistent OAI `identifier` that unambiguously identifies the metadata item within the OAI data provider repository. Syntactically, each OAI `identifier` must follow the grammar specified for Uniform Resource Identifiers (URIs, see Berners-Lee et al. 1998). The ubiquitous Uniform Resource Locator (URL) used on the Web is another example of a class of identifiers that employ URI grammar for their syntax. Each OAI metadata item `identifier` must be unique across at least the OAI data provider repository that contains the item. OAI `identifiers` must be persistent. An OAI metadata item `identifier` may not change over time. OAI `identifiers` may not be reassigned at a later time to another metadata item in the repository (that is, a metadata item describing a different resource), even if the original metadata item and associated resource are deleted. (While the only formal requirement in the protocol as to the format of OAI metadata item `identifiers` is that they conform to the URI specification, OAI maintains a recommended implementation guideline for the format of OAI identifiers.[4] This guideline provides additional suggestions regarding the `identifier` format and a scheme for ensuring the global uniqueness of a data provider's OAI `identifiers`.)

The distinction between metadata items and metadata records is important in the OAI-PMH universe. The metadata item represents the complete set of all descriptive properties available in the OAI data provider repository to describe a particular resource. A metadata item does not have to be expressed in XML. It does not have to conform to a publicly available XML schema. (It may, but it is not required.) A metadata record, on the other hand, is a valid XML instantiation of a particular metadata item in a specific, named metadata format. A metadata record might include only a subset of the information included in the corresponding metadata item. From a protocol perspective, metadata items are conceptual (that is, virtual) constructs wholly internal to an OAI data provider application. Metadata items may exist only as rows in a database, as plain-text format metadata files on a file server, or as parts of larger files (for example, the collection of HTML `<meta>` elements within a page on a Web server). Metadata records are what are disseminated, harvested, and then aggregated by OAI service providers. Because a metadata item can be disseminated in more than one metadata format, this means that there may be multiple OAI metadata records, each in a different metadata format, associated with a single OAI metadata item maintained in a repository. The distinction OAI-PMH makes between metadata items and metadata records allows for this without confusion or ambiguity.

OAI-PMH anticipates that the contents of both metadata items and metadata records may change over time. Depending on how a given metadata item is transformed into a specific metadata format for dissemination, it is possible for an OAI metadata record to change independently of its associated OAI metadata item, and vice versa.

Consider modifying a metadata item in a library's OAI data provider repository by altering a single descriptive property, one that is not used when disseminating the metadata item in simple DC format (that is, the property being altered does not map to any of the fifteen DC elements listed in Table 2-1). The OAI metadata item has changed, but the simple DC format metadata record disseminated from the item has not changed. (Other metadata records disseminated from the item in metadata formats that do incorporate the altered property will be changed.)

Or consider changing the way specific metadata properties are mapped to simple DC—for example, a metadata item property value previously mapped to the DC element "source" is now mapped to the DC element "relation." In such an instance, the metadata item remains unchanged, but the associated metadata record in simple DC format is altered (because of the change in how the item is transformed to simple DC format for dissemination).

Knowing when a metadata record last changed supports *selective harvesting* (discussed below) and allows service providers to track multiple versions or editions of metadata records. Since OAI-PMH is concerned with harvesting metadata records (not items), the protocol requires only that each OAI metadata record must have associated with it an OAI `datestamp` which indicates when the metadata record last changed. (Knowing when the metadata item last changed is not necessary for proper functioning of the protocol. It is required information for correct internal functioning of an OAI data provider, but that is outside the scope of the protocol itself.)

OAI-PMH specifies that data providers must express OAI metadata record `datestamps` in a consistent date-time granularity for all records contained in a particular repository. Allowed granularities are day (format YYYY-MM-DD) and second (format YYYY-MM-DDThh:mm:ssZ, where the hour value is between 00 and 23 inclusive). An example of a day granularity `datestamp` would be 2006-10-08 (that is, October 8, 2006). An example of a second granularity `datestamp` would be 2006-06-22T17:11:21Z (that is, 5:11 and 21 seconds in the afternoon on June 22, 2006). In both cases the `datestamp` must be provided in Coordinated Universal Time (UTC, synonymous for our purposes with Greenwich Mean Time and Zulu time) rather than in the local time zone of the data provider repository. This requirement ensures that there is no ambiguity worldwide about when an OAI metadata record was last altered.

Table 4-1 summarizes the key terms defined and discussed above. By meticulously defining the meaning of and requirements for OAI metadata items, `identifiers`, metadata records, `metadataPrefixes`, and `datestamps`, OAI-PMH is able to declare that a metadata record from a given OAI data provider repository is uniquely and unambiguously identified by the combination of its associated OAI metadata item `identifier`, the `metadataPrefix` of the record, and the `datestamp` of the record. This definitive ability to uniquely identify the version of a harvested metadata record allows multiple different service providers to determine if they have all harvested the same version of the same metadata record from a given data provider.

Two other important OAI-PMH concepts are worth mentioning at this stage—*OAI sets* and *OAI deleted records policy*. In the context of OAI-PMH, sets

TABLE 4-1 The building blocks of an OAI-PMH transaction defined.

Term	Meaning in context of OAI-PMH
Resource	The information object of interest; the "stuff" described by a *metadata item*.
Metadata item	All the metadata held in the repository about a given *resource*; may be a virtual construct only.
OAI identifier	The persistent identifier by which the *metadata item* may be referenced. The *OAI identifier* must be unique at least within the repository; properly constructed, it is globally unique.
Metadata record	A dissemination of the *metadata item* in a particular metadata format and at a particular point in time; a *metadata record* is uniquely defined by its *identifier*, *metadata prefix*, and *datestamp*.
metadataPrefix	A label for the format of a *metadata record*; the "oai_dc" *metadata prefix* must be supported by all repositories. All other *metadata prefixes* should be assumed to be repository specific.
OAI datestamp	The UTC date and optionally the time of day when a *metadata record* was last modified; this value changes when the underlying *metadata item* changes and also when the mapping of the *metadata item* to *metadata record* in the metadata format of the *metadata record* changes.
datestamp granularity	There are two allowed granularities for *OAI datestamps*: YYYY-MM-DD (that is, day granularity) and YYYY-MM-DDThh:mm:ssZ (seconds granularity).

exist as a way for a metadata repository to subdivide or otherwise organize the collection of metadata items it contains. The reason for sets in OAI-PMH is to facilitate selective harvesting of only a portion of a repository's metadata. As described below, a metadata harvester can optionally request dissemination of only one set of items in a repository containing multiple OAI sets. However, beyond that implication, the meaning of sets in OAI-PMH is intentionally vague. A repository can contain any number of sets. OAI sets can be arranged in a hierarchical structure (that is, with subsets and parent sets) or in a flat, no-hierarchy structure. Sets can be mutually exclusive or can overlap. Multiple arrangements of sets are allowed in a single repository. Even when sets are used, not all metadata items in a repository need to belong to any set. Any arrangement of sets that makes sense to the data provider can be used. The set or sets of which a metadata item is a member can even change over time. Nonetheless, the concept of OAI sets can be powerful and useful when used purposefully.

OAI-PMH also requires that data providers follow a consistent policy regarding the treatment of any and all metadata records deleted from a repository over time. As mentioned above, an OAI `identifier` associated with a deleted item cannot be reused. This is a mandatory requirement and is not optional. Obviously, when a metadata item has been deleted from a repository, all associated metadata records, that is, all disseminations of that item previously available for harvest, regardless of metadata format, also are deleted. Or, a data provider can delete a previously available metadata record in one particular metadata format without deleting the associated metadata item simply by discontinuing the repository function that transforms that metadata item to the particular metadata format. (Other records in different formats associated with the metadata item will still exist.) Either way, the end result for a service provider is that a metadata record previously available for harvest suddenly is no longer available. (OAI-PMH does not preclude un-deleting a metadata record at a future point in time.) Data providers must adhere to one of three policies for tracking deleted metadata records, but it is their option which of the three policies to follow, as long as they follow one and only one policy consistently for all records disseminated by their repository. The policies are designated in OAI-PMH as:

- `no`—meaning the repository does not report to metadata harvesters any information about records it has previously deleted, not even that the records once existed;
- `persistent`—meaning the repository will report records as being deleted and will continue to do so for as long as the repository is active; and
- `transient`—meaning the repository will report records as being deleted and will continue to do so for an arbitrary period of time, but likely not for as long as the repository is active.

If implementing a `persistent` or `transient` deleted-record policy, the data provider must track not only the `identifier` and format associated with the record that has been deleted, but also when the deletion occurred. This becomes the deleted OAI record `datestamp` value. Which policy an OAI data provider chooses to implement has implications for metadata harvesters. If the policy followed by a data provider is `no` or `transient`, then the metadata harvester cannot count on knowing when a metadata record has been deleted from the repository, that is, the metadata harvester may not know for sure when a metadata record in its aggregation has gone stale.

VERBS AND ARGUMENTS USED IN OAI-PMH REQUESTS

OAI-PMH defines six *OAI verbs* that can be used when harvesting metadata. The list is not extensible. OAI verbs are used by metadata harvesters to request information from data providers. A valid OAI request made by a service provider must contain one and only one of these six verbs. The six verbs are shown in Figure 4-1.

Each OAI verb has a distinctive meaning and purpose. The `Identify` and `ListSets` verbs solicit information pertaining to the repository as a whole. `Identify` is used by a metadata harvester to solicit general information about a data provider repository and its policies. In response to an `Identify` OAI request, the data provider tells the service provider about itself, giving the human-readable name of the repository, the e-mail address(es) of the repository administrator(s), the version of OAI-PMH implemented by the repository, and the `datestamp` value of the record in the repository having the earliest `datestamp`. In response to an `Identify`

FIGURE 4-1   The six OAI-PMH verbs and a depiction of how OAI-PMH works.

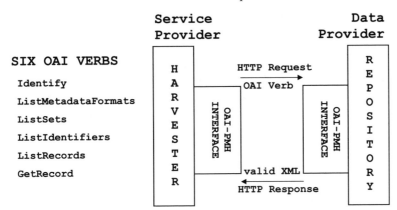

verb request, the repository must also declare its deleted-record-tracking policy and `datestamp` granularity. Optionally, the data provider may give additional information about the repository by including one or more `<description>` nodes. These nodes can contain any valid XML (that is, in a format and structure conforming to a publicly available XML schema).

The `ListSets` verb is used to solicit a listing of all sets in a repository. For each set, the data provider must provide both a `setSpec` and a `set-Name`. The `setSpec` must be unique within that repository. There are also special rules used in constructing a `setSpec` value to show hierarchical relationships between sets (if such relationships exist). The `setSpec` is used in certain other OAI-PMH requests to designate which set a metadata harvester wishes to harvest. The `setName` is the human-readable name of the set. Optionally, a data provider may elaborate by including a `<setDescription>` node. This node can contain any valid XML. If a `ListSets` verb request is made of a repository not organized into sets, the data provider will return what is technically classed as an OAI-PMH error message indicating that sets are not supported by the repository.

`ListMetadataFormats` can be used to solicit information pertaining to the entire repository, that is, a list of all metadata formats used by the repository (even if a format is used only for a single record), or it can be used to solicit information about just one metadata item. When used in the latter fashion, `ListMetadataFormats` returns all the metadata formats in which a given metadata item can be disseminated from the repository.

The `ListIdentifiers` verb is used to retrieve from the data provider a listing of identifiers for metadata items contained in a repository. This might be useful if a metadata harvester then wants to go back and check metadata formats for each item one by one, or even go back and harvest metadata records one at a time. The `ListRecords` verb functions in a similar fashion, but in this instance complete metadata records are retrieved, not just the item identifiers. Both verbs can be used to harvest all `identifiers` or metadata records in a repository, or just to harvest selectively, based either on record `datestamp` values or on `setSpec` values.

The `GetRecord` verb is used to harvest an individual metadata record from a repository. To use this verb, the metadata harvester must specify an OAI metadata `identifier` and a `metdataPrefix`. If possible, the OAI data provider must then disseminate the metadata item requested as a metadata record in the requested metadata format.

The precise meaning of four of the OAI verbs (`ListMetadataFormats`, `ListIdentifiers`, `GetRecord`, and `ListRecords`) can be elaborated or modified by the inclusion of *OAI arguments*. OAI arguments can be optional or required. A special OAI argument, `resumptionToken`, is an exclusive argument—that is, one that cannot be used in combination with any other argument. Use of `resumptionToken` overrides requirements for any other arguments. The `Identify` and `ListSets` verbs do not allow any optional or required arguments, although the exclusive `resumptionToken` argument can be used in conjunction with `ListSets`. (The `resumptionToken` argument is used as a way to manage the computing workload of an OAI data provider service; details of how to use `resumptionTokens` are provided later in this chapter.)

The list of allowed OAI arguments is finite and all can be used with more than one OAI verb. The OAI `identifier` argument is used with verbs that always or sometimes pertain to an individual OAI metadata item or metadata record. It explicitly tells the data provider the OAI `identifier` of the metadata item of interest to the harvester. The `identifier` argument is required for all `GetRecord` verb requests. It specifies the metadata item that the metadata harvester wants disseminated. The `identifier` argument is an optional argument for `ListMetadataFormats` verb requests. When present, it tells the data provider that the metadata harvester is interested only in the list of metadata formats in which a particular item in the repository can be disseminated.

The OAI `metadataPrefix` argument is used with verbs that retrieve metadata records or metadata item identifiers. For those OAI verbs with which `metadataPrefix` can be used, it is always required. Thus `ListRecords` and `GetRecord` verb requests require the `metadataPrefix` argument—it tells the data provider in which metadata format the metadata item(s) retrieved should be disseminated to satisfy the harvester's request. The `metadataPrefix` argument is also a required argument for all `ListIdentifiers` verb requests. The reason here is a little subtler. Even though the `ListIdentifiers` verb does not solicit dissemination of metadata records in a particular format, it does solicit OAI `identifiers` for metadata items. The logic of the protocol is that in response to a `ListIdentifiers` verb request, data providers should list only OAI `identifiers` which can be disseminated in the metadata format of interest to the metadata harvester. The only way for the data provider to know the metadata format of interest to the metadata harvester is for the metadata harvester to include the `metadataPrefix` with its `ListIdentifiers` verb request. In this sense, `metadataPrefix` functions much like the selective harvesting arguments discussed next.

The `from`, `until`, and `set` arguments defined in OAI-PMH are used exclusively for selective harvesting and as such are always optional. They are allowed with `ListRecords` and `ListIdentifiers` verb requests. The first two arguments, `from` and `until`, support selective harvesting by record `datestamp`. They can be used singly or together. The `from` argument is used to request dissemination of items or `identifiers` having a date-stamp greater than or equal to the value of the argument specified by the metadata harvester in its request. If absent, then items from the earliest `datestamp` in the repository should be included. The `until` argument is used to request dissemination of items or `identifiers` having a date-stamp less than or equal to the value of the argument specified by the meta-data harvester in its request. If absent, then items up until and including the most current `datestamp` in the repository should be included. All data pro-viders must support valid OAI requests that specify `from` or `until` argu-ment values with day granularity. Data providers supporting `datestamp` granularity of seconds also must support valid requests that specify `from` or `until` argument values with second granularity. However, if a repository supporting only day granularity receives an OAI request using a `from` or `until` argument value in second granularity, the repository must treat the argument value as invalid and return an error message. Mismatched `from` and `until` arguments used in the same request also are not allowed—that is, if the `from` date is later in time than the `until` date, the data provider must issue an error response.

The `set` argument supports selective harvesting of a repository by OAI set. The value of the `set` argument is the `setSpec` of the OAI set to be har-vested. A harvester must make a `ListSets` verb request (to discover valid `setSpec` values) before performing a selective harvest by `set`. To yield maximum benefit, data providers should consider the likely interests of serv-ice providers when organizing a repository into sets. An OAI set arrange-ment that reflects only the administrative or maintenance structure of a repository may not be all that useful.[5]

Selective harvesting conditions are applied cumulatively. If all of `set`, `from`, and `until` arguments are included with an appropriate OAI verb (for exam-ple, `ListRecords`), then only metadata records satisfying all three conditions will be returned. In other words, the only metadata records returned by the data provider will be those that are members of the OAI `set` specified, have `datestamps` greater than or equal to the `from` argument value, and have `datestamps` less than or equal to the `until` argument value.

Selective harvesting by date using the `from` argument alone allows service providers to periodically refresh records harvested from a particular data provider without having to harvest all records from that data provider each refresh cycle. This is referred to as incremental harvesting. However, if the data provider has a `no` or `transient` deleted records policy, incremental harvesting will not reliably reveal records that have been deleted by the data provider. To discover these, full harvests must be done to identify previously harvested metadata records that have been deleted from the data provider

TABLE 4-2   Required and optional arguments for OAI-PMH verbs.

OAI verb	Required and optional arguments
Identify	No arguments are allowed.
ListMetadataFormats	*identifier* (O): Used to discover available dissemination metadata formats for a specific item.
ListSets	*resumptionToken* (X): If the data provider provides an incomplete list of results in response to a ListSets request, additional ListSets which include a resumptionToken are allowed.
GetRecord	*identifier* (R): The OAI identifier of the item the service provider (harvester) wants disseminated.
	metadataPrefix (R): Specifies the metadata format in which the item should be disseminated.
ListIdentifiers	*metadataPrefix* (R): The service provider only wants identifiers of items available in specified format.
	from (O): The service provider only wants identifiers for records last modified on or after this date/time.
	until (O): The service provider only wants identifiers for records last modified on or before this date/time.
	set (O): The service provider only wants identifiers for records contained in a specified set.
	resumptionToken (X): If the data provider provides an incomplete list of results in response to a ListIdentifiers request, subsequent ListIdentifiers which include a resumptionToken are allowed.
ListRecords	*metadataPrefix* (R): Specifies the format in which records should be disseminated.
	from (O): The service provider only wants records last modified on or after this date/time.
	until (O): The service provider only wants records last modified on or before this date/time.
	set (O): The service provider only wants records contained in specified set.
	resumptionToken (X): If the data provider provides an incomplete list of results in response to a ListRecords request, subsequent ListRecords which include a resumptionToken are allowed.

Notes:
(R) denotes an argument that is required (except when including a *resumptionToken*).
(O) denotes an optional argument.
(X) denotes an exclusive argument, that is, *resumptionToken*; when *resumptionToken* is used, no other arguments are allowed.

repository. Table 4-2 summarizes the use of arguments in OAI-PMH, listing required and optional arguments by verb.

OAI-PMH SYNTAX AND RESPONSE SEMANTICS

OAI-PMH requests are submitted as HTTP requests. Either the HTTP POST or the HTTP GET method can be used. It is easiest to illustrate OAI request syntax by considering the HTTP GET method. When using the GET method, OAI requests devolve to the familiar form of a URL

TABLE 4-3 Illustrations of OAI-PMH requests (`baseURL` shown is for illustration only and is not real).

Illustrations of URLs containing OAI-PMH verbs and arguments

---

http://myDataProvider.org/oaiHandler?verb=Identify
http://myDataProvider.org/oaiHandler?verb=ListSets&resumptionToken=req1234567
http://myDataProvider.org/oaiHandler?verb=ListMetadataFormats&identifier=oai:
  myDataProvider.org:AP-3N-190-UNKN
http://myDataProvider.org/oaiHandler?verb=ListIdentifiers&meatadataPrefix=oai_dc
http://myDataProvider.org/oaiHandler?verb=ListRecords&metadataPrefix=oai_dc&from=
  2004-03-02&until=2005-10-08&set=Images
http://myDataProvider.org/oaiHandler?verb=GetRecord&metadataPrefix=oai_dc&identifier=
  oai:myDataProvider.org:AP-3N-190-UNKN

Notes:
Fictitious baseURL for all examples is http://myDataProvider.org/oaiHandler.
HTTP requires that colons in query strings (the part after the "?" character) be escaped. For readability, this is not done here.

---

containing query information. Specifically, for OAI, such a URL would consist of the data provider repository `baseURL`, concatenated with the '`?`' character, concatenated with a string that includes the OAI verb being used and any OAI arguments, either required or optional. The OAI verb and arguments are included as name value pairs separated by the '`&`' character, as is standard for query information included in a URL. Thus, for a data provider repository having a `baseURL` of:

`http://myDataProvider.org/oaiHandler`, the URL `http://myDataProvider.org/oaiHandler?verb=Identify` would be the OAI request asking the data provider to provide information about itself. Table 4-3 gives illustrative examples of OAI requests using each OAI verb (and assuming this same hypothetical `baseURL`).

Note that character case is meaningful in the query information part of an OAI request. Thus, `verb=GetRecord` is correct; `verb=getrecord` or `verb=getRecord` is not correct. Capitalization rules for OAI-PMH verbs and arguments differ. The initial character of all OAI verbs is uppercase. The initial character of all OAI arguments is lowercase. For both, uppercase characters within the verb or argument name imply the start of a new word for those verb and argument names constructed by concatenating together more than one English-language word. This is known as camelCase. Thus, `verb=ListRecords&metadataPrefix=oai_dc`.

The syntax of all OAI responses is valid XML conforming to the XML Schema for Validating Responses to OAI-PMH Requests.[6] This XML schema is considered part of the protocol proper. It provides separate XML container nodes for each OAI verb (plus one for error responses, discussed in the next section). The verb response containers defined for `GetRecord`, `ListRecords`, `Identify`, and `ListSets` allow for the inclusion of valid XML from any other XML namespace. For `GetRecord` and `ListRecords`, this XML is contained in an element called `<metadata>` and is provided to allow inclusion of XML metadata records expressed in formats defined by XML

FIGURE 4-2   Data provider response to an OAI `Identify` request.

```
<?xml version='1.0' encoding='UTF-8'?>
<OAI-PMH xmlns='http://www.openarchives.org/OAI/2.0/'
    xmlns:xsi='http://www.w3.org/2001/XMLSchema-instance'
    xsi:schemaLocation='http://www.openarchives.org/OAI/2.0/
        http://www.openarchives.org/OAI/2.0/OAI-PMH.xsd'>
 <responseDate>2006-08-13T17:24:00Z</responseDate>
 <request verb="Identify">
    http://aerialphotos.grainger.uiuc.edu/oai.asp</request>
 <Identify>
  <repositoryName>University of Illinois Library at Urbana-Champaign,
    Historic Illinois Aerial Photo Imagebase</repositoryName>
  <baseURL>http://aerialphotos.grainger.uiuc.edu/oai.asp</baseURL>
  <protocolVersion>2.0</protocolVersion>
  <adminEmail>thabing@uiuc.edu</adminEmail>
  <earliestDatestamp>1998-07-27</earliestDatestamp>
  <deletedRecord>transient</deletedRecord>
  <granularity>YYYY-MM-DD</granularity>
  <description>
   <oai-identifier
      xmlns="http://www.openarchives.org/OAI/2.0/oai-identifier"
      xmlns:xsi="http://www.w3.org/2001/XMLSchema-instance"
      xsi:schemaLocation="http://www.openarchives.org/OAI/2.0/oai-identifier
         http://www.openarchives.org/OAI/2.0/oai-identifier.xsd">
    <scheme>oai</scheme>
    <repositoryIdentifier>aerialphotos.grainger.uiuc.edu</repositoryIdentifier>
    <delimiter>:</delimiter>
    <sampleIdentifier>
         oai:aerialphotos.grainger.uiuc.edu:AP-1A-1-1940</sampleIdentifier>
   </oai-identifier>
  </description>
 </Identify>
</OAI-PMH>
```

schemas having non-OAI target namespaces. In responses to `Identify` and `ListSets` verbs, the elements which may contain XML from non-OAI namespaces are `<description>` and `<setDescription>`. These elements allow for the optional inclusion of repository and set descriptions as described above.

The OAI response schema includes a required sub-container XML node, the `<header>` element, which is common across `GetRecord`, `ListIdentifiers`, and `ListRecords` verbs and which is used to contain metadata item and record administrative information. This `<header>` node provides explicit XML semantics for including OAI `identifier` and `datestamp` values, for a listing of any `setSpecs` to which the item belongs, and for a special optional attribute named `status`, which can be used to indicate if a record has been deleted (for repositories with `persistent` or `transient` deleted-records policies). Returned `<records>` with the attribute-value pair `status='deleted'` include only the XML `<header>` node; for obvious reasons there is no node in such records to contain metadata.

An optional sub-container level XML node `<about>` may be used when providing OAI records in response to either `GetRecord` or `ListRecords`. This element is a sibling level node of `<header>` and `<metadata>`, can hold any valid XML child node, and is intended to provide a place for information pertaining to the metadata record itself (as opposed to the resource described by the metadata record). Provenance and intellectual property rights information pertaining to the metadata record itself goes here.

The HTTP response message body shown in Figure 2-2 is an actual OAI data provider XML response to a `ListMetadataFormats` request. Figures 4-2 and 4-3 show valid responses from this same data provider to an

FIGURE 4-3 Data provider response to an OAI `GetRecord` request.

```
<?xml version='1.0' encoding='UTF-8'?>
<OAI-PMH xmlns='http://www.openarchives.org/OAI/2.0/'
    xmlns:xsi='http://www.w3.org/2001/XMLSchema-instance'
    xsi:schemaLocation='http://www.openarchives.org/OAI/2.0/
      http://www.openarchives.org/OAI/2.0/OAI-PMH.xsd'>
  <responseDate>2006-08-13T17:24:31Z</responseDate>
  <request verb="GetRecord"
    identifier="oai:aerialphotos.grainger.uiuc.edu:AP-1A-1-1940"
    metadataPrefix="oai_dc">http://aerialphotos.grainger.uiuc.edu/oai.asp</request>
  <GetRecord>
   <record>
    <header>
     <identifier>oai:aerialphotos.grainger.uiuc.edu:AP-1A-1-1940</identifier>
     <datestamp>1998-07-27</datestamp>
     <setSpec>AP</setSpec>
     <setSpec>1940</setSpec>
     <setSpec>AP:1940</setSpec>
    </header>
    <metadata>
     <oai_dc:dc xmlns='http://purl.org/dc/elements/1.1/'
       xmlns:oai_dc='http://www.openarchives.org/OAI/2.0/oai_dc/'
       xmlns:xsi='http://www.w3.org/2001/XMLSchema-instance'
       xsi:schemaLocation='http://www.openarchives.org/OAI/2.0/oai_dc/
         http://www.openarchives.org/OAI/2.0/oai_dc.xsd'>
      <title>Champaign County, Illinois</title>
      <creator>United States. Agricultureal Adjustment Administration</creator>
      <creator>Woltz Studios, Inc. Aerial Survey</creator>
      <subject>Counties: Champaign</subject>
      <subject>Counties: McLean</subject>
      <subject>Highways: IL 119</subject>
      <subject>Quadrangles: Bellflower</subject>
      <subject>Quadrangles: Foosland</subject>
      <subject>Railroads: Wabash</subject>
      <subject>Towns: Lotus</subject>
      <subject>Water Bodies: Lone Tree Creek</subject>
      <publisher>U.S. Dept. of Agriculture, Agricultural Adjustment
        Administration, North Central Division, Washington, D.C.</publisher>
      <contributor>Scanning, indexing, and description sponsored by the Illinois
        State Library and the University of Illinois at Urbana-Champaign Library.
        Geo-referencing sponsored and performed by the Geographic Modeling Systems
        Laboratory, University of Illinois at Urbana-Champaign.</contributor>
      <date>Created: 1940-06-19</date>
      <date>Issued: 1940-01-01</date>
      <date>Scanned and Processed: 1998-06-01</date>
      <type>image</type>
      <format>image/jpeg</format>
      <identifier>http://images.library.uiuc.edu/projects/aerial_photos/searches/view.asp?
        PhotoID=2897&amp;amp;View_Type=large</identifier>
      <identifier>AP-1A-1</identifier>
      <coverage>northlimit=40.34749;southlimit=40.30505;eastlimit=-88.44968;
        westlimit=-88.50645</coverage>
      <rights>Copyright &#xA9; 1997-2003 the University of Illinois Board of Trustees.
        Images cannot be re-distributed in this form for any commercial purpose.</rights>
     </oai_dc:dc>
    </metadata>
   </record>
  </GetRecord>
</OAI-PMH>
```

OAI `Identify` request and an OAI `GetRecord` request. In addition to providing response information specific to the OAI request verb, all OAI data provider responses also include an element indicating the date and time the response was generated (in Coordinated Universal Time, UTC) and an XML node echoing the `baseURL` of the repository and including as attributes the verb used and arguments provided by the OAI harvester.

OAI-PMH APPROACH TO ERROR HANDLING

The OAI response schema includes semantics to handle OAI-PMH errors. Errors are issued in response to OAI requests having invalid syntax, verb names, or arguments, and for OAI requests that fail to include all required arguments or include argument values that individually or in combination are

TABLE 4-4   OAI-PMH error codes and their causes.

OAI error code	Can occur with	Cause
badArgument	All verbs	A required argument is missing; an argument not allowed for the verb is included; an argument is repeated; or the syntax of the argument value is illegal.
badResumptionToken	ListIdentifiers, ListRecords, ListSets	The resumptionToken value is invalid or expired.
badVerb		The verb used was not one of the six allowed by OAI-PMH.
cannotDisseminate Format	GetRecord, ListRecords, ListIdentifiers	The item or items are not available in the metadata format specified.
idDoesNotExist	GetRecord, ListMetadataFormats	The repository does not contain (or no longer contains) an item having the identifier specified.
noRecordsMatch	ListRecords, ListIdentifiers	No records matched the combination of constraints specified using from, until, and/or set arguments.
noMetadataFormats	ListMetadataFormats	The identifier specified is for a deleted item—that is, an item that can no longer be disseminated in any metadata format.
noSetHierarchy	ListSets, ListIdentifiers, ListRecords	The repository does not use sets. For ListIdentifiers and ListRecords, this error occurs only if the optional set argument is used.

not allowed by the protocol. OAI error responses also are issued for OAI requests that fail to return results or that ask for a list of sets from a repository not using OAI sets. OAI-PMH defines a non-extensible list of eight specific error codes (shown in Table 4-4).

A properly written harvesting application should never trigger some of these errors. The errors `badVerb` and `badArgument`, for instance, should never occur during an automated harvest process since OAI verb and argument semantics can (and should) be checked before an OAI request is submitted and are independent of the data provider repository's data or configuration. Other OAI errors such as `noSetHierarchy` and `noRecordsMatch` are common and will occur in the normal course of automatic harvesting. These errors can provide information about the repository configuration (for example, it is not subdivided into OAI sets) or the data in the repository (for example, no metadata records have been updated or added to the repository since the last harvest).

Although not required, OAI data provider repositories can elaborate on these basic eight error codes in the error responses they give. In an OAI error response, the error code itself always appears as an attribute value of the XML `<error>` node (for example, `<error code="badVerb">`). Including content within the XML `<error>` node is optional, but can be a way to provide a human-readable error message elaborating on the generic error code. Such elaboration can prove useful in debugging a metadata harvester application problem when the reason for an error response is not immediately obvious. For instance, including in the returned error node content such as, "The `from` argument is later than the `until` argument" makes the problem with the request more clear. OAI data provider repositories are also encouraged (but not required) to provide a complete list of all errors encountered for a given request (rather than just the first one encountered during processing). Again, this facilitates debugging of metadata harvester applications.

OAI-PMH errors are distinct from HTTP errors that a metadata harvester may encounter. An OAI error response indicates that the metadata harvester client reached an active and running OAI data provider service. This confirms that at least the `baseURL` part of the OAI request was valid. Other conditions can generate an HTTP status error code, and OAI metadata-harvesting clients must respond to such conditions appropriately. In some cases, an HTTP status error code may be issued in combination with an OAI error response. In such cases, the OAI error XML response is more informative, and the HTTP error can safely be ignored. As described in the next section, an OAI data provider repository may use HTTP status error control as part of a flow-control strategy (Web server resource management). It is important that metadata-harvesting clients understand and respect this use of HTTP status error codes.

As another example, OAI-PMH does not provide authorization and access-control mechanisms of its own. Some OAI data provider repositories use HTTP authorization mechanisms for purposes of access control. In such instances, metadata harvesters will initially receive an HTTP status error response indicating that HTTP credentials are required to access the data provider repository. Metadata harvesters may then provide their credentials via HTTP if so desired.

OAI-PMH STATE MANAGEMENT AND TRANSACTION FLOW CONTROL

Dissemination of metadata records using OAI-PMH is not especially demanding of computer resources, but neither are the demands on server resources nil. OAI-PMH has all of the overhead of Web serving, plus a little bit more (that is because it has to parse and respond correctly to specific OAI requests submitted on top of HTTP). Resource demand grows with the number of metadata items in a repository and the number of different metadata formats (implies multiple metadata transformations) supported by a repository. The frequency of metadata item update and addition also can add to server load. To ensure scalability of OAI-PMH and to give OAI data providers adequate ability to manage demands on their servers, the protocol provides multiple ways to implement flow control and manage server load.

The most powerful way to manage server load is to implement `resump-tionTokens`, an optional protocol feature. Since HTTP itself is stateless, OAI-PMH provides the `resumptionToken` argument as a simple, pseudo-state maintenance feature. The `resumptionToken` argument can be used with the `ListSets`, `ListIdentifiers`, and `ListRecords` verbs. The availability of the `resumptionToken` argument allows data providers to respond to those three OAI verbs with partial list responses. Consider a `ListRecords` verb request designed to retrieve in simple DC format all of the metadata items in a data provider repository containing 10,000 items. The complete response to this request would be a large XML file containing 10,000 metadata records. While this is certainly doable, the resources a server would have to dedicate to dynamically create this large XML file are considerable. If the same server is also simultaneously providing Web services to other clients and servicing other metadata harvesters, it may not be able to fulfill such requests in a timely manner without adversely affecting responsiveness to other service demands. Large XML files also can be troublesome for the harvesting agent to process.

In such an instance, OAI-PMH allows the data provider to divide its full response into segments. Continuing with the illustration above, each partial list segment returned might include only 500 of the 10,000 total records requested. Thus, in response to the original request, the data provider sends back only the first segment of the full response (that is, only the first 500 records). When doing so, the data provider must include a `resumptionTo-ken` value in a special XML node of that name at the end of its response. The metadata harvester then can repeat its previous request, but this time including the `resumptionToken` value from the initial incomplete response as the one and only (that is, exclusive) argument. (The OAI verb must still be provided as part of the request.) The data provider recognizes the `resump-tionToken` given with the new harvest request, prepares the second segment of the response, and sends it to the metadata harvester, this time with a new `resumptionToken` value. The metadata harvester repeats the request with this new `resumptionToken` value, gets the third segment in reply, and so on. For the illustration of 10,000 records segmented in 500 record chunks, the metadata harvester will receive all records after 20 round trips, that is, after making 20 `ListRecords` requests, 19 with `resumptionToken` arguments.

The use of `resumptionTokens` to implement statefulness and manage server utilization is optional. Indeed, the use of `resumptionToken` arguments adds significant complexity to the implementation of OAI-PMH, but experience has shown that `resumptionTokens` are necessary for repositories having more than ten- or twenty-thousand metadata items. Early efforts to implement OAI data provider repositories on that scale without the use of the `resumptionToken` option failed.

OAI-PMH requires that `resumptionToken` arguments be *idempotent* (the term is borrowed from mathematics). In practical terms, this means that if a metadata harvester issues a request that includes a `resumptionToken` value as an argument and then fails to receive the expected response correctly for whatever reason (for example, due to a transitory network problem), the metadata harvester can be confident that it can reissue the same request, that is, with the same `resumptionToken` value, and get back the exact response it would have received had not the earlier attempt failed. Idempotency of `resumptionTokens` ensures that the metadata harvester will not lose its place during a multi-step harvest because of an extraneous problem. Considered another way, `resumptionToken` idempotency means that using a `resumptionToken` value once does not negate or change its meaning. If you use it again, you should get the same result.

However, most OAI data provider repositories are not static. Metadata items are being added, subtracted, and edited on an ongoing basis. When a `ListRecords` or `ListIdentifiers` request is received by a data provider, there will be some set of metadata items in the OAI data provider repository that satisfies the request. If the set is large, the data provider will send back an incomplete list response with an embedded `resumptionToken`. Some time later, the metadata harvester will request the next response segment. What if, during the intervening time, the set of items matching the original request has changed because of metadata item addition, edit, or deletion? In such cases, OAI-PMH allows strict idempotency to be violated. The data provider may modify the next incomplete list response to reflect updates since the `resumptionToken` was originally issued, as long as the data provider does not skip any originally matching items which remain valid matches for the request. Alternatively, OAI-PMH allows data providers to unilaterally and arbitrarily declare a `resumptionToken` expired. This provides a different way to avoid idempotency issues following edits or changes to the contents of a data provider repository. Following any modification of repository contents, the data provider can simply deem any `resumptionTokens` issued prior to the modifications as null and void. If the repository is updated at a regular time each day or each week, the data provider can issue `resumptionTokens` with an explicit expiration date and time (that is, the date and time of next anticipated repository update). While declaring a `resumptionToken` expired midway through a multi-step harvesting process can be inconvenient for the metadata harvester (typically, the harvester must begin the entire harvest over from the start), this approach simplifies implementation of OAI-PMH for the data provider, an explicit objective of the protocol's authors.

Use of `resumptionTokens` allows data providers to manage some aspects of server load, but they do not address other load-balancing issues which can arise when a harvester sends OAI-PMH requests too close together or when multiple harvesters make requests of the data provider repository simultaneously. OAI-PMH recommends two other optional strategies to cope with these load-balancing issues, both of which exploit intrinsic features of HTTP.

The first approach recommends responding to metadata harvester requests coming too close together by issuing an HTTP status code of `503`

(Service Unavailable). This HTTP response can include a HTML retry-after value that instructs the metadata harvester how long to wait before trying its request again. When employing this technique, the data provider repository does not even parse or process the OAI request. It does not have to formulate any XML response. It simply instructs the Web server to respond with the HTTP status code of 503 and goes on to deal with other OAI-PMH requests which it is prepared to handle. Conforming metadata harvesting applications must observe the retry-after value and delay further requests of the data provider until the specified time period has elapsed. This technique works well when incidents of high harvest activity are relatively infrequent (as is usually the case).

For more severe overload problems, the other alternative is to distribute the OAI data provider service across multiple machines. This creates a server farm to deal with OAI harvesting requests. OAI requests can be redirected and balanced across such a server farm using a variety of standard HTTP Web-serving techniques, including through the use of the HTTP status code 302 (Found), a standard way to indicate temporary redirection to a new URL.

QUESTIONS AND TOPICS FOR DISCUSSION

1. As a practical matter, do you think the OAI distinction between metadata items and metadata records is important? Why or why not? Suggest concrete examples to support your opinion.
2. What are tradeoffs for the data provider when selecting deleted records policy? What are the implications for the service provider (metadata harvester)? How might a persistent deleted records policy help data providers comply with other OAI-PMH requirements?
3. Some OAI data providers derive the OAI identifiers they use for their metadata items from the URLs of the resources described by the metadata items. What are the advantages and disadvantages of this approach for the data provider? For the service provider (harvester)?
4. As described, OAI set structure can be strictly hierarchical (supersets and subsets) or can allow overlapping sets. Metadata items can be members of multiple sets or no sets. What are the advantages and disadvantages of these different options? Suggest a scenario in which non-overlapping, hierarchical sets would be advantageous. Suggest a scenario in which overlapping sets would be preferable.

SUGGESTIONS FOR EXERCISES

1. Find the baseURLs for at least three working OAI data providers. (As described in exercise 2 of chapter 2, baseURLs for working OAI data providers can be retrieved from a variety of sources, including http://oai.grainger.uiuc.edu/registry and http://re.cs.uct.ac.za/.) For each repository, construct several OAI requests (use the HTTP GET method). Use every OAI verb and every optional and required OAI argument (see Table 4-2). The validity of the OAI

requests you construct can be checked using your Web browser. Construct an intentionally invalid OAI request, submit it using your Web browser, and look at the error response you get back. Construct and submit a valid OAI request that uses a `resumptionToken` argument.

2. Select and copy several bibliographic item displays from your online catalog. (Use the fullest display available as the source for your copies.) For each of these items, create first an OAI metadata item and then a valid XML metadata record in `oai_dc` format. Optionally, create metadata records from same items for another XML metadata format, for example, MODS.

NOTES

1. http://www.openarchives.org/OAI/2.0/openarchivesprotocol.htm.
2. http://www.loc.gov/standards/mods/.
3. http://www.getty.edu/research/conducting_research/standards/cdwa/cdwalite/index.html.
4. http://www.openarchives.org/OAI/2.0/guidelines-oai-identifier.htm.
5. http://oai-best.comm.nsdl.org/cgi-bin/wiki.pl?SetPractices.
6. http://www.openarchives.org/OAI/2.0/OAI-PMH.xsd.

REFERENCES

Berners-Lee, T., R. Fielding, and L. Manister. 1998. *Uniform Resource Identifiers (URI): Generic Syntax [Request for Comments: 2396]*. Reston, VA: The Internet Society, http://www.ietf.org/rfc/rfc2396.txt.

CHAPTER 5

Implementing an OAI Data Provider

OAI-PMH is rightly touted as a technically low-barrier-to-implement protocol, especially for would-be OAI data providers. This is not to say that OAI-PMH is trivial to implement. Technically low barrier in this context is intended to signify the ease with which those organizations already having in place quality metadata workflows and existing Web-based information technology infrastructures can add an implementation of the protocol. In other words, if a library has metadata appropriate for sharing and a suitable preexisting information management infrastructure to support its collection(s) of content, adding an OAI data provider service is relatively easy. The objective of OAI-PMH is to simplify and standardize the interface for sharing metadata, but the implicit assumption is that there are metadata to share and an existing information infrastructure on top of which an OAI data provider service can be added.

This chapter begins with a discussion of issues to consider when adding support for OAI-PMH to an existing digital content management infrastructure. From there, key points of the OAI guidelines for repository implementers[1] are reviewed, four common OAI data provider implementation scenarios are described, and the most frequently encountered issues and challenges for OAI data providers are highlighted and discussed. Throughout these discussions, the reader is encouraged to reflect on the OAI data provider as one half of the bilateral collaboration between OAI data provider and OAI service provider (harvester). OAI-PMH works best only when each partner in this metadata-sharing collaboration keeps in mind the needs and requirements of the other partner. Subsequent chapters look at the issues associated with creating, enriching (post-harvest), and using descriptive metadata in the context of OAI-PMH and discuss the issues encountered by service providers when aggregating harvested metadata.

ADDING SUPPORT FOR OAI-PMH TO EXISTING INFRASTRUCTURE

Libraries implementing OAI-PMH often have one or more preexisting systems in place for managing local digital resources. These range from locally developed, "home-grown" systems, to fully turnkey, third-party vended or open source (a type of free-to-use software) solutions. If existing infrastructure does not include OAI-PMH already, there are several strategies for adding support for OAI-PMH. An OAI data provider can be implemented as a wholly external add-on to existing system(s) or can be integrated into existing infrastructure. As an alternative to either of these approaches, the library can chose to migrate to a turnkey solution with integral support for OAI-PMH (several such systems were discussed in chapter 3). If integrating support for OAI-PMH into preexisting infrastructure, third-party software modules are available which can facilitate the process (notably OAICat,[2] developed by the research arm of OCLC Online Computer Library Center). Regardless, an OAI data provider repository is rarely implemented in a vacuum. Existing metadata workflow, Web infrastructure, and XML competencies must be examined carefully, especially if the intent is to integrate support for OAI-PMH directly into preexisting digital content management infrastructure.

Metadata Workflow

The way in which a content provider manages metadata—that is, creates, stores, updates, adds, and deletes metadata objects—can have significant impact on how easy or hard it is to implement OAI-PMH. While the OAI data provider repository defined in the protocol can be added to an existing metadata workflow as only a virtual construct, that workflow must support the model of metadata items and records defined in the protocol. It also should support the consistent application of well-defined metadata semantics, the tracking of metadata last-modified date, and the implementation of persistent metadata item identifiers.

Several questions about existing metadata workflow should be asked. How are metadata stored? Is there a one-to-one correspondence between the metadata item and the information resource? Are metadata items maintained separately from information resources (for example, as separate files), or if not, are metadata items easily detachable from information resources in real time? Storing the descriptive metadata for each information resource as an individual file on the OAI data provider repository file system can be convenient for the purposes of OAI-PMH. Maintenance of metadata properties and attributes for an information resource within the resource itself, in a relational database structure, or in a turnkey content-management system can also work, as long as the complete metadata item for any single information resource can be quickly and efficiently identified and extracted in real time for processing and dissemination as a metadata record.

In the context of OAI-PMH, metadata item identification and last-modified date-time are especially critical. Are all metadata items in existing workflow uniquely and persistently identified, and is the date (and optionally the time) recorded whenever metadata items are modified? If not, it is advisable to add these features to the existing workflow when feasible, although technical protocol compliance can usually be achieved by having item OAI `identifier` and `datestamp` values maintained solely by an external OAI data provider application.

Confusion between metadata item identifiers and resource identifiers is a common problem for OAI data providers. These are not synonymous. A resource identifier is used to identify and often locate the resource (for example, as in the case of a URL). Digital Object Identifiers (DOIs), International Standard Book Numbers (ISBNs), library-specific accession numbers, and URLs are examples of resource identifiers. Each has special properties and uses. The OAI metadata item `identifier` is defined in the protocol, identifies the OAI metadata item (not the resource), and is designed for use in the context of OAI-PMH and related services. While the OAI `identifier` value may be derived from a resource identifier, they typically are not identical. A change in a resource identifier does not have to result in a change in OAI `identifier`. The same OAI `identifier` is meant to be retained throughout the life cycle of an information resource, even as that resource is moved (implying a new URL) or altered in other ways (for example, given a new library-specific accession number). OAI `identifiers` must not be reused for a new or different resource, even after the original resource associated with an OAI `identifier` no longer exists.

Resource datestamp and metadata `datestamp` also are not synonymous. Modification of metadata does not always mean a change in the resource. For instance, a cataloging update might change the class number or subject heading assigned to a resource (that is, it might change the metadata), but it would not change the resource itself. Ideally, workflow should support separable last-modified datestamps for resources and metadata.

Finally, it is important to consider how metadata items are added to, removed from, and updated in the OAI data provider repository. OAI-PMH assumes the existence of a data provider repository containing metadata items. It does not address how metadata items come into or are deleted from the repository. In practice, metadata are used by an institution for a number of purposes, both internal and external. It may be necessary or desirable to maintain copies of metadata in more than one place. Care must be taken in such instances. Proper processes must be implemented to synchronize metadata changes across all copies. The way these processes are managed can impact the selection of OAI data provider `datestamp` granularity (that is, days versus seconds) and policies regarding when updates to metadata are allowed in the workflow. (See the discussion below regarding `datestamp` accuracy and hidden updates.)

Web Infrastructure

As previously mentioned, OAI-PMH is made to leverage existing investments in Web infrastructure. General-purpose Web servers (for example, Apache[3] and Microsoft Internet Information Services[4]) provide a suitable infrastructure onto which an OAI data provider service can be added easily. Standard server-side scripting and Common Gateway Interface (CGI) technologies have been used extensively to implement OAI data provider services. A variety of scripting languages (for example, Perl, PHP, VBScript, and Java/Java server pages) have been used by developers of OAI data provider services.

Leveraging an existing Web server implementation simplifies the work that must be done by the OAI data provider application. The Web server receives a request for the OAI data provider service. The Web server handles the HTTP aspects of the OAI request, and passes the substance of the HTTP GET or POST message (that is, the OAI request verb and arguments) to the OAI data provider application. The OAI application formulates the appropriate XML response to the OAI request, interacting with a database or other store of metadata as necessary, and passes the OAI response (as XML) back to the Web server application. If necessary, the OAI service may also instruct the Web server to issue special HTTP headers or an HTTP response status code with the XML response sent back to the OAI harvester. The Web server constructs a valid HTTP response, embedding the XML generated by the OAI service, and replies to the OAI harvester.

While the construction of an OAI data provider application as outlined is not especially difficult, it does assume a capacity and competency within the organization to create and manage server-side scripting applications. An OAI data provider service is a dynamic Web application. An alternative for those not wishing to implement and maintain a homegrown OAI data provider application is to utilize a vended turnkey system which includes support for OAI-PMH. For instance, CONTENTdm,[5] a popular content-management system for modest-sized collections of digital content, includes built-in support for OAI-PMH. Making metadata already entered into CONTENTdm available for harvesting by OAI service providers can be as simple as changing one value in the CONTENTdm configuration settings file. Other library system vendors have added or are adding support for OAI-PMH to some of their products. Additionally, open source and other freely available library system software, especially software supporting institutional repositories (see chapter 3), are now including support for OAI-PMH. Free-to-use applications may require more customization to fit local environments and workflows than custom-vended solutions, but are still less difficult than starting from scratch.

Support for XML

Finally, a would-be OAI data provider must consider the capacity of his or her organization to work with XML. Errors in character encoding are among the most common mistakes made by new OAI data provider services (Warner 2005). These errors trace back to inadequate implementations of XML by content providers. Even when a data provider relies on vended or third-party software to implement OAI-PMH, XML-related errors embedded in metadata items at any stage can be propagated through the turnkey implementation and cause XML well-formedness or *validation* errors. In some cases, errors in source data can cause an otherwise technically correct and robust

OAI data provider implementation to fail, even one that has been widely implemented and successfully used by others. Ultimately, the raw metadata delivered to the OAI data provider service must be correct and consistent with XML requirements or the OAI data provider service will fail or at least generate errors during full harvesting.

As described in chapter 2, organizations planning to implement OAI-PMH must have some local understanding of XML character-encoding requirements—specifically UTF-8 (8-bit Unicode Transformation Format), the use of XML schemas, and the use of XML namespaces (discussed in chapter 2). By design, responses to valid OAI-PMH requests from a service provider (harvester) must be both well formed and valid XML. OAI responses must not only follow XML syntax and character-encoding rules, but also conform to the semantics defined in the XML schemas included in the OAI protocol. OAI responses which contain <metadata> nodes (for example, responses to a GetRecord or ListRecords verb) must conform to a publicly available XML schema that defines the semantics of the metadata format used. Simultaneous conformance to both OAI-defined XML schemas and community-defined XML metadata schemas is enabled by the correct use of XML namespaces in OAI responses.

RECOMMENDED GUIDELINES FOR REPOSITORY IMPLEMENTERS

The OAI-PMH specification is relatively sparse on how-to-implement details. The primary intent of the protocol itself is to articulate unambiguously the rules to which OAI data providers and service providers must adhere. To supplement the protocol and facilitate its adoption, OAI has released separate implementation guidelines.[6] These are linked from the online copy of the protocol and cover technical implementation issues. Separate guidelines are given for data providers (repository implementers),[7] for service providers, and for other special protocol features and implementation scenarios. Selected recommendations from the OAI implementation guidelines are discussed below.

Optional Features of the Protocol

OAI-PMH includes a number of optional features which can be implemented or not at the discretion of the OAI data provider. Several of these have been discussed in earlier chapters. As stated in the guidelines, these features are made optional so they do not have to be implemented in "situations when these constructs are not needed or implementation would be too difficult."[8] It is important to remember that the converse is also intended. If technically practical for the data provider, OAI-PMH optional features should be implemented when doing so will facilitate better, more complete, and more useful interaction with service providers. OAI data providers should always show a preference for implementing optional protocol features relevant to their community of users, and should take into account likely needs of and benefits to

TABLE 5-1   OAI-PMH optional features and reasons to implement them.

Optional OAI-PMH feature	Reason to implement or select a turnkey solution that supports the feature
Multiple metadata formats	To expose additional, richer, or more community-specific metadata than can be exposed using simple Dublin Core metadata format alone.
description, setDescription, and/or about containers	To provide a service provider with added, useful information about the data provider repository, about set organization of the repository, and/or about individual metadata records.
OAI sets	So that a service provider can choose to harvest only a portion of the metadata items contained in the full repository; especially desirable for larger repositories containing multiple collections.
resumptionTokens	To facilitate handling of OAI responses involving large numbers of identifiers or metadata records, that is, more than a few thousand. (Discussed in chapter 4.)
Persistent deleted records policy	To allow a harvester to better know when a record has been removed; this facilitates incremental harvesting and obviates the need for frequent full harvests. (Discussed in chapter 4.)
datestamp granularity of second	To allow a harvester to perform more precise incremental harvesting based on a more granular datestamp; essential when used that implementation is correct. (Discussed later in this chapter.)

service providers when deciding how much effort for implementation of optional features is reasonable. The availability of optional protocol features is a useful way to distinguish one third-party OAI-PMH software solution from another and to help decide which third-party solution is the best fit for an institution wanting to implement OAI-PMH.

Table 5-1 summarizes important optional features of OAI-PMH and suggests rationales for when implementation of an optional feature is especially desirable. For instance, the protocol requires an OAI data provider to implement simple Dublin Core (DC). However, if the OAI data provider has richer metadata available in an alternative format, the OAI data provider also should make metadata records in that richer format harvestable via OAI—especially if that richer scheme is well established within their community of practice. The need to do this cannot be overstated.

Similarly, OAI data providers should implement optional `<description>`, `<setDescription>`, and `<about>` containers allowed for by the protocol whenever practicable and deemed potentially informative for likely harvesters. As illustrated in the protocol, and expounded on in the implementation guidelines, the optional `<description>` container allowed in responses to OAI `Identify` requests is an effective way to convey information to OAI service providers regarding the OAI `identifier` scheme used by the data provider. The optional `<description>` container of a response to an OAI `Identify` request also can be used to share repository descriptive information considered especially useful within a specific community or subject domain. Lastly, the `<description>` container of a response to an OAI `Identify` request can be used as a way to inform harvesters about other, related OAI data providers of potential interest.

When sharing individual metadata records, the protocol allows the inclusion of an optional `<about>` container (that is, an XML node). While this container has great potential value, it also has been the source of some confusion. The OAI record-level `<about>` container is intended to convey information only about the metadata record itself—not about the information resource described by the metadata record. Thus, the OAI `<about>` container may contain information about the provenance of the metadata record (for example, indicating whether the record was previously harvested from some other site and whether it has been modified before being made available for re-harvest), but not about the provenance of the information resource itself. OAI provides an XML schema that may be used for conveying metadata record provenance information in the `<about>` container.[9] The OAI record-level `<about>` container also can be used to convey information about rights asserted over the metadata record by the OAI data provider, but should not be used to express rights asserted over the information resource itself. The OAI provides suggested guidelines for asserting rights over individual metadata records.[10]

Finally, two optional protocol features, flow control and sets, were previously discussed in chapter 4. Although it comes with a cost of increased complexity, flow control can be useful in some situations for the technical reasons described in chapter 4. Regarding sets, the OAI guidelines recommend that they be implemented in response to "a particular community-specific situation or deployment scenario that needs sets."[11] Experience has suggested that OAI data providers should be proactive and implement sets in anticipation of potential utility for service providers. However, OAI data providers should stop short of trying to use sets as a substitute for search functionality. OAI sets are assumed by the protocol to have predetermined membership, existing prior to and independent of any service provider request. A data provider must be able to list available sets when requested. Some service providers will request a set listing from a data provider and manually evaluate it before deciding which sets to harvest on a routine basis, so sets should not change frequently, or change dynamically in response to a harvester's request. With regard to the verb `ListSets`, the OAI response may optionally include a `<setDescription>` element. The `<setDescription>` element can be used to inform OAI harvesters regarding the characteristics of a set—for example, to declare set update frequency, the scope of the set, its relation to other sets, etc. Again, if sets are implemented, the OAI data provider should make use of the `<setDescription>` element to ensure maximum utility and benefit.

Recommendations Regarding OAI `Identifiers`

OAI-PMH specifies that OAI `identifiers` must be persistent and must uniquely identify a single metadata item within a given repository. While minimally adequate for the essential requirements of OAI-PMH, a way to guarantee global uniqueness (rather than just local uniqueness within a single repository) and to resolve the source or owner of a metadata record based solely on inspection of the record's OAI `identifier` is desirable. For example, it is common for OAI service providers (harvesters) to broker or re-disseminate metadata records they have harvested via OAI-PMH, either unchanged or enriched in some manner. In doing so, the harvesting agent takes on the additional role of OAI data provider. When re-disseminating a previously harvested record, the harvester-turned-data provider should include the original OAI `identifier` of the brokered metadata record (for example, in the `about/provenance` container as discussed above). This allows the next harvester in the chain of custody to recognize the origin of the records. This is especially helpful for eliminating duplicate records. Global uniqueness of all OAI `identifiers` in the chain of custody facilitates this process. In combination with a reliable way to recognize the owner (that is, the data provider) of a metadata record from the OAI `identifier` scheme used, global OAI `identifier` uniqueness can also facilitate the implementation of OAI metadata item `identifier` resolution services.[12]

In recognition of these considerations, OAI has issued implementation guidelines for OAI `identifiers`.[13] These guidelines include an optional XML schema and a recommendation that OAI `identifiers` consist of three string components concatenated with colons. The first string is always `oai` and represents the general OAI `identifier` scheme as defined in the requirements for URIs (Berners-Lee et al. 1998). The second string, the `namespace-identifier` component, should be a domain name owned and registered by the OAI data provider institution (for example, `library.uiuc.edu`). Most often this string will be the domain name of the Web server on which the OAI data provider has been implemented. Case (capitalization) of the `namespace-identifier` should be consistent in all OAI `identifiers` using that `namespace-identifier`. The third string, the `local-identifier` component, is a locally unique identifier for the metadata item. Given anticipated variations in repository architectures, the OAI stops short of recommending any format for the `local-identifier` component (beyond requiring compliance with the URI specification as discussed in chapter 4). OAI service providers (harvesters) should not assume anything about the meaning of the `local-identifier` component of an OAI `identifier`. It is not necessary for the `namespace-identifier` to be unique for each OAI data provider repository (though this is a common practice and was the recommendation during beta testing of the protocol). It is required, however, that the `local-identifier` component of an OAI `identifier` be unique across all repositories which share the same `namespace-identifier`. This ensures global uniqueness of OAI `identifiers` conforming to the implementation guidelines. Examples of valid OAI `identifiers` conforming to the implementation guidelines are embedded in the OAI responses shown in Figures 5-3 and 5-4.

COMMON IMPLEMENTATION SCENARIOS

One of the attractive features of OAI-PMH is that it does not dictate metadata storage design. Metadata items disseminated via OAI-PMH can be stored in a variety of ways within the local architecture of the data provider. While implementers appreciate the flexibility this allows, this lack of specificity can make it difficult to describe OAI data provider implementations in concrete terms. An approach to understanding OAI-PMH in more concrete terms is to look at scenarios illustrating commonly used approaches. Four such scenarios are given below.

The first two scenarios assume metadata item storage options that might match a preexisting metadata-management infrastructure. Alternatively, these scenarios also could describe OAI-PMH implementations that have been added external to the local content-management system (in which case a process would be needed to synchronize or periodically refresh contents of the OAI-PMH data provider repository). Scenario 3 assumes that OAI-PMH has been integrated into an existing Web server infrastructure in order to expose metadata describing a collection of HTML Web resources. Scenario four, an *OAI static repository* scenario, assumes support has been added external to the primary local metadata-management infrastructure. Keep in mind that these scenarios represent only a few of the viable ways an OAI data provider may be implemented. For simplicity, it is assumed for these scenarios that each repository natively uses a single repository-wide set of semantics (that is, a single metadata scheme) for storing metadata items. (This is not a requirement of OAI-PMH but is the norm except for large OAI data providers having metadata describing the content of multiple heterogeneous collections.)

Scenario 1: Metadata Items Stored as XML Files

The repository architecture assumed for this scenario stores metadata items separate from the resources they describe in a dedicated portion of the server file system. Metadata items are maintained as stand-alone, valid XML files. That is to say, metadata item files are both well formed and conformant to an XML schema defining the metadata semantics intrinsic to the repository. The OAI data provider application, running as an extension of the repository Web server application, has permission to enumerate, read, and manipulate the stored XML metadata items (files). Figure 5-1 depicts such an arrangement of metadata items. In the figure, the root folder containing the complete store of metadata files is `C:\InetPub\MetadataItems`. This root folder in turn contains two subfolders, `\Set1` and `\Set2`, each of which contains metadata items in the form of XML files.

FIGURE 5-1   A depiction of how metadata items might be stored as individual XML files on an OAI data provider's Web server file system.

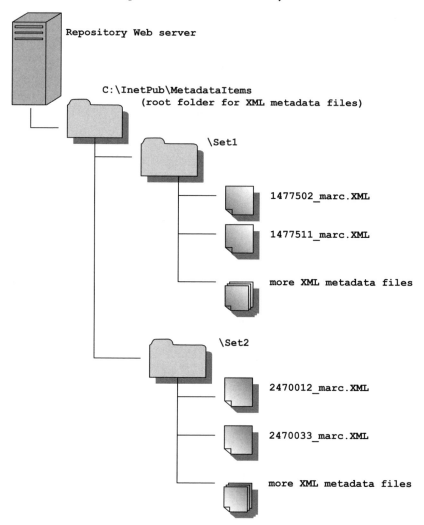

For the purposes of OAI-PMH, this is a convenient arrangement. Since each metadata item exists as a distinct file on the file system of the server, each metadata item is guaranteed to have a unique name (composed of the filename prefixed with the names of the folders in the file system hierarchy containing the file). Each metadata item also has a last-modified datestamp maintained by the Web server's file-management system. If the metadata items as stored on the local file system conform to the simple DC metadata format, then all that is needed to disseminate a metadata item via OAI is to encapsulate the metadata item XML file within the correct OAI-namespace nodes as defined in the OAI-PMH namespace schemas maintained by the OAI. In this instance, the metadata item and the metadata record are synonymous.

Dissemination of metadata items stored in a different metadata format, or dissemination of items in multiple metadata formats, is possible through the

FIGURE 5-2   The XML for a metadata item as stored on an OAI data provider's Web server file system.

```
<?xml version="1.0" encoding="UTF-8"?>
<record xmlns="http://www.loc.gov/MARC21/slim"
    xmlns:xsi="http://www.w3.org/2001/XMLSchema-instance"
    xsi:schemaLocation="http://www.loc.gov/MARC21/slim
        http://www.loc.gov/standards/marcxml/schema/MARC21slim.xsd" >
  <leader>01012nam  2200265 a 4500</leader>
   <controlfield tag="001">1477502</controlfield>
   <controlfield tag="005">20020808050439.0</controlfield>
   <controlfield tag="008">920623s1959    meua         s000 0 eng d</controlfield>
   <datafield tag="035" ind1=" " ind2=" ">
     <subfield code="a">(OCoLC)ocm26068200</subfield>
   </datafield>
   <datafield tag="100" ind1="1" ind2=" ">
     <subfield code="a">Trevett, M. F.</subfield>
     <subfield code="q">(Moody Francis),</subfield>
     <subfield code="d">1907-</subfield>
   </datafield>
   <datafield tag="245" ind1="1" ind2="0">
     <subfield code="a">1959 chemical weed killers /</subfield>
     <subfield code="c">by M.F. Trevett and H.J. Murphy.</subfield>
   </datafield>
   <datafield tag="260" ind1=" " ind2=" ">
     <subfield code="a">Orono :</subfield>
     <subfield code="b">Maine Extension Service :</subfield>
     <subfield code="b">Maine Agricultural Experiment Station</subfield>
     <subfield code="c">1959</subfield>
   </datafield>

     ... additional datafields not shown to preserve space ...

</record>
```

dynamic application of *transforming XML stylesheets* (XSLTs). XSLTs are special XML files that provide the instructions necessary for the automated transformation of XML files conforming to one schema into XML files conforming to a different schema. In an OAI-PMH context, XSLTs can be used to transform metadata items dynamically from the repository-intrinsic metadata schema to the desired dissemination metadata schema(s). The OAI record `datestamp` is then the later of the metadata item file's last-modified date and the XSLT file's last-modified date.

OAI sets can be supported to a limited extent by assuming that each folder below the metadata root folder is an OAI `setName`. Any subfolders below that level can be treated as subsets in the OAI set hierarchy of the repository, and so on. Metadata items can be added to or subtracted from the repository simply by adding or deleting files from the file system (but notice that the OAI deleted-records policy must be `no`, information about deleted items is not maintained by the OAI data provider after file deletion).

If the collection of metadata items is large enough to warrant it, `resumptionTokens` may be supported. It is easiest to support `resumptionTokens` by disseminating each folder in the metadata store individually. The value of `resumptionToken` is then just a token indicating the next folder in sequence to disseminate and the time that the `resumptionToken` was issued. Issue time is checked against the folder's last-modified time to recognize stale `resumptionTokens` and ensure idempotency (as discussed in chapter 4).

Figure 5-2 shows a metadata item XML file as it might be maintained on the repository Web server in this scenario. The intrinsic metadata format of

FIGURE 5-3 Metadata item shown in Figure 5-2 disseminated as an `OAI record` in MARC XML metadata format.

```
<?xml version="1.0" encoding="UTF-8"?>
<OAI-PMH xmlns="http://www.openarchives.org/OAI/2.0/"
    xmlns:xsi="http://www.w3.org/2001/XMLSchema-instance"
    xsi:schemaLocation="http://www.openarchives.org/OAI/2.0/
        http://www.openarchives.org/OAI/2.0/OAI-PMH.xsd">
<responseDate>2006-01-28T18:27:52Z</responseDate>
<request verb="GetRecord"
        identifier="oai:grainger.uiuc.edu:Set1/1477502_marc.xml"
        metadataPrefix="marc">
    http://myserver.library.uiuc.edu/ASPOAIDP-FS/oai.asp</request>
<GetRecord>
 <record>
  <header>
   <identifier>oai:grainger.uiuc.edu:Set1/1477502_marc.xml</identifier>
   <datestamp>2004-05-10</datestamp>
   <setSpec>Set1 </setSpec>
  </header>
  <metadata>
   <record xmlns="http://www.loc.gov/MARC21/slim"
       xmlns:xsi="http://www.w3.org/2001/XMLSchema-instance"
       xsi:schemaLocation="http://www.loc.gov/MARC21/slim
           http://www.loc.gov/standards/marcxml/schema/MARC21slim.xsd" >
    <leader>01012nam  2200265 a 4500</leader>
    <controlfield tag="001">1477502</controlfield>
    <controlfield tag="005">20020808050439.0</controlfield>
    <controlfield tag="008">920623s1959    meua         s000 0 eng d</controlfield>
    <datafield tag="035" ind1=" " ind2=" ">
     <subfield code="a">(OCoLC)ocm26068200</subfield>
    </datafield>
    <datafield tag="100" ind1="1" ind2=" ">
      <subfield code="a">Trevett, M. F.</subfield>
      <subfield code="q">(Moody Francis),</subfield>
      <subfield code="d">1907-</subfield>
    </datafield>

        ... additional datafields not shown to preserve space ...

   </record>
  </metadata>
 </record>
</GetRecord>
</OAI-PMH>
```

the repository is U.S. MARC 21. Figure 5-3 shows how that metadata item might look when disseminated as a record via an OAI data provider service. Notice the use of XML namespaces. Figure 5-4 shows how that metadata item might look when transformed to simple DC (metadata format `oai_dc`) and disseminated as an OAI record. (The stylesheets used to transform the metadata item from U.S. MARC 21 to simple DC are based on XSLT stylesheets maintained by the Library of Congress.[14])

This scenario is easy to implement and in its simplest form does not require the use of databases. However, for performance reasons, this scenario is often implemented with a database cache that contains a listing of metadata items currently available on the file system and their properties (such as file name, last-modified date stamps, and location on the file system). The use of a database cache facilitates quicker responses to `ListIdentifiers`, `ListRecords`, and `ListSets` OAI requests. Caching requires implementation of update rules to insure synchronicity between the file system and the caching database. An open source, simple-to-implement illustration of this file-based scenario (with and without the caching database) is available for Microsoft Windows platforms from SourceForge.org.[15]

FIGURE 5-4   Metadata item shown in Figure 5-2 disseminated as an `OAI record` in `oai_dc` (Dublin Core) XML metadata format.

```
<?xml version="1.0" encoding="UTF-8"?>
<OAI-PMH xmlns="http://www.openarchives.org/OAI/2.0/"
     xmlns:xsi="http://www.w3.org/2001/XMLSchema-instance"
     xsi:schemaLocation="http://www.openarchives.org/OAI/2.0/
        http://www.openarchives.org/OAI/2.0/OAI-PMH.xsd">
  <responseDate>2006-01-28T18:03:58Z</responseDate>
  <request verb="GetRecord"
          identifier="oai:grainger.uiuc.edu:Set1/1477502_marc.xml"
          metadataPrefix="oai_dc">
       http://myserver.library.uiuc.edu/ASPOAIDP-FS/oai.asp</request>
  <GetRecord>
   <record>
    <header>
     <identifier>oai:grainger.uiuc.edu:Set1/1477502_marc.xml</identifier>
     <datestamp>2004-05-10</datestamp>
     <setSpec>Set1 </setSpec>
    </header>
    <metadata>
     <oai_dc:dc xmlns:oai_dc="http://www.openarchives.org/OAI/2.0/oai_dc/"
          xmlns:xsi="http://www.w3.org/2001/XMLSchema-instance"
          xmlns:dc="http://purl.org/dc/elements/1.1/"
          xsi:schemaLocation="http://www.openarchives.org/OAI/2.0/oai_dc/
             http://www.openarchives.org/OAI/2.0/oai_dc.xsd">
      <dc:title>1959 chemical weed killers /</dc:title>
      <dc:creator> Trevett, M. F. (Moody Francis), 1907- </dc:creator>
      <dc:creator> Murphy, H. J. </dc:creator>
      <dc:type>text</dc:type>
      <dc:publisher>Orono : Maine Extension Service : Maine Agricultural
          Experiment Station</dc:publisher>
      <dc:date>1959</dc:date>
      <dc:language>eng</dc:language>
      <dc:subject>Herbicides</dc:subject>
     </oai_dc:dc>
    </metadata>
   </record>
  </GetRecord>
</OAI-PMH>
```

Scenario 2: Item Metadata Stored in a Relational Database

It is more common for digital library applications to store descriptive metadata in a relational database, sometimes the same database used to store the resource objects themselves. From an OAI perspective, the crucial requirement is that the database design supports a way to extract all metadata properties associated with a resource using an unambiguous, persistent identifier. The database design also must provide a field which contains the date (and optionally time) when metadata property values associated with a given identifier were last modified. It must be possible to enumerate the complete list of OAI `identifiers` for all metadata items ready for dissemination (to support `ListRecords` and `ListIdentifiers` verbs), and if OAI sets are to be used, it must be possible to list and retrieve OAI `identifiers` and items by OAI `setSpec` value.

Given such prerequisites, an OAI data provider service can be built that extracts information from the database as necessary to fulfill valid OAI requests. Depending on database design, rules for adding and deleting items from the repository, and other considerations, this approach can support most of the OAI optional features, including OAI sets, `resumptionTokens`,

FIGURE 5-5   Illustrative database schema for a relational database designed to hold an OAI data provider's metadata items.

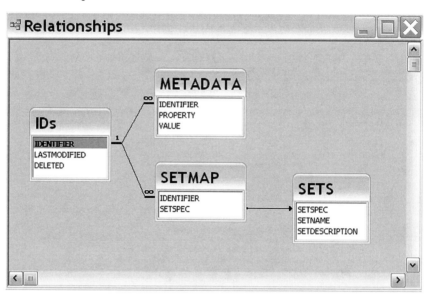

dissemination of items in multiple metadata formats, and any of the OAI deleted-records policies enumerated in the protocol.

Consider as an example a relational database design that includes four tables shown in Figure 5-5. One table, the IDs table, has as its primary key an IDENTIFIER column containing unique and persistent metadata item identifiers. Values from this column can be used to link to related tables and to construct the local-identifier component value for each OAI identifier. Each record in the IDs table also contains a date-time column, LASTMODIFIED, containing the date (and optionally time) when the metadata record was last modified, and a binary column, DELETED, indicating whether the metadata item has been deleted or not (in order to support a deleted-record policy of persistent). Each record in a second table, METADATA, consists of three columns: IDENTIFIER, as its foreign key column (links from the IDs table on a one-to-many basis); PROPERTY, to hold the name of a metadata property; and VALUE, to hold the value of the named descriptive property. Typical records in the METADATA table might look as shown in Figure 5-6. The third and fourth tables shown in Figure 5-5, SETS and SETMAP, support implementation of OAI sets. The third table describes each of the OAI sets defined for the repository, and the fourth table associates individual metadata items (via an IDENTIFIER foreign key column) with individual OAI sets in the repository. This approach supports the arbitrary implementation of OAI sets, including the implementation of overlapping sets.

Assuming that such a database design is used for storing metadata items, it is then the function of the OAI data provider application in this scenario to

FIGURE 5-6 Properties and values for a metadata item.

IDENTIFIER	PROPERTY	VALUE
5	title	1959 chemical weed killers
5	creator	Trevett, M. F. (Moody Francis), 1907–
5	creator	Murphy, H. J.
5	type	text
5	publisher	Orono : Maine Extension Service : Maine Agricultural Experiment Station
5	date	1959
5	language	eng
5	subject	Herbicides
0		

transform strings retrieved from the database into XML metadata records that can be disseminated via OAI. Given the example metadata attributes shown in Figure 5-6, and assuming that values in the SETMAP table associate this metadata item with a set having a setSpec of "Set1," the resulting record when disseminated via OAI in the oai_dc metadata format would look the same as shown in Figure 5-4 (from the previous scenario). This illustrates that the end result of disseminating metadata using OAI-PMH is independent of the way in which metadata items are stored by the OAI data provider repository. The OAI service provider harvests a metadata record that looks the same whether the metadata items are stored by an OAI data provider as XML files or as rows in a relational database. The primary concern of OAI-PMH is with the process of delivering metadata as valid XML to a service provider in response to a request from that service provider.

Dissemination of metadata items stored in a relational database in multiple metadata formats can be done by including multiple alternative mappings for translating value strings retrieved from the database into XML. Not all metadata properties associated with a given metadata item identifier in the database need to be exported for dissemination in all metadata formats supported by the OAI data provider. If a specific metadata format is not designed to expose a particular property associated with an item, then that property can be ignored when it is retrieved from the database. The same property may populate an XML node in other metadata formats.

Assuming proper database design and optimization, database-based OAI implementations can be very robust. Such implementations have scaled successfully up to hundreds of thousands of metadata items. In practice, designs for databases containing metadata will vary greatly from one digital library implementation to another. Database design will be determined more by the needs of local applications than the needs of the OAI data provider service. OAI data provider implementations must be adapted to match database design, not the other way around.

Scenario 3: Item Metadata Stored within a Resource

As a third illustrative scenario, consider a repository composed of a collection of HTML Web pages. Each page contains HTML <meta> tags which hold

FIGURE 5-7 HTML <meta> elements from Web version of a 1959 report on herbicides.

```
<META content="1959 chemical weed killers" name="DC.title" />
<META content=" Trevett, M. F. (Moody Francis), 1907- " name="DC.creator" />
<META content=" Murphy, H. J." name="DC.creator" />
<META content="text" name="DC.type" />
<META
   content=" Orono : Maine Extension Service : Maine Agricultural Experiment Station"
   name="DC.publisher" />
<META content="1959" name="DC.date" />
<META content="eng" name="DC.language" />
<META content="Herbicides" name="DC.subject" />
```

the essential metadata describing that page as an information resource. There is a one-to-one relationship between HTML pages and metadata items—that is, the metadata item for any HTML page is understood to consist of the sum of all the <meta> tags contained within that HTML page. Figure 5-7 illustrates what the complete set of <meta> elements within an HTML Web page might look like.

In this scenario, metadata items as understood for the purposes of OAI-PMH are virtual—that is, they do not exist as separate entities within the OAI data provider repository, but rather, the information that comprises each metadata item is embedded within each of the HTML objects being described. Under this scenario, the role of the OAI data provider application is to extract and deliver metadata contained in each of the resources maintained in the repository. This scenario is just a slightly more complicated variant of the first scenario discussed, in which metadata items were stored on the repository file system as discrete, valid XML files.

As in that scenario, the repository Web server file system can be used to generate unique metadata item identifiers (derived in this case from the fully qualified file names of the HTML Web pages themselves). Alternatively, the URLs of the HTML pages could be used to derive the local-identifier component of the OAI identifier. The Web server file system also provides last-modified date stamps for both metadata items and resource objects. Note that this assumption is made for simplicity and is not rigorous. It is possible, for instance, to modify the HTML of an information resource, thus changing the file system last-modified date stamp, without changing any of the <meta> values contained within the HTML page. In such an instance, the OAI data provider would indicate a metadata update that had not really happened. In practical terms, however, the impact of the additional harvesting that this would engender is unlikely to be significant.

The main difference from the metadata-items-as-XML-files scenario is that the OAI data provider cannot rely simply on XSLTs to prepare metadata items for dissemination as OAI records (unless the HTML pages conform to the XHTML standard). Instead, the application must extract metadata in the form of HTML <meta> tags and then translate <meta> tag content and name attributes into appropriate XML structures within the XML OAI record being disseminated. This additional workload can have performance implications. For that reason, the use of an intermediate database to cache some of all of the information used to respond to OAI requests is very common with this type of scenario.

Scenario 4: An OAI Static Repository

The three scenarios described above all assume an OAI data provider application which can interact dynamically with a Web server—that is, can respond to OAI requests as they are received by creating on-the-fly the appropriate OAI responses. For some organizations, such as those which contract with outside vendors to maintain their organizational presence on the Web or otherwise do not directly maintain and manage their own Web servers, this may not be feasible. To address this problem, OAI has promulgated a *Specification for an OAI Static Repository and an OAI Static Repository Gateway*[16] (Hochstenbach et al. 2003). An OAI static repository is intended as a lower barrier alternative to full conformance with OAI-PMH and is meant for data providers with static or infrequently changing collections of less than 5,000 metadata items. Metadata, XML expertise, and Web access are still prerequisites, but in lieu of a requirement to implement a dynamic Web-accessible service, the specification only requires an OAI data provider to make a static XML file accessible at a persistent URL.

A compliant OAI static repository is a single XML file containing: i) pre-coordinated responses to OAI Identify and `ListMetadataFormats` requests; and ii) all of the metadata records which the data provider wishes to be able to disseminate (that is, all metadata items in `oai_dc` and also in any additional metadata formats supported by the data provider). The OAI static repository specification includes a special XML schema that defines elements to contain all of this information, properly arranged. Most optional features of OAI-PMH, including OAI sets and `persistent` or `transient` deleted-record policies, cannot be supported by static repositories.

OAI harvesters do not directly harvest XML static repository files. To make the contents of an OAI static repository available for harvesting, the data provider must first arrange intermediation with an OAI static repository gateway, such as the one maintained by the Open Language Archives Community.[17] This can be done through a registration process set up by the gateway, or through the use of the static repository `initiate` verb as defined by the specification. (The specification also defines a `terminate` verb for the opposite purpose.) As part of the process of initiating a static repository, the gateway application retrieves the XML static repository file from the URL provided by the data provider and validates that it conforms to the static repository XML schema. The gateway then provides the dynamic application support necessary to make the static repository harvestable—that is, it dynamically extracts information from the XML static repository file as necessary to respond to OAI harvester requests. Usually the gateway relies (for performance reasons) on a locally cached copy of the XML static repository file to fulfill OAI requests. Each time before responding, the gateway

FIGURE 5-8 OAI static repository architecture.

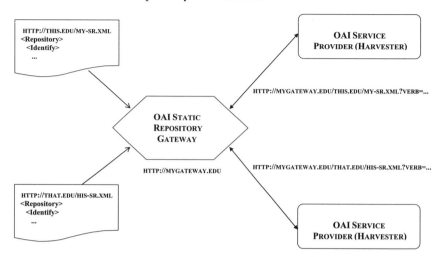

double-checks with the Web server where the original XML static repository file resides to verify that the locally cached copy is still current. If not, it retrieves and caches a new copy. The baseURL for the static repository is a concatenation of the baseURL for the gateway application and the URL for the XML static repository file. Figure 5-8 depicts the architecture.

COMMON ISSUES AND CHALLENGES FOR DATA PROVIDERS

As clear from the illustrative scenarios discussed above, OAI data provider implementations, regardless of underlying repository architecture, share certain functional characteristics. First, the data provider application must include some way to implement metadata record datestamps, unique and persistent OAI identifiers, and (optionally) organization of metadata items into sets. Depending on how metadata items are stored and accessed in the local repository architecture, the local-identifier component of OAI identifiers can be derived from a range of sources, for example, file system information, appropriate database table key columns, or the URL (or other persistent identifier) of the resource being described. Second, an OAI data provider application needs a reliable means by which to enumerate available metadata items, available sets, supported metadata formats, and an on-demand way to obtain the contents of individual metadata items, whether stored as XML files, as values in a database table, or as elements (for example, <meta> tags) contained in the information resource being described. Third, an OAI data provider application must be able to translate or transform the contents of stored metadata items into XML conformant with the desired dissemination metadata format schema(s), and must be able to encapsulate the XML form of the metadata record within the appropriate OAI-namespace XML structures.

Conceptually, the process is reasonably straightforward. Practical experience, however, reveals a number of opportunities for mistakes along the way. Described below are several frequently encountered OAI data provider implementation errors. Errors typically stem either from systematic mistakes in repository architecture and application code design or from errors in the actual metadata being processed. The errors discussed below include those reported frequently by the data provider validation and registry service maintained by the OAI (Warner 2005).

XML Validation

From the earliest introduction of OAI-PMH, the most frequently occurring OAI data provider problems have had to do with XML validation. Character-encoding problems are common, especially for implementers who rely on legacy, non-Unicode applications as the source for the metadata being disseminated. The default character encoding for XML and the character encoding required by OAI-PMH is *UTF-8*, a specific standard for encoding characters defined by the Unicode Standard.[18] Some legacy applications make use of earlier encoding standards. For example, some libraries still have large bodies of descriptive metadata with MARC-8 character encoding embedded. Other applications may use older versions of extensions to ASCII, such as ISO-8859 or Microsoft Windows code page 1252 character encodings. Characters encoded in any of these legacy, non-Unicode-compliant character encodings must be translated into UTF-8. Additionally HTML allows for special character entities not supported in well-formed XML (for example, the © entity, which is used in HTML to encode the © symbol, is not supported intrinsically by XML). Use of HTML-allowed entities in OAI responses will lead to XML character-encoding errors. Character-encoding problems can be difficult to isolate, since they may occur only in a few metadata records. However, the presence of one invalid character in a ListRecords response invalidates the entire response.

Failure to validate against schema is another common error encountered with OAI data provider implementations. XML validation errors vary from the obvious, mistakes in spelling of an XML metadata element name, to the subtler, for example, incorrect ordering of metadata elements. Data providers also have been known to inadvertently include elements from their repository-native metadata schema not allowed by the dissemination metadata record-format schema.

Commercial and open source XML-validating parsers allow OAI data providers to identify and resolve XML well-formedness and validation issues, but for large volume OAI data providers, the routine requirement to check all records that can be disseminated from a repository may be demanding. The continuing high frequency with which XML validation errors continue to be encountered (Warner 2005) suggests that many OAI data providers fail to take full advantage of such tools, or at least fail to check every record in their repository.

Datestamp Accuracy and Hidden Updates

Metadata record `datestamp` problems can be obvious (forgetting to include a `datestamp` when disseminating an OAI metadata record) or subtle (consistently calculating OAI `datestamps` incorrectly). OAI service providers can readily detect and report back to the OAI data provider the more obvious `datestamp` errors. Other `datestamp` problems may be more difficult for service providers to detect immediately, but in the long run, these can still have an adverse impact on metadata sharing. There are two difficult-to-detect OAI `datestamp`-related problems encountered frequently, although often unknowingly, by OAI-PMH service providers.

Consider a data provider in Illinois that fails to take into account the OAI-PMH requirement to express OAI record `datestamps` in Coordinated Universal Time (UTC). Such a data provider might give a record modified at 1 AM Thursday UTC an OAI `datestamp` value of 7 PM Wednesday (that is, local time when last modified). A service provider harvesting records at 12:01 AM Thursday UTC (6:01 PM local time in Illinois) would assume incorrectly that it had obtained all records from that repository which had Wednesday `datestamps`. At the next incremental harvest, it would ask only for records modified Thursday or later (UTC). Because the data provider incorrectly calculated the `datestamp` for the record modified Wednesday evening local time, the harvester would not get this updated record.

A similar problem can arise if the master copy of metadata items is maintained separately from the copy of metadata records used by the OAI data provider application. In such a situation, it is common for the copy of metadata items used by the OAI data provider application to be refreshed on a regular schedule by an automated process, say at 1 AM UTC each morning. Under this scenario, consider a metadata item that was modified at 3 PM on Wednesday afternoon UTC. Assuming an update of the OAI data provider repository on the regular cycle, that metadata record would not be available for harvesting until 1 AM Thursday morning UTC. If no adjustment in the last-modified OAI `datestamp` was made when the record was uploaded to the OAI data provider repository (that is, if the OAI `datestamp` for the item remained set at 3 PM Wednesday), a harvester requesting records at 12:01 AM Thursday UTC, that is, before the modified metadata item had been transferred into the repository, would again assume incorrectly that it had gotten from the OAI data provider all records with a Wednesday or earlier `datestamp`. Because these sorts of hidden `datestamp` errors are so common, some OAI harvesters overlap harvests by twenty-four or forty-eight hours, deleting any duplicate records post-harvest as necessary.

Other Hidden Errors

There are other "hidden" errors that can go unnoticed (for a while) by service providers. New OAI data providers often encounter subtle difficulties when implementing OAI sets. If a metadata item is a member of set B, and all of set B is considered a subset of set A, then the metadata item must be also a member of set A. The OAI record header must reflect membership in both sets. It is all too common to find implementations that leave out of records header membership in a parent set. This can then lead to what appears to be inconsistent results when selectively harvesting all metadata items in set A. Some records returned will appear that show membership (according to OAI record header) only in set B. OAI service providers that do not explicitly harvest set A, however, will not notice anything wrong.

Similarly, difficult-to-detect errors also can show up with regard to an OAI deleted-record policy. A deleted-record policy of `persistent` can be demanding to maintain over time since it implies that once a metadata item has been disseminated and then later deleted, the OAI data provider must maintain forever a record of the deleted status of that item. Given the tendency of some digital libraries to purge, migrate to new data-management systems, or otherwise clean house over time, this can be an onerous requirement. While much appreciated by OAI service providers, data providers should claim a deleted-records policy of `persistent` only when certain that the data storage architecture they use is stable enough to fulfill the commitment this policy implies.

Finally, configuration incompatibilities between Web servers and OAI applications can be a source of errors. Because OAI-PMH is implemented over the top of HTTP, responses to OAI requests, including responses to erroneous OAI requests, are conveyed as HTTP response messages. This implies that OAI responses have HTTP response message headers, articulating MIME type (HTTP Content-Type Header), response length in bytes (HTTP Content-Length Header), date and time of response, HTTP status code, etc. OAI data provider applications leave implementation of HTTP response message headers largely to the Web server application. However, incorrect HTTP headers can confuse the OAI harvesting application. It is important that all OAI responses be disseminated by the Web server as HTTP `Content-Type=text/xml`. Correct use of HTTP status codes, especially for responses to erroneous requests, also is critical.

QUESTIONS AND TOPICS FOR DISCUSSION

1. Consider how digital content and metadata are managed at your institution's library. Would you advocate implementing the protocol by integrating support for OAI-PMH into existing digital content management infrastructure, by creating a new implementation external to existing infrastructure just for OAI-PMH, or by migrating to a new digital content management system with support for OAI-PMH already built-in? Why?

2. As an OAI service provider, which optional features of the protocol would you most want to see implemented by the OAI data providers you harvest? Why?

3. Consider the range of local digital content available at your institution. If you are using OAI-PMH to make metadata describing this content available, would you organize your OAI data provider repository into sets? If so, how might you go about doing so?

4. Of the four implementation scenarios presented, which is closest to the way your institution's library currently manages metadata for digital resources? Which would you favor as a starting point for developing a local OAI-PMH implementation for your institution's library?

SUGGESTIONS FOR EXERCISES

1. Following on suggested exercise 2 from chapter 4 (which involved creating OAI metadata records from online catalog bibliographic displays), add about nodes to your OAI records. Be as complete as possible.
2. The OAI implementation guidelines for OAI Static Repositories[19] include both a sample OAI static repository instance and an XML schema against which OAI static repositories can be validated. Create your own OAI static repository instance containing at least five metadata items, each disseminated in at least `oai_dc` metadata format.
3. Visit the Web sites for three vended or open source systems with built-in support for OAI-PMH. (To find Web addresses for such systems, see chapter 2 or the tools Web page maintained by the OAI at http://www.openarchives.org/tools/tools.html.) Compare and contrast the support of each application for OAI-PMH, for example, in terms of optional OAI-PMH features supported.

NOTES

1. http://www.openarchives.org/OAI/2.0/guidelines-repository.htm.
2. http://www.oclc.org/research/software/oai/cat.htm.
3. http://www.apache.org/.
4. http://www.microsoft.com/WindowsServer2003/iis/default.mspx.
5. http://www.oclc.org/contentdm/.
6. http://www.openarchives.org/OAI/2.0/guidelines.htm.
7. http://www.openarchives.org/OAI/2.0/guidelines-repository.htm.
8. Ibid.
9. http://www.openarchives.org/OAI/2.0/guidelines-provenance.htm.
10. http://www.openarchives.org/OAI/2.0/guidelines-rights.htm.
11. http://www.openarchives.org/OAI/2.0/guidelines-repository.htm.
12. http://www.oclc.org/research/projects/oairesolver/.
13. http://www.openarchives.org/OAI/2.0/guidelines-oai-identifier.htm.
14. http://www.loc.gov/standards/marcxml/.
15. http://uilib-oai.sourceforge.net/.
16. http://www.openarchives.org/OAI/2.0/guidelines-static-repository.htm.
17. http://www.language-archives.org/sr.
18. http://www.unicode.org/standard/standard.html.
19. http://www.openarchives.org/OAI/2.0/guidelines-static-repository.htm.

REFERENCES

Berners-Lee, T., R. Fielding, and L. Manister. 1998. *Uniform Resource Identifiers (URI): Generic Syntax [Request for Comments: 2396].* Reston, VA: The Internet Society. http://www.ietf.org/rfc/rfc2396.txt.

Hochstenbach, Patrick, Henry Jerez, and Herbert Van de Sompel. 2003. The OAI-PMH static repository and static repository gateway. *JCDL '03: Proceedings of the 3rd ACM/IEEE-CS Joint Conference on Digital Libraries*, 210–217. Los Alamitos, CA: IEEE Computer Society.

Warner, Simeon. 2005. OAI Data-Provider Registration and Validation Service, ed. A. Rauber, S. Christodoulakis, and A. M. Tjoa, *Research and Advanced Technology for Digital Libraries, Proceedings of the 9th European Conference, ECDL 2005, Vienna, Austria, September 18–23*, 491–492. Lecture Notes in Computer Science 3652. Berlin: Springer-Verlag. More extensive version of paper is available from arXiv. org as preprint cs.DL/0506010, http://arxiv.org/abs/cs.DL/0506010.

PART III

Sharable Metadata: Creating and Using

CHAPTER 6

Creating Metadata to Share

Metadata are structured data that facilitate librarian and library user interactions with information resources. Good and appropriate metadata can facilitate discovery, identification, selection, management, and use of information. Considered a tool for building digital libraries, OAI-PMH is only as useful as the metadata records shared by content providers via the protocol.

The records of a library's online catalog are a familiar example of metadata. They allow library users to discover and locate a book in a library's collection. In this example, the book is the information resource the user is seeking. A user typically is not interested in the catalog record itself but rather in the book; however, the catalog record can help a user understand what a book is about and can help a user decide if a specific book is more or less likely to be relevant to his or her information need. Digital library collections tend to include a wider variety and more varied granularity of resources than print or analog library collections—for example, not only digital books, but also individual digital reports, articles, images, audio recordings, videos, Web pages, and datasets, all mixed together. Nonetheless, descriptive metadata records in a digital library can serve much the same function for a digital library user as online catalog records in a traditional print-based library serve for users of that library.

Metadata play an even more central role in digital library systems than in systems designed solely for print collection management and use. Designers and architects of digital library systems are increasingly finding additional uses for metadata. Metadata can be used for a multiplicity of functions in a digital library system. *A Framework of Guidance for Building Good Digital Collections* describes metadata as supporting the "discovery, description, use, administration, and/or management" of information resources in a digital library (NISO Framework Advisory Group 2004). Metadata is one of the four core entities around which the Framework itself is organized. (The others are projects, collections, and objects.)

In 2006, almost all large *distributed digital libraries* (that is, digital libraries encompassing content distributed across multiple servers dispersed widely across the Web) relied on metadata to enable core functions and services offered. Given sufficiently rich metadata, these systems do not need to ingest the digital information resources themselves in order to provide useful services. It is enough to aggregate metadata about the resources. Quality metadata helps librarians and users comprehend and use digital information resources more efficiently and more fully. The success of OAI-PMH is evidence of the value and utility of metadata.

A metadata format specifies the syntax and semantics to be used in constructing a metadata record about a resource. As described in earlier chapters, OAI-PMH requires that each harvestable metadata record be expressed as XML (dictating the syntax of metadata formats used with OAI-PMH) conforming to a specific XML schema (declaring the semantics of the metadata format). In order to ensure a minimum level of interoperability across all OAI data provider repositories, the protocol requires that all metadata items in an OAI data provider repository be made available in the unqualified (simple) DC metadata format. Use of additional metadata formats is optional, albeit strongly encouraged.

There are different types of metadata designed to enable different types of interactions with resources. Metadata may describe the content of a resource, define rights and conditions of use, describe the structure of a resource, provide information to manage and preserve the resource, describe the technical characteristics of a resource (for example, the scanner parameters used to digitize a picture), or provide a pointer to retrieve a specific view or instantiation of a resource. *A Framework of Guidance for Building Good Digital Collections* categorizes metadata as descriptive, administrative, or structural, with further subdivisions of these top-level categories to explicitly include metadata dealing with rights, management, preservation, and so on (NISO Framework Advisory Group 2004).

Through 2006, descriptive metadata had been the kind of metadata most in demand to support the construction of distributed digital libraries. Although experiments with harvesting other categories of metadata (and even complete information objects) have been performed using OAI-PMH, the protocol has been used primarily to share descriptive metadata. However, even limiting consideration to descriptive metadata, available metadata records describing library and other kinds of information resources tend to be highly heterogeneous. There are a myriad of reasons for this, chief among them the heterogeneity of the communities and catalogers creating metadata, which in turn has led to a large array of different metadata schema (see also the discussion in chapter 2 of Intner, Lazinger, and Weihs 2006).

The heterogeneity of metadata creation practices encountered by OAI service providers has created a number of challenges. Resolution of these challenges cannot be accomplished solely by OAI service providers. Institutions that implement OAI data provider repositories have an obligation to define sensible metadata creation and dissemination strategies that are cognizant of requirements for metadata interoperability and reuse. Metadata created with sharing in mind can help ensure the effective representation of resources in the context of distributed digital library systems being built by OAI service providers. *A Framework of Guidance for Building Good Digital Collections* recommends that digital library collections, metadata, and objects "be viewed not only within the context of the projects that created them but as building blocks that others can reuse, repackage, and build services upon. Indicators of goodness must now emphasize factors contributing to interoperability, reusability, persistence, verification, documentation, and support for intellectual property rights" (NISO Framework Advisory Group 2004).

A complete treatise on metadata is beyond the scope of this text. This chapter provides a practical context for prospective OAI data providers creating or retrospectively enhancing metadata to be shared using OAI-PMH. A representative sample of metadata formats that have been used or considered for use with OAI-PMH is introduced, and format features most relevant within the context of OAI-PMH are briefly discussed. The range and diversity of metadata formats listed are indicative of the potential reach of OAI-PMH. This chapter concludes with a brief discussion of practical considerations for sharing metadata: factors bearing on the selection of metadata format(s); issues to be considered when transforming local metadata for use with OAI-PMH; and comments on *metadata quality* and the nature of *sharable metadata*. Chapter 7 considers metadata sharing from the other side of the collaboration, looking at strategies OAI service providers employ to harmonize and enrich metadata harvested using OAI-PMH.

THE DUBLIN CORE METADATA FORMATS

In her guide entitled *Using Dublin Core*, Diane Hillmann of Cornell University defines DC as a metadata standard that "is a simple yet effective element set for describing a wide range of networked resources" (Hillmann 2005). The DC standard defines two levels of description, unqualified DC (also referred to as simple DC) and qualified DC. For the purposes of OAI-PMH, the two levels of the DC standard are treated as two different metadata formats. In the syntax of OAI-PMH, the `metadataPrefix` for unqualified DC is `oai_dc`.

Hillmann goes on to state that the semantics of both qualified and unqualified DC "have been established through consensus by an international, cross-disciplinary group of professionals from librarianship, computer science, text encoding, the museum community, and other related fields of scholarship" (Hillmann 2005). The limited complexity and the broad consensus vetting of unqualified DC are among the primary reasons why it was selected as the one OAI-PMH mandatory metadata format. DC is designed to be useable by the nonspecialist, but is also perceived as useable by and useful for library catalogers as a way to create good, albeit basic, digital resource descriptions (Coleman 2005). Both unqualified DC and qualified DC have been used successfully with OAI-PMH.

The Fifteen Elements of Unqualified DC

The elements of unqualified DC were originally known collectively as the Dublin Core Metadata Element Set (DCMES) and were created as a means to express a limited set of metadata values pertaining to any digital resource. Version 1.0 of DCMES was published in September 1998 (Weibel et al.), and version 1.1 was subsequently released in 1999.[1] (Release of another version is unlikely.) Unqualified DC is intended to facilitate the description of Web pages and other Internet resources and to be used by content creators as well as by librarians and other professional curators of digital content. It is a minimal set of elements providing a basic level of semantic interoperability across distributed resources. The fifteen elements of unqualified DC were introduced briefly in chapter 2, but are listed again in Table 6-1, this time with their formal, canonical definitions and subdivided into three categories:

1. elements related mainly to the *content* of the resource,
2. elements related mainly to the resource when viewed as *intellectual property*, and
3. elements related mainly to the *instantiation* of the resource.

This categorization of the unqualified DC elements dates from the same September 1998 Internet Society Internet Engineering Task Force Request for Comments, IETF-RFC 2413 (Weibel et al. 1998), which presented version 1.0 of DCMES to the broader Internet community.

In unqualified DC, no element is mandatory. All are repeatable. This means that a metadata record containing a single element—for example, a

TABLE 6-1   Dublin Core Metadata Element Set, version 1.1.

Content elements	
Title	A name given to the resource
Subject	The topic of the content of the resource
Description	An account of the content of the resource
Relation	A reference to a related resource
Coverage	The extent or scope of the content of the resource
Source	A reference to a resource from which the present resource is derived
Type	The nature or genre of the content of the resource
Intellectual property elements	
Creator	An entity primarily responsible for making the content of the resource
Publisher	An entity responsible for making the resource available
Contributor	An entity responsible for making contributions to the content of the resource
Rights	Information about rights held in and over the resource
Instantiation elements	
Date	A date associated with an event in the life cycle of the resource
Format	The physical or digital manifestation of the resource
Identifier	An unambiguous reference to the resource within a given context
Language	A language of the intellectual content of the resource

DC title element only—is valid. It also means that it is possible to assign as many DC title elements or DC date elements as necessary (see for example Figure 6-1). While this illustrates the flexibility of the standard, it also illustrates the breadth of different usage that can be encountered by OAI service providers when harvesting unqualified DC metadata describing heterogeneous information resources from multiple sources.

The Dublin Core Metadata Initiative (DCMI) maintains the DC Web site[2] (with support from OCLC Online Computer Library Center), works to promote the use of DC, and encourages wide participation through e-mail lists, annual conferences, and the chartering of the DCMI Architecture Forum, DCMI communities, and DCMI task groups. The element names of unqualified DC are intended to be intuitive, although in practice differences over the finer points of usage have sparked many spirited discussions on DCMI group e-mail lists. Extensive documentation providing guidance on unqualified DC element usage has been developed in the years since its initial release. Documentation is maintained by the DCMI on the DC Web site. DCMES Version 1.1 has become an international standard, ISO 15836-2003.[3]

The fifteen elements of unqualified DC have their own distinct XML namespace (http://purl.org/dc/elements/1.1/). The DCMI maintains an XML schema for unqualified DC[4] as well as an RDF (Resource Description Framework) schema.[5] While the DCMI's XML schema for unqualified DC defines XML semantics for all fifteen elements of the metadata format, it does not define a root or top-level XML element to contain the fifteen elements. A separate XML schema defining such a root element is maintained by the

FIGURE 6-1 Unqualified Dublin Core metadata from a harvested OAI record describing a digitized version of an architectural floor plan drawing.

```
<oai_dc:dc xsi:schemaLocation="http://www.openarchives.org/OAI/2.0/oai_dc/
    http://www.openarchives.org/OAI/2.0/oai_dc.xsd"
  xmlns="http://purl.org/dc/elements/1.1/"
  xmlns:xsi="http://www.w3.org/2001/XMLSchema-instance"
  xmlns:oai_dc="http://www.openarchives.org/OAI/2.0/oai_dc/">
 <title>Old Main (New Design) 1929-2000</title>
 <subject>Federal-Revival Style</subject>
 <date>1929</date>
 <date>1931</date>
 <date>1931</date>
 <description>
    President's Office, Administrative Offices, Student Offices and
    Meeting Rooms</description>
 <title>Old Main Building Third Floor Plan</title>
 <date>1996</date>
 <description>Plot Plans</description>
 <creator>Penn State University Office of Physical Plant</creator>
 <relation>University Park Campus History Collection:
    http://www.psubldg.libraries.psu.edu</relation>
 <source>Pennsylvania State University Archives</source>
 <format>JPEG</format>
 <rights>This image is posted publicly for non-profit educational uses,
    excluding printed publication. Other uses are not permitted.
    For details please see:
    http://alias.libraries.psu.edu/vius/copyright/publicrightssc.htm</rights>
 <identifier>opp_bldg_old-main49A.tif</identifier>
 <identifier>UP29</identifier>
 <identifier>http://Collection1.libraries.psu.edu/u?/upchc,3</identifier>
</oai_dc:dc>
```

OAI[6] to facilitate the use of unqualified DC in the context of OAI-PMH. The OAI schema imports the canonical XML schema maintained by the DCMI and defines as new only the top-level container element required to hold the elements defined by the DCMI's XML schema. During beta testing of OAI-PMH version 1.0, the OAI maintained complete, independent XML schemas for both unqualified DC and the MARC metadata format discussed below. Subsequent release of unqualified DC and MARC XML schemas by the DCMI and the Library of Congress respectively allowed the OAI to discontinue the OAI MARC XML schema altogether and to simplify the OAI unqualified DC schema. These changes also reduced the potential for any synchronicity problems across different schemas for the same metadata format.

As of late 2006, the DCMI Architecture Forum was considering a new recommendation for expressing unqualified and qualified DC in XML. Although this work will likely lead to an alternative way to express DC in XML, Andy Powell, 2006 chair of the DCMI Architecture Forum, is on record on the group's Web site saying he does not "expect [that] the current mechanism for encoding simple DC in OAI-PMH is going to change."[7]

Qualified DC

Recognizing the need for a level of resource description beyond that possible with unqualified DC, the DCMI has added new DC elements, element refinements, and encoding schemes, and has developed a controlled vocabulary for describing resource types. Collectively and in combination with the fifteen stand-alone elements of unqualified DC, these are known as qualified DC.[8] The DCMI Usage Board reviews and ultimately makes determinations about updates and additions to DC that occur on an ongoing basis. According to the board's Web site, new stand-alone elements and element refinements can be approved as either *conforming*, "those for which an implementation community has a demonstrated need and which conform to the DCMI Abstract Model," or *recommended*, those "that conform to the DCMI Abstract Model and do not semantically overlap with other terms in DCMI namespaces."[9] For purposes of OAI-PMH as of this writing, the distinction is insignificant.

All elements of unqualified DC are understood to be part of qualified DC. Since the release of DCMES version 1.1 and through the end of 2005, the DCMI Usage Board had added one new element as recommended and six new elements as conforming. Including the fifteen elements of unqualified DC, this brings to twenty-two the total number of stand-alone elements included in qualified DC. While there was some controversy early on, *Using Dublin Core* (Hillmann 2005) and other documentation on the DCMI Web site treat as settled that all elements that have been approved by the DCMI Usage Board since the release of DCMES version 1.1 are part of qualified DC only—that is, new stand-alone elements do not become part of unqualified DC. For XML schema purposes, the seven newly added stand-alone elements are declared in an XML namespace (http://purl.org/dc/terms/)

TABLE 6-2   The additional stand-alone elements of qualified Dublin Core (as of September 2006).

	New "recommended" elements
audience	A class of entity for whom the resource is intended or useful (added May 21, 2001)

	New "conforming" elements
accrualMethod	The method by which items are added to a collection (added June 13, 2005)
accrualPeriodicity	The frequency with which items are added to a collection (added June 13, 2005)
accrualPolicy	The policy governing the addition of items to a collection (added June 13, 2005)
instructionalMethod	A process, used to engender knowledge, attitudes, and skills that the resource is designed to support (added June 13, 2005)
provenance	A statement of any changes in ownership and custody of the resource since its creation that are significant for its authenticity, integrity, and interpretation (added September 20, 2004)
rightsHolder	A person or organization owning or managing rights over the resource (added June 14, 2004)

separate from that used to declare the unqualified DC elements. Qualified DC element refinements and encoding schemes also are declared in this namespace, reinforcing the idea that the seven new stand-alone elements are part of qualified DC, but not part of unqualified DC. The qualified DC controlled vocabulary for resource types is declared in a third namespace (http://purl.org/dc/dcmitype/). Table 6-2 lists the seven stand-alone elements that have been added to qualified DC since the release of DCMES version 1.1.

Qualified DC adds a special new class of elements called element refinements. Refinements are metadata elements that refine the meaning of one of the twenty-two stand-alone elements of qualified DC. For example, the DC `date` element can be used to contain any "date associated with an event in the life cycle of the resource."[10] Sometimes it can be useful to know precisely which date (that is, the date of which event in the resource life cycle) is being provided. Qualified DC includes element refinements for that purpose, specifically: `available`, `created`, `dateAccepted`, `dateCopyrighted`, `dateSubmitted`, `issued`, `modified`, and `valid`. In qualified DC expressed as XML, these specific element refinements may appear in metadata records in lieu of the DC `date` element, that is, as a more precise form of that element. Applications processing qualified DC records understand the semantic relationship of DC `date` element refinements to the DC `date` element. As of 2006, thirty-three element refinements had been defined.[11] These are listed in order by the element refined in Table 6-3.

The mechanism of element refinements can facilitate more precise searching, browsing, identification, selection, and grouping of resources. At the same time, the relationship between element refinements and the element refined (in this example, DC date) facilitates transformation of qualified DC metadata records to unqualified DC—for example, all element refinements of DC date in a qualified DC record are transformed to DC date elements in the unqualified version of that record. The only limitation of this approach to transforming qualified DC into unqualified DC (commonly referred to as *dumbing down*) occurs when transforming element refinements which refine stand-alone elements of qualified DC that are not included in unqualified DC. For instance, element refinements `educationLevel` and `mediator` refine DC audience, but knowing this does not really help us realize where or whether the value of an `educationLevel` element refinement appearing in a qualified DC record should be included in the unqualified DC record describing the same resource. In practice, implementers must assess whether including the information contained in such an element refinement in an alternative unqualified DC element (for example, DC description) is likely to be more useful than confusing to potential users of the metadata record.

Qualified DC also supports the use of encoding schemes. There is a natural tendency when describing metadata formats used with OAI-PMH to focus on metadata element names. However, at least as important in practice when creating a metadata record to share are the rules or *metadata content standards* which are used to create the values (that is, the strings of text) that are placed within the XML nodes of the metadata record. (For a more in-depth discussion of metadata content standards, see chapter 3 of Intner, Lazinger, and Weihs 2006.) Qualified DC encoding schemes provide a way for metadata creators to explicitly label metadata values as coming from a specific terminology or controlled vocabulary or as adhering to a specific formal notation. For an OAI service provider, knowing what rules were used by an OAI data provider to create metadata values can be desirable and in some cases enabling. Knowing explicitly which DC subject elements contain values taken from a particular controlled vocabulary (for example, the Library of Congress Subject Headings) or which DC date values conform to the W3C Date Time Format (W3CDTF) allows the OAI service provider to unambiguously interpret and manipulate harvested metadata values in ways to provide enhanced services to end users (for example, by grouping, filtering, or ranking records according to specific controlled vocabularies or consistently formatted values). As of late 2006, qualified DC included eighteen encoding schemes.[12] These are listed in Table 6-3 along with the qualified DC element refinements discussed above.

While the DCMI generally encourages the use of controlled vocabularies (for example, for subjects, place names, and language names), it does not maintain controlled vocabularies of its own. The one exception is a resource-type vocabulary. The DC `type` and DC `format` elements are sometimes confused. DC `format` should be used to identify the manifestation of the resource in a way that informs as to the hardware or software required to use the resource. The recommended controlled vocabulary for DC `format` is the *Internet Media Type* list[13] maintained by the Internet Assigned Numbers

TABLE 6-3 Qualified Dublin Core element refinements and encoding schemes (as of September 2006) listed by stand-alone element qualified.

Stand-alone element	Element refinement	Encoding scheme[a]
Audience	educationLevel, mediator	
Coverage	spatial, temporal	Box, ISO3166, Point, TGN
Date	available, created, dateAccepted, dateCopyrighted, dateSubmitted, issued, modified, valid	Period, W3CDTF
Description	abstract, tableOfContents	
Format	extent, medium	IMT
Identifier	bibliographicCitation	URI
Language		ISO639-2, RFC1766, RFC3066
Relation	conformsTo, hasFormat, hasPart, hasVersion, isFormatOf, isPartOf, isReferencedBy, isReplacedBy, isRequiredBy, isVersionOf, references, replaces, requires	URI
Rights	accessRights, license	
Source		URI
Subject		DDC, LCC, LCSH, MESH, NLM, UDC
Title	alternative	
Type		DCMIType

[a] Encoding scheme may be allowed only with selected element refinements, or may be allowed only with a stand-alone element, or may be allowed with both.

Note: There are no element refinements or encoding schemes associated with the following: *accrualMethod, accrualPeriodicity, accrualPolicy, contributor, creator, instructionalMethod, provenance, publisher,* and *rightsHolder.*

Authority. Using this controlled vocabulary, the DC `format` metadata value for describing an Adobe PDF document would be `application/pdf`. DC `type` should be used to categorize the genre of the resource more broadly, independent of computer file format and in a way more meaningful to a human end user. The DC `type` of an Adobe PDF document would be `Text`. As of 2006, the DCMI-maintained controlled vocabulary for encoding DC type was: `Collection`, `Dataset`, `Event`, `Image`, `InteractiveResource`, `MovingImage`, `PhysicalObject`, `Service`, `Software`, `Sound`, `StillImage`, and `Text`.

The DCMI maintains approved recommendations for expressing qualified DC in HTML/XHTML and XML. (As of late 2006, a proposed recommendation from 2001, last updated in 2002, for expressing qualified DC in RDF/XML was still pending.) The recommended guidelines in place as of late 2006 for expressing qualified DC in XML[14] gave specific advice on syntax to use for expressing qualified DC entities in XML. In XML, stand-alone elements and element refinements are treated the same way—that is, they occur at the same level of the XML hierarchy and there is nothing in the XML instance to suggest the relationship between element refinements and the

FIGURE 6-2   Qualified Dublin Core metadata from a record harvested using OAI-PMH.

```
<dc_qual:qualifieddc
    xsi:schemaLocation="http://cicharvest.grainger.uiuc.edu/schemas/QDC/
      http://cicharvest.grainger.uiuc.edu/schemas/QDC/2004/07/14/CICQualifiedDC.xsd"
    xmlns:xsi="http://www.w3.org/2001/XMLSchema-instance"
    xmlns:dc_qual="http://cicharvest.grainger.uiuc.edu/schemas/QDC/"
    xmlns:dc="http://purl.org/dc/elements/1.1/"
    xmlns:dct="http://purl.org/dc/terms/"
    xmlns:dcmitype="http://purl.org/dc/dcmitype/">
  <dct:spatial>Juneau</dct:spatial>
  <dct:spatial>Juneau County</dct:spatial>
  <dc:description>Lantern slides</dc:description>
  <dc:description>8.1 x 10.1 cm</dc:description>
  <dct:isPartOf>American Environmental Photographs</dct:isPartOf>
  <dc:identifier>http://pi.lib.uchicago.edu/1001/dig/aep/AEP-AKS6</dc:identifier>
  <dc:relation>University of Chicago Department of Botany Records</dc:relation>
  <dc:publisher>
    University of Chicago Library, Special Collections Research Center
  </dc:publisher>
  <dct:spatial>Alaska</dct:spatial>
  <dc:subject xsi:type="dct:LCSH">Tundras</dc:subject>
  <dc:subject xsi:type="dct:LCSH">Snow</dc:subject>
  <dc:title>Mountain tundra [and] snowfields near Juneau, Alaska</dc:title>
  <dc:type>Image</dc:type>
  <dc:rights>http://pi.lib.uchicago.edu/h/2004-001</dc:rights>
</dc_qual:qualifieddc>
```

stand-alone elements they refine. (Implementers and applications must infer this from the XML schemas and from other supporting documentation.) Qualified DC encoding schemes are expressed by typing the XML element or element refinement through the use of a `type` attribute from the XSI *(XML Schema Instance)* namespace. For instance: `<dc:type xsi:type="dct:DCMIType">Image</dc:type>`.

The DCMI Web-published guidelines for expressing qualified DC in XML reference a set of XML schemas[15] declaring entities from all three of the DC namespaces mentioned above; however, as with unqualified DC, no XML schema is provided which declares an XML element to contain all the entities of qualified DC. (Note also that in a subtle way the qualified DC XML schema-declaring elements in the http://purl.org/dc/terms/namespace, that is, the stand-alone elements of unqualified DC, differs from the DCMI-recommended XML schema for unqualified DC. The two XML schemas cannot be used interchangeably.)

As with unqualified DC, it is assumed that communities will import the DCMI XML schemas for qualified DC into community-based XML schemas, declaring community-specific namespaces and container elements as needed. Unfortunately, unlike with unqualified DC, OAI does not provide such a schema. This has proven an impediment to the use of qualified DC with OAI-PMH; however, there are a few examples of general-purpose, community-based schemas for qualified DC that have been used successfully with OAI-PMH.[16, 17] Figure 6-2 shows the metadata node of a qualified DC metadata record harvested using OAI-PMH. As mentioned above, further DCMI recommendations with regard to expressing both unqualified and qualified DC in XML are anticipated. Unlike with unqualified DC, the preferred way to express qualified DC metadata in an OAI-PMH context may evolve.

DC Application Profiles

An *application profile* is a customization of a standard metadata format for a particular application or community of use (Heery and Patel 2000). Application profiles elaborate on the generic guidelines for using a metadata format. An application profile may make generically optional elements of the format required, or may disallow use of certain elements normally allowed by the format. An application profile may also provide elaboration on when or how to use a specific element and may provide guidance regarding value encoding, that is, the use of controlled vocabularies and syntactic rules for creating metadata values. An application profile also may provide guidance on how to intermingle semantics from multiple metadata formats.

DCMI has encouraged and facilitated the creation of DC application profiles by DCMI communities and task groups. DC application profiles have been created or are under construction for library resources,[18] for educational resources,[19] and for describing collections.[20] The 2004 working draft of the DC library application profile, for instance, makes use of elements from the MODS metadata format (described below) as well as from qualified DC. For each element treated by the DC library application profile, the profile specifies a level of obligation—either mandatory (M), mandatory if applicable (MA), strongly recommended (R), or optional (O). Encoding-scheme recommendations are made for many elements and element refinements used by the DC library application profile, including encoding schemes from authorities not mentioned by qualified DC (for example, the MARC code list for organizations).

DC application profiles are typically the result of large-group consensus and are often well optimized for interoperability within a broad community of practice. For this reason, DC application profiles can be extremely useful to OAI data providers seeking guidance on how to create metadata well suited for sharing within a particular domain. However, as of late 2006, XML schemas specific to DC application profiles were lacking. This means, for example, that an OAI data provider wanting to use the DC library application profile with OAI-PMH would first have to construct an XML schema that encoded the guidelines of that application profile. This is a significant undertaking, so for now DC application profiles are most often just consulted for guidance on how to create qualified DC metadata records which are optimized for use within a specific domain or community of practice. Enforcement of specific application profile rules by XML schema is not implemented. Generic qualified DC XML schemas are used instead.

OTHER METADATA FORMATS USED WITH OAI-PMH

Because unqualified DC (`metadataPrefix oai_dc`) is required by OAI-PMH, it is the most common metadata format in use among OAI data providers. However, the unqualified DC metadata format supports only a limited level of description. While it can be useful as a lowest common denominator for describing heterogeneous resources, to support more advanced functionality, and especially when sharing resources within a specific academic domain or community of practice, richer metadata is desirable. Sheila Intner, Susan Lazinger, and Jean Weihs note that, "Every organization has its own internal language, its own jargon, that has evolved over time so people within it can communicate meaning to each other. Metadata identifies an organization's own 'language' .... " (Intner, Lazinger, and Weihs 2006, p. 21). The same can be said about each community of discipline or practice, both within and external to the community of traditional libraries.

Whenever possible, OAI data providers should expose richer metadata formats. Institutions use a variety of metadata formats for their internal applications, rarely relying exclusively on unqualified DC. Metadata formats are conceived for different models of use. They can serve different types of applications. Some OAI service providers may be interested in using metadata records with more precise semantics. Major non-DC metadata formats that have been used with OAI-PMH or are being investigated for possible use with OAI-PMH are briefly introduced here. (For further discussions of these and other commonly used metadata schemas and content standards suitable for use with OAI-PMH, see also Baca 1998; Caplan 2003; Hillmann and Westbrooks 2004; Smiraglia 2005; and Intner, Lazinger, and Weihs 2006.)

MARCXML (MAchine-Readable Cataloging Bibliographic Format in XML)

MARC is a set of bibliographic metadata formats with roots dating back to the 1960s. MARC 21 is a version of the MARC bibliographic formats developed in the late 1990s as the result of successful efforts to harmonize the U.S. MARC standard and the Canadian CAN/MARC standard.[21, 22] More recently, the British Library has migrated from UKMARC to the MARC 21 standard as well.[23] MARC 21 documentation is available from the Library of Congress.[24] (The Library and Archives Canada also maintains a complementary MARC 21 standards site.[25]) The Library of Congress maintains under the name MARCXML an XML schema to encode MARC 21 records in XML.[26] A series of conversion tools to transform or *crosswalk* from MARC 21 to MARCXML and from MARCXML to unqualified DC and other metadata formats are also available on the Library of Congress Web site.[27]

For some library implementations MARCXML is an appealing format to use with OAI-PMH. Library catalogers are familiar with the format and with associated metadata content standards, for example, the *Anglo-American Cataloging Rules* (*AACR2*[28]). MARC 21 metadata may already exist for print library resources being digitized. However, the roots of MARC predate the Web and the advent of many formats and types of digital information resources. It is unlikely that MARCXML will achieve the dominance as a metadata format in the digital library domain that it enjoys in traditional print libraries.

The bodies responsible for the maintenance of *AACR2* have begun work collaboratively on a new metadata content standard, *RDA: Resource Description and Access*,[29] better suited for use in the digital realm. Meanwhile work on other formats that may supplant MARC itself for use with digital content is well along.

MODS (Metadata Object Description Schema)

MODS was created to provide an alternate way to express selected metadata from MARC 21 records in XML. MODS also facilitates the original creation of descriptive records for digital information resources. MODS includes a subset of MARC fields, but uses language-based XML element names rather than numeric names (as are used in MARCXML) to encode these fields, in some cases also regrouping elements differently from the MARC 21 bibliographic format. The top-level elements of MODS are listed in Table 6-4. As with MARCXML, MODS documentation is maintained by the Library of Congress.[30] An XML schema for the MODS format[31] and a series of stylesheets to crosswalk MODS records into MARCXML and vice versa and MODS records into simple DC and vice versa are among the MODS-related documents maintained on the Library of Congress MODS Web site.[32] As with MARCXML, the MODS XML schema defines two different root elements, one (<mods>) to use when expressing a single MODS record in an XML document instance and one (<modsCollection>) to use when expressing multiple MODS records in a single XML document instance.

Early in its history MODS was rarely used as a native format. More often the format was used as a way to share metadata records originally created in MARC. However, more recently a series of application profiles and implementation guidelines have been created for authoring metadata directly in MODS, for example, one for sharing descriptions of digital cultural heritage and humanities-based scholarly resources[33] and another to encode thesis and dissertations. The mid-2006 release of version 3.2 of the MODS format included several attributes and other entities not found in MARCXML. It is

TABLE 6-4   The top-level elements of MODS.

titleInfo	note
name	subject
typeOfResource	classification
genre	relatedItem
originInfo	identifier
language	location
physicalDescription	accessCondition
abstract	part
tableOfContents	extension
targetAudience	recordInfo

anticipated that over time the MODS format will continue to diverge from MARCXML. Original cataloging in MODS is increasing.

Formats for Works of Art, Visual Resources, and Cultural Materials

The Visual Resources Association (VRA) is an international organization of image media specialists and counts among its membership librarians and curators who manage art slide libraries and other collections of visual resources. The VRA Data Standards Committee maintains VRA Core, a descriptive standard for use with visual resources and cultural heritage materials. As of late 2006, VRA Core version 4.0 was in beta-phase release (that is, a phase of standards development designed to allow for final testing and comment prior to formal release as an approved standard). New with this version of VRA Core was an XML schema suitable for use with OAI-PMH. Schema and documentation are linked from the VRA Data Standards Committee home page.[34]

The Getty Research Institute (a part of the J. Paul Getty Trust) also maintains data standards and guidelines designed to support and facilitate access to and use of visual works and the construction of online art information systems. *Categories for the Description of Works of Art* (*CDWA*[35]) is a descriptive standard maintained on the Getty Research Institute Web site for describing works of art and material culture. CDWA-Lite[36] is an XML schema that defines an XML metadata format based on the CDWA descriptive standard and *Cataloging Cultural Objects* (*CCO*[37]), a metadata content standard promulgated and maintained by the VRA. By design, CDWA-Lite is intended for use with OAI-PMH.

CDWA-Lite and VRA Core have some similarities. As a metadata content standard, CCO is designed to inform use of terminologies and notations for both formats. Both CDWA-Lite and VRA Core include special features designed to explicitly differentiate and express relationships between images of a work and the work itself. Metadata that describe a painting as a work of art are segregated from metadata that describe a digital image (view) of that painting. Multiple images (views) may be associated with a single work. When expressed as XML, linkages between image and work metadata are maintained through the use of XML attributes created for that purpose.

This approach to descriptive granularity is potentially powerful, but also quite different from the approach taken by formats like DC, MARCXML, and MODS. This can create issues for OAI data providers and OAI service providers who want to use CDWA-Lite or VRA Core. For OAI data providers who must organize their OAI data repository into metadata items, it is unclear how best to define a single organization of items that at once supports dissemination of metadata in both unqualified DC and VRA Core or CDWA-Lite. For OAI service providers aggregating heterogeneous metadata in several formats including VRA Core and CDWA-Lite, it is unclear how best to comingle descriptions in different formats. More experimentation and experience using these formats in the context of OAI-PMH is needed.

EAD (Encoded Archival Description)

Early work on the *Encoded Archival Description (EAD)* format predated XML (initial development of the format began at the University of California at Berkeley in 1993). EAD was initially implemented as an SGML Document Type Definition (DTD). EAD is a format designed to encode descriptions of archival collections. EAD is maintained in partnership by the Library of Congress and the Society of American Archivists, and is closely related to (and was influenced during its development by) ISAD(G), the *General International Standard for Archival Description* maintained by the Committee on Descriptive Standards of the International Council of Archives.[38] As of late 2006, the current release of the format was the EAD 2002 DTD (XML compatible). An official XML schema for EAD 2002 is in beta-phase testing, with formal release expected in early 2007. In the meantime, a few implementers have begun testing EAD with OAI-PMH using locally developed XML schemas, for example, at Princeton University.[39] (For a more in-depth discussion of evolution of EAD and the related Encoded Archival Context standard, see Thurman 2005.)

An objective of EAD is to make archival resources more widely available and accessible. To achieve this objective, EAD must accommodate and reflect a wide range of archival descriptive practice. While EAD can be used to describe a single, indivisible resource, EAD records are most often used to describe archival collections, that is, groups of related resources rather than individual items. An archival collection might consist of numerous boxes of materials collected by or about a specific individual or institution or relating to a specific event. An EAD record will divide an archival collection into subordinate components, for example, groups of boxes, individual boxes, folders within a box, subfolders, and so on. Organization will be appropriate to the material, for example, chronological, topical, and types of resources. EAD records have a hierarchical structure. They contain header elements that provide a description of the overall unit of collection being described, then a description of subordinate components section that describes items of the archival collection in a hierarchical structure. Information that applies at a given level of hierarchy is not repeated at lower levels.

EAD records can be considered both metadata and resources in their own right (for example, digital versions of traditional archival finding aids). Since they contain multiple levels of descriptive granularity, complete EAD records can be difficult to mix with other metadata formats. Some early efforts to use EAD with OAI-PMH looked at creating multiple item-level metadata records from individual EAD finding aids. This approach discarded important hierarchical relationships and proved problematic for other reasons (Prom and Habing 2002). A more successful strategy has been to use truncated forms of EAD files (that is, primarily the EAD header elements) for OAI-PMH, describing either the EAD finding aid as an information resource in its own right, or describing the archival collection as a whole rather than trying to describe individual items within archival collections. Good crosswalks from EAD to unqualified DC at this level of granularity are available on the Web.[40] These approaches facilitate the inclusion of EAD records in aggregations but can leave out useful information regarding items.

TEI (Text Encoding Initiative) Header

The *Text Encoding Initiative* standard (TEI[41]) is not a metadata format but rather an encoding standard for full text. The TEI Document Type Definition (DTD) defines rules for full text structural and descriptive markup. This allows applications to understand the semantics of a text. TEI applications can facilitate browsing and manipulation of texts and can perform statistical analysis of individual texts and collections of texts. There are successful Web-based large-scale TEI-based digital text initiatives at the University of Virginia,[42] the University of Michigan,[43] Indiana University,[44] and elsewhere.

While the complete TEI standard encompasses more than metadata, the contents of the TEI header element can be thought of and are routinely treated as metadata. The TEI header includes descriptive, technical, and administrative metadata. The TEI header is composed of a `file description` which is a bibliographic description of the text, an `encoding description` which provides information on the transcription and encoding of the text, a `text profile` which contains contextual information about the text, and finally a `revision history`.[45] A major distinction compared to the metadata formats mentioned above is that the TEI header is included in the same file as the information resource described.

Like EAD, initial work on TEI predates XML. The earliest expression of the TEI standard was an SGML DTD. As of late 2006, an XML-compatible DTD was available for TEI, and tools for generating modular XML schemas for TEI are available as part of the TEI infrastructure.[46] As of 2006, TEI as a format was not being used routinely with OAI-PMH; however, because of the importance of the standard in the digital library domain, implementers have developed standard strategies and mappings for extracting metadata from the TEI headers and expressing those metadata in several formats compatible with OAI-PMH.[47]

METS (Metadata Encoding and Transmission Standard)

According to the official *Metadata Encoding and Transmission Standard (METS)* Web site maintained by the Library of Congress, METS is intended for "encoding descriptive, administrative, and structural metadata regarding objects within a digital library."[48] The METS format was initially developed as an initiative of the Digital Library Federation, following work performed during the Making of America II project (MOA II). METS is designed to encompass all metadata necessary to use and preserve objects. Because it supports transmission of structural and administrative metadata (as well as descriptive metadata), it can be used in creating submission, archival, or dissemination information packages (SIPs, AIPs, and DIPs, respectively) as defined in the *Reference Model for an Open Archival Information System* (OAIS[49]). (See also a discussion of the relationship between METS and OAIS in Cantra 2005.) The scope of METS as a metadata format is apparent from the seven major headings of the format.

A METS Document Consists of Seven Major Sections

1. METS header: The METS header contains metadata describing the METS document itself, including such information as the creator, editor, etc.
2. Descriptive metadata: The descriptive metadata section may point to descriptive metadata external to the METS document (e.g., a MARC record in an OPAC or an EAD finding aid maintained on a World Wide Web server), or contain internally embedded descriptive metadata, or both. Multiple instances of both external and internal descriptive metadata may be included in the descriptive metadata section.
3. Administrative metadata: The administrative metadata section provides information regarding how the files were created and stored, intellectual property rights, metadata regarding the original source object from which the digital library object derives, and information regarding the provenance of the files comprising the digital library object (i.e., master/derivative file relationships and migration/transformation information). As with descriptive metadata, administrative metadata may be either external to the METS document or encoded internally.
4. File section: The file section lists all files containing content which comprises the electronic versions of the digital object. Such `<file>` elements may be grouped within `<fileGrp>` elements, to provide for subdividing the files by object version.
5. Structural map: The structural map is the heart of a METS document. It outlines a hierarchical structure for the digital library object, and links the elements of that structure to content files and metadata that pertain to each element.
6. Structural links: The structural links section of METS allows METS creators to record the existence of hyperlinks between nodes in the hierarchy outlined in the structural map. This is of particular value in using METS to archive Web sites.
7. Behavior: A behavior section can be used to associate executable behaviors with content in the METS object. Each behavior within a behavior section has an interface definition element that represents an abstract definition of the set of behaviors represented by a particular behavior section. Each behavior also has a mechanism element which identifies a module of executable code that implements and runs the behaviors defined abstractly by the interface definition.

SOURCE: Excerpted from *METS: An Overview and Tutorial*. Available at http://www.loc.gov/standards/mets/METSOverview.v2.html (Web page accessed December 15, 2006). Used with permission of the author.

As compared to the formats described above, METS is more a skeleton than a fully realized descriptive format. METS defines where in its hierarchy descriptive metadata should appear, but does not define the elements that should be used for expressing description. For example, a METS record can contain as descriptive metadata a DC record or a MODS record or both. As a result, even if harvested metadata records conform to the METS standard, this says very little about their semantic similarity and their capacity to be used in concert by any OAI service provider application. For this reason, METS is of most interest for OAI-PMH when used with application profiles that specify descriptive metadata format (among other things).

As of late 2006, METS was not being used routinely with OAI-PMH. The potential advantage of METS as a format for use with OAI-PMH lies in its inclusion of structural and administrative metadata alongside descriptive metadata. As digital library services and resources become increasingly complex (see also the discussion in chapter 8), structural metadata will become increasingly important. As a simple example, consider a digital version of a book having ordered page images. To present this digital resource to an end user via a page-turning application requires knowledge of structural metadata (that is, the sequence of page images that comprise the resource). In this instance, general descriptive metadata on its own is not enough. It is likely that METS records aligned with specific application profiles will be used with OAI-PMH in the future.

PRACTICAL CONSIDERATIONS WHEN SHARING METADATA

Metadata may represent digital content in multiple contexts and enable a range of interactions with digital objects. When content providers decide to share metadata with others, either for a specific collaborative project or for general use, they must take into account the ways they want their resources represented and the scope of interactions with their content they want to enable. As part of that process they must decide what metadata in what format(s) they wish to share.

Which Format(s) to Share?

In the first year following the introduction of OAI-PMH, nearly all OAI data providers exclusively shared unqualified DC records. This contributed to a misunderstanding that OAI-PMH was an extension of DC and that OAI-PMH could transfer only unqualified DC records. Communities of practitioners, notably those participating in the National Science Digital Library, the Digital Library Federation, the Networked Digital Library of Theses and Dissertations, and the Open Language Archives Community, must be credited with helping to overcome these misunderstandings and with encouraging other OAI data providers to provide metadata in multiple formats.

The metadata formats enumerated above are community based. Sometimes they are implemented verbatim for local applications. More often, however, local variants of these formats are used in the context of a local application. It may not be optimal to share via OAI-PMH metadata records exactly as they exist in the data provider's local system. The local metadata format may be nonstandard and/or there may not be the required XML schema for the local format at hand. Local metadata records may include information useful or meaningful only in a local context. Essential contextual information may be implicit, that is, not included in metadata records as they exist in the local system. There may be a highly interpreted description included in local metadata records that the data provider does not want to share. Practically, OAI service providers cannot be expected to harvest unique, repository-specific, idiosyncratic metadata formats. For these pragmatic reasons, OAI data providers are encouraged to share only that subset of their metadata which they can reasonably anticipate will be of interest and useful to service providers, and to share it using standard metadata schemas likely to be of interest to OAI service providers aggregating content across a community of practice.

Why share anything more than unqualified DC? There is a chicken-and-egg sort of issue here. Initially, OAI data providers provided only unqualified DC, and OAI service providers only harvested unqualified DC. This began changing not long after the advent of OAI-PMH. For most data providers it is a painful process to have to dumb down precise and well-elaborated metadata into a less expressive generic format such as unqualified DC. Such crosswalks are highly lossy (that is, entailing an irrecoverable loss of information—the term is borrowed from electrical engineering). The original rich metadata structure and precision cannot be recovered from the transformed unqualified DC record. Some data providers do not want to share metadata only in a format that fails to reflect the quality of their descriptive cataloging. Often unqualified DC does not do justice to the resources described. Fortunately, the tools and options available for sharing metadata have improved since the initial release of OAI-PMH. The choice of community-standard metadata formats for use with OAI-PMH, while still not overly large, is growing as more communities create XML schemas for their formats (partly in response to the popularity of OAI-PMH). VRA Core 4.0 and CDWA-Lite are examples of this. Another phenomenon is that service providers have begun to harvest richer metadata formats with more regularity. As long as no service was available to take advantage of richer metadata format, the incentive for data providers to share rich metadata was limited. However, service providers, wanting to build services of a sort enabled by richer metadata, have begun to harvest richer formats. As of 2006, harvesting of qualified DC, MODS, and MARCXML was commonplace.

Ultimately, the decision of which metadata formats to expose via OAI-PMH requires the OAI data provider to consider not only the scope and richness of metadata on hand, but also the likely needs of OAI service providers. Given the resources described by the OAI data provider's metadata, who are the likely OAI service providers and with what other metadata is the OAI data provider's metadata most likely to be aggregated? To know this it is essential to engage the broader community and participate in community-based initiatives.

Transforming Local Metadata

Since metadata are typically not shared in exactly the same format as is used for local purposes, OAI data providers often must implement metadata transformations. Sometimes, the transformation to a format appropriate for OAI-PMH is hidden from view within the bowels of the turnkey or other application used to implement the OAI data provider service. In other cases, the cataloger or metadata librarian may need to be involved in creating the crosswalk from local metadata format to metadata formats used for OAI-PMH. Technically, such crosswalks may be accomplished through scripting or XML transforming stylesheets (XSLT). Intellectually, there are several factors that may need to be taken into account, depending on the formats involved.

At a very basic level, it may be necessary to transform into Unicode local character encodings not compatible with XML (for example, MARC character encodings). Metadata field mapping must be defined (for example, from author element in local format to DC creator in unqualified DC). Often this will not be a one-to-one mapping. Mapping of terminologies and other locally coded information into terminologies or human-readable values compatible with target metadata format may be needed (for example, from Dewey Decimal Class Number into a human-readable subject string). Specific terminologies, codes, and other vocabularies may be implicitly assumed in a local application. These must be labeled and expanded as necessary to ensure that disseminated metadata records stand well on their own. In a similar vein, it may be appropriate to add explicit information about the collections(s) to which an item belongs and about any relations to other objects—again, to help make sure that the record can be understood outside its local context. In some cases, specific transformations may be implemented in order to follow a specific OAI service provider's guidelines. Finally, metadata quality control should be reviewed both for local metadata records and for those being disseminated via OAI-PMH. Encoding errors can arise when transforming metadata from local format into XML. Scripts to map and concatenate values can leave unexpected artifacts, for example, semicolons at the beginning or end of values. (For a thoughtful, more high-level discussion of the intellectual underpinnings of the relationships between and among metadata schemes and a proposal for a framework to facilitate cross-schema analysis, see Greenberg 2005.)

Metadata Quality and the Nature of Sharable Metadata

Librarians sometimes fall prey to the notion that resource descriptions are inherently monolithic. The prescriptiveness of the MARCXML format and the AACR2 metadata content standard can make one feel that for every information resource, there is one and only one perfect descriptive metadata record. This is not true. The metadata record is not an end in itself. Metadata records are created for a purpose, that is, to be used. MARCXML is a fine format for describing bibliographic resources and for enabling delivery of traditional library services (for example, see discussion of the historical functions of bibliographic records in Svenonius 2000, chapter 2). However, MARCXML is less well suited for use with other kinds of resources and in other contexts. Metadata cannot be fully evaluated without reference to purpose. Creating metadata records without considering how they are to be or might be used is nonsensical.

The major difficulty in deciding how to transform or create metadata for sharing using OAI-PMH is that OAI data providers may expose their metadata to multiple service providers implementing multiple types of applications. Not all OAI service providers are interested in the same metadata format. They sometimes have distinct or even divergent requirements. Their systems may use different metadata fields for different digital library functions. For instance, one service provider may display for each record in a list of results only DC title and DC relation, whereas another service provider may choose to display DC title, DC subject, DC creator, DC description, and DC type. For the first service provider, it is essential that the OAI data provider include a DC title element in every metadata record, even if that means duplicating for some records part of the DC description field as DC title. For the second service provider, doing this is unnecessary and actually creates redundancy in displays generated by that service provider.

In a closed collaboration, this tension can be resolved. The OAI data provider learns the requirements and preferences of the OAI service provider and adapts his or her metadata accordingly. However, in the more general case, the OAI data provider must adopt a more flexible and less precise approach. There are two keys. First, assess the content being shared, likely users and uses of that content, and the metadata available, and appreciate how those metadata can be used to represent the content to best effect. This requires that the OAI data provider consider who might harvest his or her metadata and why. Second, consider what can or cannot be done reasonably by the harvesting agent, that is, the OAI service provider, to normalize or mediate harvested metadata. The OAI data provider should focus first on ensuring quality for facets of metadata records that cannot be mediated for a specific use by OAI service providers.

While metadata quality is impossible to judge fully without reference to purpose, general principles of information quality offer a useful starting point for evaluating metadata quality (Stvilia et al. 2004). More specific to digital libraries, Thomas Bruce and Diane Hillmann of Cornell University suggest seven metrics as especially useful for measuring digital library metadata quality: accuracy, completeness, provenance, conformance to expectations, logical consistency and coherence, timeliness, and accessibility (Bruce and Hillmann 2004). However, by taking into account the specifics of metadata sharing via OAI-PMH, these metrics can be refined further and augmented.

In the summer of 2004, the Digital Library Federation (DLF), in collaboration with the National Science Digital Library (NSDL), convened a working group to develop best practices for OAI and sharable metadata. This working group brought together experienced OAI data providers and service providers, yielding results informed by both perspectives. A draft of the working group's recommended best practices for sharable metadata was released on the Web in August 2005 and remains available online in updated form.[50] Sarah Shreeves and her coauthors summarized results from the working group regarding sharable metadata in an article appearing in *First Monday* (Shreeves et al. 2006). The DLF/NSDL working group found that even metadata of high quality for local use may not be well suited for sharing. They concluded that, over and above the metadata quality attributes proposed by Bruce and Hillmann, the key features of quality sharable metadata records are:

1. metadata content which is optimized for sharing;
2. metadata which include essential context;
3. metadata which are coherent and self-explanatory;
4. metadata created according to consistent application of descriptive practice; and
5. metadata which conform to technical standards and rely on appropriate data content standards.

The common sense behind each of these recommendations is readily apparent. Metadata content appropriate for sharing speaks to which metadata elements should be included—for example, URLs or other metadata values supporting unambiguous identification and access to the described resource are essential in a sharable metadata record. It also speaks to appropriate use of controlled vocabularies, the inclusion and completeness of fields useful in a shared metadata environment (and the exclusion of fields not useful), and the appropriateness of descriptive granularity. Coherence and the inclusion of essential contextual information within individual metadata records are especially important when sharing metadata records because each metadata record must be self-sufficient and complete within an aggregation of records harvested from several disparate sites. Information assumed or implicit in a local application environment will not be present to help users and machine applications interpret metadata records in the OAI service provider's environment. Metadata must be self-explanatory and make sense, even to relatively naive users. Information meaningful only in a local application environment must be removed to avoid confusing users seeing the record in an aggregated metadata environment. Because it is impossible when sharing metadata to anticipate all the ways records will be reused and repurposed, consistency of descriptive practice is essential in order to facilitate normalization or mediation of harvested metadata records by the service provider. This extends to consistent use of metadata elements, controlled vocabularies, and value-encoding schemes. Finally, because the whole proposition of OAI-PMH and similar protocols is based on technical agreements between the data provider and the service provider, technical conformance—that is, conformance to XML syntax, metadata format schemas, and XML encoding rules—is critical.

Beyond the general advice embodied in the above recommendations, the DLF/NSDL working group also provides specific advice regarding the description of versions and reproductions, linkages from metadata to resource and to other entities, selection of metadata formats, descriptive granularity, documentation of descriptive practices, and the population of specific metadata fields and classes of metadata elements. These range from advice that should be obvious to most catalogers to advice that is subtler, even for experienced cataloger. At the naive end of the spectrum, there should be advice to include language as a metadata field when describing textual resources, but typically not when describing image resources. Subtler is advice that no title element is better than including a title element with a placeholder string value such as "[title not available]." OAI service providers develop strategies to deal with records lacking certain fields. A service provider will overcome a missing title field more easily than he or she will recognize all the possible idiosyncratic strings meaning not available or not applicable.

Ultimately, delivering sharable metadata requires an OAI data provider to assess critically the utility of his or her existing metadata in a shared metadata context and to commit to make the necessary changes, consult with OAI service providers, and iterate as necessary to improve metadata quality and suitability for sharing. Most of all it requires truly understanding and appreciating how metadata enables and facilitates interaction with content.

QUESTIONS AND TOPICS FOR DISCUSSION

1. What is your opinion of the usefulness of DC application profiles? For an OAI data provider what are the advantages and disadvantages of opting to use a DC application profile as compared to simply using a non-DC metadata format?
2. In the longer term, do you think that both MARCXML and MODS are needed? If so, why? If not, why not?
3. What are the most important distinctions between a metadata format, for example, MODS, VRA Core, or CDWA-Lite, and a metadata content standard, for example, CCO or AACR2? Which is the DCMI library application profile?[51]
4. What are some examples of resources that would best be described using VRA Core or CDWA-Lite metadata formats? Resources best described using METS?
5. What are some examples of metadata records which are of high quality when considered for a local application, but which are not well suited for sharing via OAI-PMH?

SUGGESTIONS FOR EXERCISES

1. Identify an OAI data provider service that disseminates metadata items in multiple formats (for example, the Library of Congress OAI data provider at baseURL <http://memory.loc.gov/cgi-bin/oai2_0>). Harvest at least a dozen

metadata items in at least two metadata formats (for example, oai_dc, marc21, mods). Analyze how the crosswalk was done. What information was lost in dumbing-down records to unqualified DC? Would you have done the crosswalk differently? < /http://memory.loc.gov/cgi-bin/oai2_0 >

2. Retrieve a dozen records from your institution's online catalog. Transform these retrieved records into MARCXML. Crosswalk the records into MODS. Crosswalk the records into qualified DC and then unqualified DC (that is, oai_dc). What information was lost in the process as went from each metadata format to the next?

3. Select a number of images available online (at least ten), preferably from several different sources and collections. Select at least two metadata formats and create metadata records for the resources in each metadata format. Repeat the process this time selecting images of two or three specific buildings and using as one of the formats VRA Core or CDWA-Lite. What problems might you anticipate if you tried to combine all these image-related records into one metadata aggregation?

NOTES

1. http://dublincore.org/documents/dces/.
2. http://www.dublincore.org.
3. http://www.niso.org/international/SC4/n515.pdf.
4. http://www.dublincore.org/schemas/xmls/simpledc20021212.xsd.
5. http://dublincore.org/2003/03/24/dces.
6. http://www.openarchives.org/OAI/2.0/oai_dc.xsd.
7. http://www.jiscmail.ac.uk/cgi-bin/webadmin?A2=ind0609&L=dc-architecture&T=0&P=255.
8. http://www.dublincore.org/documents/dcmi-terms/.
9. http://dublincore.org/usage/documents/process/.
10. http://www.dublincore.org/documents/dcmi-terms/.
11. Ibid.
12. Ibid.
13. http://www.iana.org/assignments/media-types/.
14. http://www.dublincore.org/documents/dc-xml-guidelines/.
15. http://www.dublincore.org/schemas/xmls/.
16. http://www.pictureaustralia.org/schemas/pa/picture.xsd.
17. http://cicharvest.grainger.uiuc.edu/schemas/QDC/2004/07/14/CICQualifiedDC.xsd.
18. http://www.dublincore.org/documents/2004/09/10/library-application-profile/.
19. http://dublincore.org/educationwiki/DC_2dEducation_20Application_20Profile.
20. http://www.dublincore.org/groups/collections/collection-application-profile/2006-02-24/.
21. http://www.collectionscanada.ca/obj/s19/f2/01-e.pdf.
22. http://www.loc.gov/marc/annmarc21.html.
23. http://www.bl.uk/services/bibliographic/marc21move.html.
24. http://www.loc.gov/marc/.
25. http://www.collectionscanada.ca/6/19/.
26. http://www.loc.gov/standards/marcxml/.

27. http://www.loc.gov/marc/.
28. http://www.aacr2.org/.
29. http://www.collectionscanada.ca/jsc/rda.html.
30. http://www.loc.gov/standards/mods/.
31. http://www.loc.gov/standards/mods/v3/mods-3-2.xsd.
32. http://www.loc.gov/standards/mods/.
33. http://www.diglib.org/aquifer/DLF_MODS_ImpGuidelines_ver4.pdf.
34. http://www.vraweb.org/datastandards/VRADS_Main_page.htm.
35. http://www.getty.edu/research/conducting_research/standards/cdwa/.
36. http://www.getty.edu/research/conducting_research/standards/cdwa/
    cdwalite.html.
37. http://www.vraweb.org/ccoweb/index.html.
38. http://www.icacds.org.uk/eng/standards.htm.
39. http://diglib.princeton.edu/ead/dtd/2002/ead.xsd.
40. http://www.getty.edu/research/conducting_research/standards/intrometadata/
    dc_ead.html.
41. http://www.tei-c.org/.
42. http://etext.lib.virginia.edu/.
43. http://www.hti.umich.edu/.
44. http://www.letrs.indiana.edu/web/w/wright2/.
45. http://www.tei-c.org.uk/release/doc/tei-p5-doc/html/html/HD.html.
46. http://www.tei-c.org.uk/release/doc/tei-p5-doc/html/html/ST.html.
47. http://www.tei-c.org.uk/release/doc/tei-p5-doc/html/html/SH.html.
48. http://www.loc.gov/standards/mets/.
49. http://ssdoo.gsfc.nasa.gov/nost/isoas/.
50. http://oai-best.comm.nsdl.org/cgi-bin/wiki.pl?PublicTOC.
51. http://www.dublincore.org/schemas/xmls/.

REFERENCES

Baca, Murtha, ed. 1998. *Introduction to Metadata: Pathways to Digital Information*. Los Angeles: Getty Information Institute, http://www.getty.edu/research/conducting_research/standards/intrometadata/index.html.

Bruce, Thomas R., and Diane I. Hillmann. 2004. The Continuum of Metadata Quality: Defining, Expressing, Exploiting. *Metadata in Practice*, ed. Diane I. Hillmann and Elaine L. Westbrooks, 238–256. Chicago: American Library Association.

Cantra, Linda. 2005. The Metadata Encoding and Transmission Standard. *Metadata: A Cataloger's Primer*, ed. Richard P. Smiraglia, 237–253. Binghamton, NY: Haworth Press.

Caplan, Priscilla. 2003. *Metadata Fundamentals for All Librarians*. Chicago: American Library Association.

Coleman, Anita S. 2005. From Cataloging to Metadata: Dublin Core Records for the Library Catalog. *Metadata: A Cataloger's Primer*, ed. Richard P. Smiraglia, 153–181. Binghampton, NY: Haworth Press.

Greenberg, Jane. 2005. Understanding Metadata and Metadata Schemes. *Metadata: A Cataloger's Primer*, ed. Richard P. Smiraglia, 17–36. Binghamton, NY: Haworth Press.

Heery, Rachel, and Manjula Patel. 2000. Application profiles: mixing and matching metadata schemas. *Ariadne* 25 (September 24), http://www.ariadne.ac.uk/issue25/app-profiles/.

Hillmann, Diane. 2005. *Using Dublin Core.* Dublin, OH: Dublin Core Metadata Initiative, http://www.dublincore.org/documents/usageguide/.

Hillmann, Diane I., and Elaine L. Westbrooks, eds. 2004. *Metadata in Practice.* Chicago: American Library Association.

Intner, Sheila S., Susan Lazinger, and Jean Weihs. 2006. *Metadata and Its Impact on Libraries.* Library and Information Science Text Series. Westport, CT: Libraries Unlimited.

NISO Framework Advisory Group. 2004. *A Framework of Guidance for Building Good Digital Collections*, 2nd edition. Bethesda, MD: National Information Standards Organization, http://www.niso.org/framework/framework2.pdf.

Prom, Christopher J., and Thomas G. Habing. 2002. Using the Open Archives Initiatives Protocols with EAD. *Proceedings of the 2nd ACM/IEEE-CS Joint Conference on Digital Libraries*, 171–180. New York: Association for Computing Machinery.

Shreeves, Sarah L., Jenn Riley, and Liz Milewicz. 2006. Moving towards Shareable Metadata. *First Monday* 11 (8), http://www.firstmonday.org/issues/issue11_8/shreeves/.

Smiraglia, Richard P., ed. 2005. *Metadata: A Cataloger's Primer.* Binghamton, NY: Haworth Press. Simultaneously published as *Cataloging & Classification Quarterly* 40 (3/4).

Stvilia, Besiki, Les Gasser, Michael Twidale, Sarah L. Shreeves, and Timothy W. Cole. 2004. Metadata quality for federated collections. *Proceedings of ICIQ04—9th International Conference on Information Quality*, ed. Shobha Chengalur-Smith, Jennifer Long, Louiqa Raschid, and Craig Seko, 111–125. Cambridge, MA: Massachusetts Institute of Technology, http://www.iqconference.org/ICIQ/iqpapers.aspx?iciqyear=2004.

Svenonius, E. 2000. *The Intellectual Foundation of Information Organization.* Cambridge, MA: MIT Press.

Thurman, Alexander C. 2005. Metadata Standards for Archival Control: An Introduction to EAD and EAC. *Metadata: A Cataloger's Primer*, ed. Richard P. Smiraglia, 183–212. Binghamton, NY: Haworth Press.

Weibel, Stuart, J. Kunze, Carl Lagoze, and M. Wolf. 1998. *Dublin Core Metadata for Resource Discovery, IETF #2413.* Reston, VA: The Internet Society, http://www.ietf.org/rfc/rfc2413.txt.

CHAPTER 7

Post-Harvest Metadata Normalization and Augmentation

Each institution, each cataloger, and each metadata librarian take a distinctive approach to digital resource description. These distinctions reflect, among other things, local variations in purpose and context. As discussed in chapter 6, metadata records are created by individual catalogers or metadata librarians according to professional and institutional practices to make sense for use in a specific, usually local, application.

However, OAI-PMH is about the sharing and reuse of metadata. This means that metadata records created to describe resources in a local context must be made rich enough and comprehensible enough outside of that context to be included in other, larger applications that bring together metadata from distributed and disparate sources. Metadata must make sense in different contexts and must be manageable and importable in a standard way.

Chapter 6 describes the ways in which OAI data providers can facilitate the reuse of the metadata they disseminate, but the obligation to facilitate metadata sharing does not lie solely with the data provider. In order to cope with the heterogeneity of harvested metadata records and to facilitate their reuse in the context of a metadata aggregation, the OAI service provider also can reprocess metadata post-harvest, *normalizing records* to allow more effective and complete integration of metadata and *augmenting records* with additional information to make implicit context explicit.

Normalization is designed to standardize record structures and values across an aggregation. For instance, some metadata records may contain dates in the form of month, day-of-month, and year, with varying punctuation and with month as a numerical value or an English language string—for example, "January 5, 2004" or "1-5-2004." It is possible to transform (normalize) such dates into World Wide Web Consortium Date Time Format (W3CDTF[1]) compliant strings of the pattern YYYY-MM-DD, that is, with the year expressed as four digits, the month as two digits, and the day of the month as two digits—for example, "2004-01-05." Such normalization greatly facilitates searching, browsing, and the ordering of search results by date.

Post-harvest augmentation is the process of adding information to harvested metadata to facilitate integration and interoperability of records across an aggregation. Augmentation allows for inclusion of metadata provenance and other implicit contextual information. For instance, it might be helpful for search and discovery and for user interpretation of retrieved record displays to know which records in an aggregation came from a collection of metadata describing digitized images of U.S. President Theodore Roosevelt, particularly if the metadata records do not otherwise make this clear, that is, if the metadata author assumed this context was understood implicitly (for such an example, see Wendler 2004). Implicit contextual information may be hard to recover once all harvested metadata records have been integrated into a single aggregation, but can be added relatively easily through metadata processing done immediately post-harvest on collection-by-collection basis.

This chapter gives a sense of how OAI service providers approach metadata normalization and augmentation. The chapter begins with a brief consideration of metadata aggregations as collections. What is the collection-development policy of the OAI service provider and how is it implemented? Aspects and examples of metadata normalization and augmentation are then examined. The chapter closes with a discussion of the shared responsibilities of data providers and service providers and a few thoughts about the trade-offs between having rich, normalized metadata records and preserving absolutely the integrity of harvested metadata. The specific metadata processing applied in any given instance is determined both by the characteristics of the metadata harvested and by the requirements for the services that the OAI service provider seeks to implement. Chapter 8 continues with more about services implemented over aggregations of metadata harvested using OAI-PMH.

THE METADATA AGGREGATION AS A COLLECTION

A service provider's metadata aggregation should be coherent and should have all the characteristics of a good collection. Typically, some initial post-harvest processing by the OAI service provider is required to achieve the desired degree of collection identity and coherence. These tasks should be performed before metadata normalization and augmentation is attempted.

Defining a Collection-Development Policy for a Metadata Aggregation

Just as it is for more traditional library collection building, an explicit collection-development policy is an essential prerequisite for any successful OAI service provider implementation. Such a policy can be useful and informative for OAI data providers and for end users of a service as well. An OAI service provider collection-development policy should follow from service objectives and should in turn inform metadata selection. What is the intended scope of the services that will be provided? What are the interests of the target audience? How might these limit resource types, formats, and/or subjects of interest? Do the planned services require the presence of specific metadata fields, a certain level of metadata completeness, or specific metadata granularity? Is resource availability, access restrictions, or terms of use a consideration? An OAI service provider's collection-development policy does not have to be lengthy. Simple and succinct statements are the norm.[2, 3] The brief OAI service provider collection-development policy below was created by the authors for an ongoing metadata sharing collaboration of the Committee on Institutional Cooperation (CIC).

CIC Metadata Portal Collection-Development Policy[4]

This site provides access to digital collections developed in CIC institutions. Each of these universities has defined its own collection-development policies, their own digitization policy, and their own priorities for sharing their content with the CIC-OAI metadata portal and other information services.

   The CIC metadata portal itself also has adopted a series of principles to aggregate metadata from partner institutions. Metadata "shared" with the OAI protocol by partner institutions are systematically made available within the metadata portal in accordance with the following principles.

Collection-Development Principles

- *Included resources are limited to those produced or developed, at least in part, by CIC institutions.*
   This excludes external content simply aggregated by partner CIC institutions.
- *Included metadata describe a digital or physical resource.*
   This excludes any metadata record aimed at cross-referencing, for example (only containing the information on the relationship between two resources).
- *Included metadata refer to resources of interest to academic/research communities.*
- *Included metadata facilitate resource discovery and representation.*
   Metadata facilitates resource discovery and representation within the CIC portal, and can be in any relevant format. Most partner institutions make their content available in simple or qualified Dublin Core.

Metadata selection guidelines follow from collection-development policy and define record inclusion and exclusion criteria. In the context of OAI-PMH, metadata selection criteria can manifest in three ways:

1. in the selection of which repositories to harvest;
2. in whether and how to perform selective harvesting of a particular repository; and
3. in whether and how to filter records post-harvest.

Implementing Metadata Record-Selection Criteria

The above criteria for selecting metadata records are progressively more sophisticated, requiring increasingly more effort. Some individual OAI data provider repositories are cohesive and homogeneous when considered as collections. These repositories will either fit or not within the selection criteria for a metadata aggregation. The OAI service provider simply harvests relevant repositories of this sort in their entirety.

If only a specific subset of a repository is of interest, sometimes the service provider can meet aggregation-selection criteria by using the selective harvesting mechanisms built into OAI-PMH. As discussed in earlier chapters, the protocol supports selective harvesting by OAI set. This is a viable option only if the data provider makes use of OAI sets (which are optional) and has divided his or her repository into sets that match or map effectively to the selection criteria of the service provider. (Keep in mind that OAI-PMH does not support search functionality or other forms of dynamic selection.)

To fulfill aggregation selection criteria using OAI selective harvesting, the service provider must use the `ListSets` verb to investigate and track over time the sets arrangement of the data provider repository. If the `setDescriptions` given by the data provider in response to `ListSets` requests are insufficient to judge the relevance of a particular OAI set, then the service provider must contact the data provider directly (that is, outside the scope of the protocol) for additional details.

If the data provider does not support OAI sets or if the available sets do not correspond to the service provider's selection criteria, selection of which metadata records to include in an aggregation may be managed post-harvest through the implementation of *record-selection filters*. Such filters, which can be implemented programmatically (that is, in code or script) or through the application of transforming XML style sheets (XSLTs), open and read each harvested metadata record to determine whether it (or the resource it describes) matches the service provider's metadata-selection criteria (as derived from collection-development policy). Based on this determination, the filter either passes a metadata record on for further processing and inclusion in the aggregation, or removes it from the workflow. Such an approach works only if harvested metadata records are rich enough and properly structured to apply the service provider's selection criteria. For example, if the service provider's selection criterion is to include only metadata records describing resources of a certain type (such as textual), then selection by filtering is viable only for harvested metadata records which include explicit, well-labeled, machine-understandable metadata values describing resource type.

De-Duplication

Record duplication is of particular concern for collections of metadata aggregated from disparate distributed repositories. Duplicative metadata records can clutter search-results lists and have long been identified by end users as a significant concern in the context of both harvested (for example, OAI-PMH) and broadcast (for example, Z39.50) approaches to cross-repository searching (Payette and Rieger 1997). However, automated, post-harvest de-duplication of large metadata aggregations is challenging.

In the context of digital library metadata aggregations, duplication is typically understood to encompass multiple occurrences of metadata records describing variant digital instances of the same manifestation or closely related manifestations of a given work. It is not essential that the metadata records themselves be identical, or even that the digital object instances described by each record be identical. Two metadata records may be considered duplicative if both describe digitized versions of the same document, even if one record describes a PDF version of the document as digitized by institution A, and the other record describes an HTML version of the document as digitized by institution B. Consider the example of World War II posters printed and distributed by the U.S. government. Several libraries have overlapping collections of such posters, have digitized these collections, and independently have created metadata records for each poster digitized. As a result, it has become commonplace to harvest multiple metadata records from different institutions all describing the same World War II poster. For some purposes, for example, search and discovery services, these metadata records are duplicative and in need of reconciliation and merging.

In practical terms, this means that the Web URL included in a metadata record may be inadequate for identifying duplicative metadata records. URLs as conclusive evidence of metadata record duplication can also be problematic because not all URLs included within metadata records necessarily point to the individual resource being described. For example, some content providers will include a URL to a collection home page or some other collection-level entry page—for example, as a related item or to facilitate authentication and/or require users to view collection-level information and conditions of use before proceeding to a view of the individual resource (Shreeves and Kirkham 2004).

For digital versions of traditional text resources, inclusion of ISBNs (International Standard Book Numbers) and ISSNs (International Standard Serial Numbers) within metadata records can help with automated discovery of duplicative metadata records. Unfortunately, there are no universally recognized identifiers of similar scope for resources such as digitized images and digitized audio, or for certain types of resources initially created in digital form. As of this writing, de-duplication and reconciliation of metadata describing digital resources remain an active area of research within the domain of cross-repository search and discovery generally, that is, both among OAI service providers (Harrison et al. 2004) and among implementers of Z39.50 (Sfakakis and Kapidakis 2004).

NORMALIZING METADATA

Metadata normalization is done to ensure that all records of the metadata aggregation express the same concepts and values in the same way. Both record semantic structures, and the value strings contained in metadata records may be normalized. Because normalization strategies sometimes must take into account specific metadata practices followed by a particular OAI data provider, normalization, in whole or in part, may be done on a repository-by-repository basis.

General Record Cleanup

Elimination of Empty Metadata Elements and Meaningless Values

Empty elements, that is, XML nodes within metadata records containing neither content nor any informative attributes, are encountered surprisingly often. The CIC collaborative OAI-based metadata sharing project mentioned above found that more than one in six harvested records contained at least one empty element (Foulonneau and Cole 2005). Although easy to accommodate in theory, in practice the presence of empty elements in metadata records can confuse search implementations and degrade the quality and consistency of record display. Empty elements are easy to automatically recognize and remove when normalizing metadata records.

Metadata values meaningful in a local context or system implementation may not be meaningful when metadata are aggregated. This is the case with institution- or implementation-specific codes. For example, the metadata value PXPX in a particular OAI data provider's local implementation means, "access not restricted." When encountered by an OAI service provider, the code should be replaced by a more standard and more human-readable form. If the service provider has not yet or is unable to determine the meaning of coded values encountered, they should be eliminated or otherwise hidden from view.

Similarly, OAI data providers use a variety of ways to indicate the absence of specific information. Value strings such as "not applicable," "n/a," and "—" are not useful for information retrieval and generally should not be indexed. Because data providers are inconsistent about which strings to use for this purpose (or whether to use any at all), the presence of such strings in merged results lists also can be confusing to the end user. An OAI service provider may reasonably choose to eliminate or suppress such values; however, when doing so, the service provider should be careful to account for forms that may carry some informational value in specific contexts. The fact that the author of a resource has been determined to be unknown or that a resource is undated can be informative in certain contexts. However, when offering a list of distinct authors or when ordering search results by author, a value of "unknown" is less useful.

OAI service providers should also be cognizant of artificial value strings that may carry no real information. An interesting case is the date value of "1970-01-01." This happens to be the so-called UNIX date of birth, that is, it is the default date embedded in many UNIX operating systems. Multiple occurrences of this date in a set of metadata records are suspicious, suggesting that default date values were automatically generated by the system. It may be necessary to contact the OAI data provider to determine if such values are actually meaningful.

Value Splitting

Some OAI data provider implementations concatenate values for metadata fields such as subject rather than include multiple instances of the metadata field (for example, subject) within their disseminated metadata records. In the following example eight distinct subject headings have been concatenated together, delineated one from another by the semicolon character.

```
<subject>Lincoln, Abraham, 1809-1865; Coles County,
Illinois; Cabins; Pioneers; Politics & Government; Kyser;
Chesebro Blacksmith Shop; Chicago, Illinois;</subject>
```

Concatenated subject terms can adversely impact search and discovery and can detract from the clarity and consistency of search result displays. An OAI service provider should consider splitting such values in order to facilitate indexing and display of results. Delineators may be OAI data provider specific, so this must be done on a repository-by-repository basis.

Consideration should also be given to parsing even valid multiword subject headings. In the following example, the value comes from a hierarchical thesaurus or subject-heading scheme.

```
<subject>Nicaragua—Politics and government</subject>
```

While the implicit spatial coverage term (that is, Nicaragua) is perfectly valid as part of a compound subject heading, an OAI service provider may wish to repeat it in the coverage field (if it is not already present) in order to facilitate search recall.

Normalizing Semantic Structure

An OAI service provider must adopt a strategy for storing and indexing harvested metadata that is optimized to support service objectives. There are two basic options. Metadata may be stored in as-harvested metadata formats. Alternatively, the service provider may choose to crosswalk and store all harvested metadata in a normalized, service provider-specific format that is well adapted to both the metadata being harvested and the services being implemented.

The first approach requires the service provider to implement services that can recognize and work with metadata values of interest as expressed in multiple metadata formats. For example, such a service would be able to fulfill a request to show URLs for a selection of resources by looking simultaneously in DC `identifier` elements, MODS `location` elements, and MARCXML `varfield` elements having `id` attribute values of 856. Metadata record cleanup and value normalization (see below) is still required when using this approach. It also is essential to verify consistency of usage across the entirety of each set of records expressed in each metadata format. However, it is not necessary to transform or crosswalk harvested records to a single, normalized semantic structure. The implementation of sophisticated services can be more complex when using this approach. This is because services must be built to utilize metadata records maintained in multiple formats

FIGURE 7-1   Fragment of a metadata format crosswalk strategy.

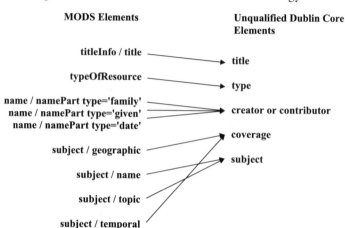

seamlessly and dynamically. The complexity of such implementations is dependent on the range and diversity of metadata schemas accommodated.

The second approach requires that the service provider crosswalk or transform harvested metadata records to a normalized, service-provider-specific metadata format during post-harvest processing. As of 2006, this was the more common approach used by OAI service providers. (Service providers are well advised to create an XML schema and application profile defining in detail the common format to be used and the rules and encodings to be followed.) To implement this approach, the service provider begins by mapping elements found in harvested metadata records to the common, normalized format. Figure 7-1 illustrates how a service provider might map selected MODS metadata format elements to unqualified DC metadata format elements. Note that information can be lost in this process; for example, the distinction between temporal and spatial coverage is lost in the semantic mapping illustrated in Figure 7-1. Service providers should prefer mappings that minimize loss of information relevant to services being implemented. Canonical crosswalks exist for transforming between standard metadata formats,[5, 6] and these are good starting points for service providers.

Transforming harvested metadata to a common, normalized metadata format can have advantages for the service provider. Such an approach can help avoid ambiguities that may arise when OAI data providers use metadata fields in inconsistent and contradictory ways. For example, data providers may follow different practices when describing digital resources derived from physical entities, for example, a digital view of a painting or other cultural artifact. Some data providers will describe the physical artifact and provide the URL to the digital view only in the DC relation element (that is, in the sense that the digital view is a specific format or version of the original physical resource). Another data provider may prefer a composite description of the digital view and physical artifact, and may provide the URL to the digital view in the DC identifier element. This data provider may use the DC relation element to provide the URL to a thumbnail version of the digital view.

Among data providers, unique differences in semantic usage can be dealt with by normalizing metadata record semantics on a provider-by-provider basis. This requires that the service provider apply a distinct semantic normalization mapping for each data provider. Data-provider-specific mappings are determined by analyzing records harvested from each data provider and/or by communicating with each data provider to learn usage rules being applied by that data provider. Where usage rules are applied at the level of the OAI set, semantic normalization can also be done on a set-by-set basis rather than uniformly across an entire data provider repository.

Additionally, a service-provider-specific metadata format can include metadata fields to facilitate description of attributes of special interest to a service provider. The service provider format, for example, may provide one distinct field for thumbnail URLs and another for a service-provider-specific taxonomy of described resource granularity. Inclusion of such added fields also can facilitate the metadata augmentation process described below.

Normalizing Values

Metadata value strings also can be normalized. For example, as described in chapter 6, the preferred encoding scheme for the DC format element (and equivalent elements in other metadata formats) is the Internet Media Type list maintained by the Internet Assigned Numbers Authority.[7] Not all OAI data providers adhere to this recommendation; however, if a data provider at least follows consistent practice and uses an equally rich, locally controlled vocabulary, the potential for normalization is increased. Consistent use of a DC format element value of JPG across a repository facilitates transformation of format values to the normalized value image/jpeg for records from that repository. Normalizing values against larger, hierarchical thesauri (for example, *Library of Congress Subject Headings*) is more ambitious but is theoretically possible and potentially powerful. Here again, potential for success is heightened if it can be determined that a controlled vocabulary of some sort was used and if that vocabulary is of similar richness to the target for normalization.

For some steps in the normalization process it can be useful to inspect the form or structure of a metadata value string—that is, in an effort to guess the implicit encoding scheme. Consider a case where an OAI data provider is known to include both resource URLs and Digital Object Identifiers (DOIs) in the DC identifier field. Values matching the format for URIs (Berners-Lee et al. 1998) can be normalized one way; those matching the format of DOIs[8] can be normalized another way.

Normalization of Date Metadata

Normalizing encoding scheme and value format is especially useful for metadata elements relied on as search and/or browse access points, for example, temporal and spatial information. Unfortunately, these values can be difficult to normalize. Table 7-1 shows examples of values seen in the DC date element of metadata records harvested by the University of Illinois at Urbana-Champaign Library and illustrates the challenge of normalizing date values.

TABLE 7-1   Values found in date fields of metadata records harvested using OAI-PMH.

September 29–October 28, 51 AD; 1970
second half of IXth century AD; 1978
Rebuilt 1984
Possibly Vth/VIth century AD; 1935
Planted 1985
n/a
n.d.
Mid IInd century AD; 1973
Jul-51
circa 900 AD
ca. 701 BC
Begun 14th century
184-?
1839
18–?
August 23, 2000
between 1827 and 183
VIIIth/IXth century AD ? (TC);1965
Vth-VIth century AD (McNamee); IVth century AD (Cribiore); 1982
XVIII Dynasty
Winter 2003
era of redevelopment
various
2002-00
1980, refurbished 1997
China: Neolithic Period (5000 BCE-ca 1600 BCE)?
19691968
21. Nouemb. Anno. 1564.
And finisshed on the euen of thanunciacion of our said bilissid Lady falling on the
    wednesday the xxiiij daye of Marche. in the xix yeer of Kyng Edwarde the fourthe
    [1479]]
19193
xxxx Oct xx
Various
1938-05-38
1963 to 1953
[not after 1579]
163[5?]

There are several factors to consider when normalizing date values. Dates present in metadata records are associated with different events in the life cycle of a resource—for example, the temporal period the resource is about, the date the resource was first published, or the date the resource was digitized. Metadata formats such as unqualified DC do not support explicit labeling of which date value relates to which event in the resource life cycle. Another difficulty, especially for cultural heritage metadata, is the relation of date to culture and place. Antique Roma and Ming Dynasty include both spatial and temporal information (albeit imprecise). The meaning of XVIII

`Dynasty` is uncertain when considered on its own. The precise temporal meaning of such terms may vary according to context and across different academic communities. Temporal value strings in metadata records may also conflate information. `Possibly Vth/VIth century A.D.; 1935` most likely expresses both the temporal coverage of the resource described and its original date of publication, although this should not be assumed without further investigation.

Selecting a target-encoding scheme for normalized date values is not trivial. Date normalization should support both machine processing of metadata and clarity of presentation to human end users. Depending on scope of the aggregation, the date encoding scheme selected may need to support both BCE and AD dates. (The widely implemented W3CDTF encoding scheme[9] mentioned above and in chapter 6 does not support BCE dates.) Typically, the normalized date format also must support expression of temporal periods and uncertain dates. The DC-Library Metadata Application Profile[10] and several other application profiles recommend expressing date information using W3C-DCTF or the broader, more comprehensive International Standard ISO-8601.[11] Metadata content standards (for example, CCO, DACS, and AACR2/RDA; see chapter 6) provide guidance, although they do not offer complete date-encoding schemes as such. As of this writing, no solution covers all possible cases. ISO-8601 is by far the broadest approach, but its very breadth allows a multiplicity of encodings with attendant potential for confusion. Ideally, any encoding approach that is designed for normalized temporal information should provide means to express unambiguously:

- uncertainty of dates;
- approximate dates;
- the absence of dates;
- date intervals and named periods (for example, `Spanish Civil War`);
- both BCE dates and AD dates;
- dates from Julian, Gregorian, and other culture-specific calendars;
- temporal range of cultures (for example, `Ming Dynasty`); and
- pre-history eras, epochs, and other dates that do not translate well into calendar dates.

As of 2006, the accuracy and completeness limits of post-harvest date normalization were still being evaluated. Early anecdotal experience of OAI service providers (the CIC OAI-PMH-based metadata sharing project[12] and the California Digital Library American West project[13]) suggests that although difficult, date normalization is possible with an acceptable confidence of accuracy for a significant range of as-harvested metadata. However, a complete post-harvest date-normalization solution is unlikely. Temporal metadata is an example of where both the data provider and service provider need to invest effort.

Normalization of Spatial Metadata

Normalization of spatial coverage requires an approach that recognizes the presence of relevant place name information as it occurs throughout a metadata record and then transforms it into a normalized vocabulary and locates it in a normalized metadata element. The International Standard ISO-3166 parts 1 and 2[14] provide a list of place names at the level of country and country subdivision (for example, states) and can be used as the basis for a normalized place name vocabulary. Two letter codes are provided for all country names. *The Getty Thesaurus of Geographical Names* (TGN[15]) is a much more comprehensive and extensive hierarchical thesaurus containing more than one million place names. TGN provides greater granularity as well as vernacular and historical forms of place names, but is also more complex to implement and (as of 2006) must be licensed for use of the sort described here. Precise numerical formats (for example, longitude and latitude) can also be used to express normalized spatial coverage metadata.

Generally, the challenge is less with choosing the normalized formats than with the diversity of where and how spatial coverage information appears in harvested metadata. As noted above, spatial coverage is often conflated with subject. Place names may also appear in other fields such as titles and description. Several practical difficulties may be encountered as described below.

- Names and territories change over time. Rhodesia was renamed Zimbabwe when the country gained independence. In antiquity, locations might have had multiple spellings; many names may have been associated with the same location, varying according to the author's region of origin and when he or she was writing. (For a more extensive discussion of these issues and research into practical ways to address them, see Buckland and Lancaster 2004.)
- Metadata creators do not always follow forms used in place names standards, especially when embedding place names in free text metadata fields such as description. Informal forms such as "North Korea" or "South Korea" are more likely to appear in metadata records than more formal forms such as "Korea, Democratic People's Republic of." (This may adversely impact browsing, but is not all bad. End users as well tend not to search on standard forms of place names.)
- Place names encountered might be ambiguous: Is New York a state or a city? What about Washington? Where is Springfield exactly in the United States? Is Georgia a U.S. state or a country?

As with date normalization, the objective for a service provider when normalizing spatial references should not be complete success, but rather a significant improvement in the percentage of aggregated metadata records containing spatial references that can be used to support services implemented. Value normalization is resource intensive and time consuming. The level and complexity of effort made by the service provider should be consistent with the importance of value normalization to the services.

AUGMENTING METADATA

Post-harvest augmentation or enrichment of records adds metadata to enhance records for use with the particular service or services being implemented by the metadata harvester. In practice, metadata may be added to harvested records, including general-purpose metadata concerning provenance and implicit context and more specific metadata especially helpful for supporting target services and the presentation of aggregated metadata to end users.

The OAI-PMH Provenance Node

It is the responsibility of the OAI service provider to ensure the provenance of harvested metadata records, especially if services implemented will allow the further reharvesting and reuse of metadata records by others. This can require adding provenance information to harvested metadata records. OAI-PMH provides recommended guidelines and an XML schema useful for adding OAI-related provenance metadata to harvested records.[16] These guidelines anticipate that some OAI service providers will implement metadata-brokering services—that is, services that reorganize, normalize, and/or enrich harvested metadata and then make processed records available for reharvesting again by others. These guidelines also have value for service providers who simply want to keep track of harvested record provenance in order to facilitate or protect the integrity of their own internal processing and workflow. (Alternatively, service providers may maintain harvested record provenance needed for local use in other ways, for example, within the database used locally to aggregate and index harvested metadata.)

As alluded to in earlier chapters, the OAI-PMH <provenance> element is implemented in XML as a child of the <about> node of an OAI metadata record. The OAI-PMH <about> node is optional and repeatable. Each <about> node must have one and only one child node. If no <about> node is present or if all <about> nodes present in the harvested record contain children other than <provenance>, then the service provider simply adds another, new <about> node containing as its child a <provenance> node. If an <about> node in the harvested record already includes a <provenance> child node, then the service provider should merge into that <about> node the additional OAI provenance metadata required.

The provenance node contains only one immediate child, <originDescription>, which includes one attribute giving the date and time when the metadata record was last harvested and a second attribute indicating whether the harvesting service provider has altered the record. The <originDescription> element in turn contains the baseURL of the originating repository from which the record was disseminated, the OAI datestamp of the record as disseminated by the originating repository, the OAI identifier of the associated item in the originating repository, and the XML metadataNamespace of the format in which the record was disseminated. In order to be able to track the identity and authenticity of a record, and to update it as necessary, it is important to maintain this information as part of managing harvested metadata records.

The OAI-PMH provenance schema allows the nesting of <originDescription> nodes. If a metadata record is harvested first by OAI service

FIGURE 7-2   OAI-PMH provenance node for a twice-harvested metadata record.

```
<about>
  <provenance xmlns="http://www.openarchives.org/OAI/2.0/provenance"
      xmlns:xsi="http://www.w3.org/2001/XMLSchema-instance"
      xsi:schemaLocation="http://www.openarchives.org/OAI/2.0/provenance
          http://www.openarchives.org/OAI/2.0/provenance.xsd">
    <originDescription harvestDate="2006-10-04T21:46:21Z" altered="true">
      <baseURL>http://wolfram.grainger.uiuc.edu/oai.asp</baseURL>
      <identifier>
        oai:wolfram.grainger.uiuc.edu:(Mathworld):oai:mathworld.wolfram.com:2D3130312D4D61747269782E68746
      </identifier>
      <datestamp>2003-03-29</datestamp>
      <metadataNamespace>http://www.openarchives.org/OAI/2.0/oai_dc/</metadataNamespace>
      <originDescription harvestDate="2006-09-04T21:50:30Z" altered="false">
        <baseURL>http://nsdl.grainger.uiuc.edu/WolframMathworld/oai.asp</baseURL>
        <identifier>oai:mathworld.wolfram.com:2D3130312D4D61747269782E68746</identifier>
        <datestamp>2003-03-29</datestamp>
        <metadataNamespace>http://www.openarchives.org/OAI/2.0/oai_dc/</metadataNamespace>
      </originDescription>
    </originDescription>
  </provenance>
</about>
```

provider A, then later harvested from A by service provider B, and then sub-sequently reexposed by B for possible harvest yet again by another service provider C, the record as disseminated by service provider B will contain a single `<provenance>` node with nested `<originDescription>` nodes, the innermost detailing the harvest by service provider A, and the outermost detailing the harvest by service provider B. Figure 7-2 illustrates this scenario, showing the `<provenance>` node for a twice-harvested metadata record. As illustrated, the `<provenance>` node can become complex.

Collections, Context, and Relationships

In the OAI-PMH model, metadata records may be harvested in bulk by repository or by OAI set. Although not a requirement of the protocol, in practice metadata records harvested in such groupings nearly always exhibit a measure of cohesiveness (Foulonneau in press). They may exhibit similar semantic and structural characteristics—for example, the same value encoding schemes, the presence of the same optional fields, and the similar use of elements. If the character of repository or OAI set cohesiveness is well understood, OAI service providers can exploit this cohesion when processing harvested metadata, making it possible to clean and normalize records more efficiently and effectively on a repository-by-repository or set-by-set basis.

OAI data provider repository and set configuration also may correspond to the organization of digital resources into cohesive collections of content, for example, collections of resources related topically, pertaining to the work of a particular individual, pertaining to a particular place or historical event, or curated by the same individual. In such instances, the item-collection relationship represents a critical form of implicit context at risk when item-level metadata are removed from a local context and added to an aggregation. Service providers should inspect harvested records to ensure that essential contextual information inherited from a parent collection is present and that item-collection relationships are explicitly expressed. At a minimum, a collection name or title and/or an is-part-of relationship value pointing back to the parent collection should be present somewhere in every item-level metadata record. If it is not present, the service provider should add such information to the metadata record during post-harvest processing. Failure to do so may adversely impact the quality of services provided.

A librarian at Harvard University, Robin Wendler (see also chapter 1), offered a real-world illustration of the potential problem, citing a collection of metadata records describing digitized photographs of Theodore Roosevelt (Wendler 2004). These metadata records were created for use in a local application dedicated to this single collection. Subject headings were assigned which assumed this local-use context. For example, "On a horse" was assigned as a subject heading for one image. As long as the metadata record was to be used only within the local context, such a subject heading was adequate—an end user could recognize that Theodore Roosevelt was implied. However, taken out of local context, for example, harvested, and added without modification to a larger aggregation including metadata describing resources not related to Roosevelt, the subject heading "On a horse" became nonsensical and not at all helpful to understanding the nature of the resource described.

A slightly subtler illustration (Foulonneau et al. 2005) from the CIC collaborative metadata sharing project mentioned above[17] considered a selection of metadata records harvested from multiple collections and included in the CIC aggregation, all of which described digitized works by or about Harriet Beecher Stowe. All would be relevant in response to a general query about Stowe. However, one subset was more relevant in response to a query about the poetry of Stowe, while a different subset was more relevant in response to a query about Stowe as a factor in antebellum social history. Inspection of the item-level metadata records alone did not allow this level of differentiation. Only by referencing the relevant collection descriptions, and noting that some records came from collections of resources associated with American poetry while other records came from collections dealing with American nineteenth-century social history, was it possible to uncover such distinctions.

This second illustration also demonstrates that it is not necessary to replicate collection-level description within the item-level metadata record of each collection member. In the CIC model as implemented, it was found sufficient to maintain a link between item-level and collection-level descriptions. Excessive replication of collection-level information in item-level metadata records can result in redundancy and blur useful distinctions between item-level metadata records (Foulonneau 2007).

Item-to-item relationships also are useful and should be preserved. Service providers should inspect relation elements within metadata records for such information and insure that references used can be resolved. Some data providers may use local, shorthand notation to indicate sibling, parent, or child relationships among items, collections, and subcollections—for example, as between an archival record set, box, folder, and item. This may be difficult to resolve once metadata records have been added to a larger aggregation, so service providers should augment relation element values as required to preserve linkages between records and related resources. Encoding relationships either with globally unique OAI `identifiers` or with persistent, absolute URLs can help to preserve important relationships between resources.

Enriching and Normalizing for Specific Services

Metadata normalization and augmentation are performed by OAI service providers in order to adapt harvested records for specific uses and to support specific service objectives. Both human-readable and machine-understandable metadata may need to be considered. Standard codes and controlled vocabulary terms that can be easily processed by computer applications are well suited to support automated filtering, ranking, and browsing of harvested metadata records, but may not be easily and intuitively interpretable by end users, nor of optimum granularity to allow end users to quickly identify and select records of interest. Free-text metadata may be better suited for display to end users and for indexing to support keyword searching. When processing harvested records that make extensive use of codes and controlled vocabularies designed for machine consumption, the service provider will want to add human-readable values to records during processing. When processing metadata records well suited for display to end users but lacking in code and controlled vocabulary optimized for automated processing, the service provider will want to enrich and normalize records by adding standard, machine-understandable codes and terminology.

In order to accomplish this phase of metadata normalization and augmentation, it is essential to inventory available metadata fields and metadata content-encoding options and assess how metadata elements will be used in context of the services being implemented. For example, if implementing a cross-repository search-and-browse portal, a service provider might begin by asking:

- Which metadata elements and value encodings will support search and discovery?
- Which elements and value encodings will be relied on for filtering and ranking search results?
- Which facets will be enabled for browsing, and what terminologies will be used for browsing?
- How will relationships between items and between items and collections be exploited?
- Which metadata elements will appear in displays?
- What end-user actions and functions will portal displays support, and which metadata elements will be required to enable those actions and functions?
- How will the absence of useful elements in some records be managed?

Tables 7-2, 7-3, and 7-4 illustrate how the answers to such questions might inform the metadata-processing steps undertaken by the service provider.

End-user displays may include both as-harvested metadata elements and values and metadata elements and values that have been created during post-harvest processing. End-user displays—for example, search-results lists,

TABLE 7-2 Examples of metadata processing to support search.

Search criteria	Search targets	Processing required
Full text of metadata record	Entire record except rights and other administrative metadata.	Clean all values except rights and other administrative metadata fields.
Title	Title, alternate titles, subtitles, series titles.	Clean and map all relevant values to title.
Author	Author, creator, other equivalent fields; may choose to include contributor.	Clean and map all relevant values to author.
Subject	Subject, other relevant fields; may choose to include temporal and spatial coverage fields.	Clean and split (for example, if semicolon separated) all relevant values. Potentially transform to common vocabulary (for example, LCSH).
Type	Type, resourceType, other equivalent fields.	Transform relevant values to selected type vocabulary. For records lacking explicit type, it may be implicit in format value.
Collection	Collection title; may be recognizable in relation, isPartOf, or other equivalent field.	Clean and map relevant fields if present, but typically this value is added by service provider during metadata augmentation based on either the OAI repository or an OAI set.

TABLE 7-3 Examples of metadata processing to support browse.

Browse by	Metadata element	Processing required
Institution	Provenance	Field added by the service provider according to the repository or OAI set from which the record has been harvested
Geographic representation	Spatial coverage	Normalized values of the spatial information from coverage, subject, and other relevant fields
Type	Resource type	Values from type, resourceType, and other relevant fields transformed to type vocabulary used by the service; type information may be implicit in format or other metadata fields

browse listings, and displays describing individual resources—need not (usually do not) include all elements present in metadata records. The objective is to present metadata describing a resource in a manner that is clear,

TABLE 7-4   Examples of metadata processing to support display.

Display label	Metadata element	Processing required
Title	Title only; if a title does not exist or contains a meaningless value such as "no title," then alternative titles; if no alternative titles, then subject; if no subject, nothing	Clean and map all relevant values to title
Creator/contributor	Creator, author, contributor, and other equivalent fields	Clean and map all relevant values to the creator/contributor
Lock symbol (that is, restricted access)	Rights	Binary mapping of rights value to open or restricted access
Type, sometimes represented by icons	Resource type	Values from type and other relevant fields transformed to type vocabulary used by the service; type information may be implicit in format or other metadata fields

human readable, and easy to grasp and use. Metadata elements and value encodings intended solely for machine processing should be suppressed. Some elements that were separated during record cleaning in order to facilitate indexing and machine use may be concatenated again. Selected values may be converted to standard icons for display purposes. Values may be truncated to facilitate generation of results lists and the like. Alternative fields may be used for display if a preferred field is not present (for example, the first several words of a DC description field may be displayed for presentation of a given record in lieu of an absent DC title field).

At the same time, it is vital to not misrepresent harvested metadata records. Original, unmodified metadata values from the as-harvested metadata record should be used whenever feasible, especially when displaying metadata records to end-users. This requires that the service provider preserve the values, semantics, and structure of the as-harvested metadata. Mechanically, in XML-based processing this can be accomplished through the use of XML attributes and/or maintenance of as-harvested elements within a different XML node than the one used to record normalized and augmented metadata elements and values.

COLLABORATION BETWEEN DATA AND SERVICE PROVIDER

The ultimate quality and utility of services implemented using OAI-PMH are limited by the combined quality of data provider and service provider implementations. This is an inescapable consequence of the OAI-PMH interoperability model.

FIGURE 7-3   Summary of post-harvest metadata processing steps.

Select	Cleanup	Normalize	Augment	Adapt for Display
Exclude records not matching aggregation collection development policy.	Delete artifacts of concatenation (e.g., punctuation delimiters at start or end of a value).	Rename fields and/or map values from one field to another.	Add values and/or fields detailing provenance and containing default values assigned to all members of repository or set.	Select fields for service display(s).
				Select alternative display strategies, e.g., fields to display when first choice not present.
	Remove empty fields.	Modify / transform values to preferred vocabularies and/or add normalized values.	Add collection title and other fields and values relating record to other records or entities.	Decide on strategies for truncating long values and listing multiple values (e.g., concatenate multiple authors, delimiting with semi-colons).
Remove as duplicates or reconcile metadata records describing objects at same URL.	Split values that have been concatenated.		Relate to external authorities.	

Figure 7-3 summarizes in generic terms the steps available to an OAI service provider during post-harvest metadata processing. Using automated approaches, the OAI service provider can go a long way toward adapting harvested metadata to support specific service objectives; however, it is not practical for a service provider to fully re-catalog a data provider's collection of resources. Service providers want data providers to give them as much as possible to work with—that is, to include as much relevant metadata as possible and to implement service provider-preferred standard metadata value encodings and terminologies to the maximum extent feasible.

Data providers, while they want to see their metadata reused (why else implement OAI-PMH?), tend to focus first on their local metadata requirements and context. They may be limited by local system infrastructure (a number of commercially available systems that incorporate support for OAI data provider implementations allow only a limited range of metadata formats). Data providers also may not be aware of the specific needs of service providers harvesting them.

Good two-way communication between service provider and data provider is critical to maximize success. As described in chapter 6, data providers should document metadata creation practices so that service providers can better understand how specific fields are being used and know which value vocabularies and encoding schemes are being used. For their part, service providers need to inform data providers about aggregation collection development policies, post-harvest processing approaches being used, and ultimate services being implemented. Communication of this sort can lead to improvements on both sides of the collaboration. For instance, knowing more about the collection-development policies of OAI service providers can lead OAI data providers to modify repository OAI set organization.

OAI service providers should clarify expectations and preferences and the rationale for those expectations and preferences. For example, to facilitate resource discovery, a service provider might encourage data providers to describe intellectual resources as a whole rather than just the digitized surrogates of resources. In practice, this might lead a data provider to include in the DC creator field the name Pablo Picasso in lieu of or in addition to the name of the photographer who created a digitized image of Picasso's *Guernica* mural. In particular, service providers should document preferences regarding descriptive granularity, metadata formats, and metadata content-encoding schemes and terminologies. Good examples of service provider guidelines are available (for example,[18, 19]). Data providers should consider such guidelines as supplemental to the more generic sharable metadata best practices described in chapter 6.

OAI service providers also have an obligation to protect the integrity of harvested metadata records. Metadata are always created for a purpose. Reuse of metadata in a different context necessarily raises issues. When processing harvested metadata records, OAI service providers run the risk of introducing inaccuracies and/or reducing the precision of the original metadata. On the other hand, incomplete metadata records or metadata values expressed in formats incompatible with service implementations can undermine service quality and utility.

For example, the metadata portal for the CIC OAI-PMH-based metadata sharing project mentioned above[20] offers the option to filter searches by resource type. Only 77 percent of as-harvested metadata records contained a normalized type value usable for this search filter. Any search using this filter would consider only 77 percent of the records in the aggregation. Too many potentially useful resources would be overlooked, and search results would be misleading. Post-harvest normalization and enrichment of metadata records dramatically increase the percentage of records in the aggregation containing a type value useable for filtering. Sampling of processed records indicates that a very small, albeit non-zero error was introduced during normalization and augmentation of type values. For this application, the level of potential degradation in search precision generated by this error was deemed an acceptable trade-off for the improvement in search recall (Foulonneau and Cole 2005).

QUESTIONS AND TOPICS FOR DISCUSSION

1. What is different about creating a collection-development policy for an aggregation of harvested metadata as compared to creating a collection-development policy for a traditional library print collection?
2. Creating a crosswalk to transform harvested metadata records from a format such as MODS to a less-rich format such as unqualified DC involves trade-offs. Semantic information may be lost (for example, the distinction between parts of a name, as illustrated in Figure 7-1). Some data values present in the richer record may not fit well in the less-rich record. When is it better to leave out a value from the rich-format record altogether rather than try to force the value into a not-entirely-appropriate element of the less-rich format?

3. What approaches would you suggest for normalizing name values? Do you think it viable to normalize all names present in harvested metadata records, or only those in certain fields?
4. What are the potential hazards and issues associated with harvesting for the same metadata aggregation from multiple OAI data providers having metadata records exhibiting very different descriptive granularities?
5. What specific metadata-quality problems would compel you as an OAI service provider to exclude records from a specific OAI data provider? What specific metadata-quality problems might you overlook if the records provided by an OAI data provider describe resources relevant to the service you want to implement?

SUGGESTIONS FOR EXERCISES

1. As described in previous chapters, use your Web browser to submit a `GetRecord` or `ListRecords` OAI request and harvest a sample metadata record from the Library of Congress OAI data provider. (`baseURL` as of this writing is < http://memory.loc.gov/cgi-bin/oai2_0 >, or you can visit the University of Illinois OAI-PMH Data Provider Registry at < http://gita.grainger.uiuc.edu/registry/ > and search for "Library of Congress.") Assume you wanted to reexpose this record for subsequent harvesting by other OAI service providers. Construct the appropriate OAI <provenance> XML node that you would need to add to the record before making available for reharvest.
2. Use your Web browser to harvest in the `oai_dc` metadata format (that is, in unqualified Dublin Core) at least ten sample records each from at least three different OAI data provider repositories. Examine the date, type, and format elements if present. Based on your sample, can you deduce whether the values in these fields conform to consistent community vocabularies? Are values for these metadata attributes consistent across each individual repository? Is enough information present to allow automatic transformation of these values to conform to the W3CDTF, DC Type, and Internet Media Type encoding standards?
3. Use your Web browser to harvest metadata sample records (at least a dozen) from an OAI data provider repository that supports the MODS metadata format. (A candidate repository would be the Library of Congress OAI repository, but there are several others as well.) Harvest the same items in both the MODS format and in unqualified DC (that is, `oai_dc` metadata format). Compare each metadata item as harvested in the two formats. Describe what information was lost in the crosswalk from MODS to unqualified DC? As an OAI service provider, would you prefer to harvest the records in MODS or in unqualified DC? If you were creating a service that required you to crosswalk harvested metadata to unqualified DC anyway, would that change your answer?

NOTES

1. http://www.w3.org/TR/NOTE-datetime.
2. http://oaister.umdl.umich.edu/o/oaister/restricted.html.
3. http://nsdl.org/about/index.php?pager=collection_policy.

4. http://cicharvest.grainger.uiuc.edu/collection.asp.
5. http://www.getty.edu/research/conducting_research/standards/intrometadata/crosswalks.html.
6. http://www.loc.gov/standards/mods/mods-dcsimple.html.
7. http://www.iana.org/assignments/media-types/.
8. http://www.doi.org/handbook_2000/toc.html.
9. http://www.w3.org/TR/NOTE-datetime.
10. http://dublincore.org/documents/library-application-profile/index.shtml.
11. http://www.iso.org/iso/en/prods-services/popstds/datesandtime.html.
12. http://cicharvest.grainger.uiuc.edu/collection.asp.
13. http://www.cdlib.org/inside/projects/amwest/.
14. http://www.iso.org/iso/en/prods-services/iso3166ma/index.html.
15. http://www.getty.edu/vow/TGNSearchPage.jsp.
16. http://www.openarchives.org/OAI/2.0/guidelines-provenance.htm.
17. http://cicharvest.grainger.uiuc.edu/collection.asp.
18. http://metamanagement.comm.nsdlib.org/outline.html.
19. http://cicharvest.grainger.uiuc.edu/dcguidelines.asp.
20. http://cicharvest.grainger.uiuc.edu/.

REFERENCES

Berners-Lee, T., R. Fielding, and L. Manister. 1998. *Uniform Resource Identifiers (URI): Generic Syntax [Request for Comments: 2396].* Reston, VA: The Internet Society, http://www.ietf.org/rfc/rfc2396.txt?number=2396.

Buckland, Michael, and Lewis Lancaster. 2004. Combining Place, Time, and Topic: The Electronic Cultural Atlas Initiative. *D-Lib Magazine* 10 (5), doi: 10.1045/may2004-buckland, http://www.dlib.org/dlib/may04/buckland/05buckland.html.

Foulonneau, Muriel. 2007. Information Redundancy across Metadata Collections. *Information Processing & Management.* 43 (3): 740–51. Preprint available, doi: 10.1016/j.ipm.2006.06.004.

Foulonneau, Muriel, and Timothy W. Cole. 2005. Strategies for Reprocessing Aggregated Metadata. *Research and Advanced Technology for Digital Libraries, Proceedings of the 9th European Conference, ECDL 2005, Vienna, Austria, September 18–23,* ed. A. Rauber, S. Christodoulakis, and A. M. Tjoa, 290–301. Lecture Notes in Computer Science 3652. Berlin: Springer-Verlag.

Foulonneau, Muriel, Timothy W. Cole, Thomas G. Habing, and Sarah L. Shreeves. 2005. Using Collection Descriptions to Enhance an Aggregation of Harvested Item-Level Metadata. *Digital Libraries: Cyberinfrastructure for Research and Education. Proceedings of the Fifth ACM/IEEE-CS Joint Conference on Digital Libraries [Denver, June 7–11],* 32–41. New York: Association for Computing Machinery.

Harrison, Terry L., Aravind Elango, Johan Bollen, and Michael Nelson. 2004. *Initial Experiences Re-Exporting Duplicate and Similarity Computation with an OAI-PMH Aggregator.* arXiv Technical Report [preprint], cs.DL/0401001, http://www.arxiv.org/abs/cs.DL/0401001.

Payette, S. D., and O. Y. Rieger. 1997. Z39.50 the User's Perspective. *D-Lib Magazine* 3 (4), http://www.dlib.org/dlib/april97/cornell/04payette.html.

Sfakakis, M., and S. Kapidakis. 2004. An Architecture for Online Information Integration on Concurrent Resource Access on a Z39.50 Environment. *Research and Advanced Technology for Digital Libraries, Proceedings of the 7th European Conference,*

ECDL 2003, Trondheim, Norway, August 17–22, ed. T. Koch and I. Torvik, 288–299. Lecture Notes in Computer Science 2769. Berlin: Springer-Verlag.

Shreeves, S. L., and C. M. Kirkham. 2004. Experiences of educators using a portal of aggregated metadata. *Journal of Digital Information* 5 (3), Article No. 290, 2004-09-09, http://jodi.ecs.soton.ac.uk/Articles/v05/i03/Shreeves/.

Wendler, Robin. 2004. The Eye of the Beholder. *Metadata in Practice*, ed. Diane I. Hillmann and Elaine L. Westbrooks, 51–69. Chicago, IL: American Library Association.

CHAPTER 8

Using Aggregated Metadata to Build Digital Library Services

As described in chapter 1, OAI-PMH is designed to enable greater interoperability between digital libraries and to facilitate the more efficient dissemination of digital information resources. In practice, such goals are accomplished through the implementation of digital library services. OAI-PMH is successful only to the extent that it enables or facilitates the implementation of useful digital library services which further interoperability across digital collections and lead to more efficient dissemination and use of digital information resources.

The understanding of what is meant by a digital library service is not precise and can vary by context. Any comprehensive definition must encompass not only macro services to end-users—for example, online interlibrary loans, e-reserves, and other computer-mediated forms of traditional library services—but also more granular services targeting automated applications that rely on and manipulate digital content. A good working definition, one appropriate to the context of OAI-PMH, was offered by the Digital Library Federation Services Framework Group (Lavoie, Henry, and Dempsey 2006): "A service is a discrete piece of functionality, manifested in the form of a technical implementation, and deployed for use, usually on a network (e.g., as a Web service). Looking ahead, there is every indication that more and more library processes and workflows will take the form of automated systems built by combining a variety of services." Digital library services are *modular* and *layered*, and high-level macro services can be decomposed into finer-grained services. An OAI-PMH-based search-and-discovery service might be separable into a harvesting service, a metadata normalization and enrichment service, an indexing service, a search interface service, and a service that manages and presents search results to end users.

While a wide range of services can be built over aggregated metadata, there are unique challenges and considerations that must be taken into account when building services based on aggregations of metadata. A good digital library service built using OAI-PMH considers not only the metadata records harvested, but also the information resources represented by those metadata records. Initially, OAI service providers focused on basic cross-repository search-and-discovery services—that is, portals and gateways "to make cataloging and related metadata about scholarly collections more visible to Internet users" (Waters 2001). The University of Michigan's OAIster portal[1] is one of the oldest and most prototypical examples of a search-and-discovery portal based on OAI-PMH. In the years since the introduction of OAI-PMH, cross-repository services built atop harvested metadata have evolved and become broader in scope and more sophisticated, encapsulating additional functions. As of 2006, the newest OAI-PMH-based services go well beyond basic finding functionality to emphasize user-mediated organization, navigation, manipulation, and utilization of full-content digital information resources.

This chapter examines issues that must be considered when implementing digital library services over aggregations of metadata. The chapter begins with a consideration of the kinds and range of end-user tasks and library operations that define the essential functions of a digital library and drive the development of digital library services. Anecdotal examples of how OAI service provider implementations have evolved over time to support a broader range of end-user tasks are cited. The chapter continues with a discussion of the ways in which the intrinsic heterogeneity of metadata aggregations shape the nature and identity of OAI-PMH-based services. Ultimately, resources, not metadata, are the focus of user-oriented digital library services. The chapter closes with a brief look at the issues of using aggregated metadata to facilitate access to and use of digital information resources.

SUPPORTING THE NEEDS OF DIGITAL LIBRARY USERS

As discussed in earlier chapters, implicit in the design of OAI-PMH is the idea that *metadata are created for a purpose*—for example, to enable the implementation of metadata-mediated services that address user and institutional needs. In undertaking to implement a digital library service based on an aggregation of metadata, a natural first question to ask is what library function(s) and/or end-user task(s) can be enabled or facilitated by metadata-based services?

This is not a new question, at least not within the library community. The nature of library services based on metadata in the form of bibliographic records has been extensively studied. The role of bibliographic records has evolved and continues to change and expand. In 1998, the International Federation of Library Associations and Institutions (IFLA) released the final report of a multi-year examination of the Functional Requirements for Bibliographic Records (FRBR). This landmark study had as its aim "to produce a framework that would provide a clear, precisely stated, and commonly shared understanding of what it is that the bibliographic record aims to provide information about, and what it is that we expect the record to achieve in terms of answering user needs" (IFLA Study Group on the Functional Requirements for Bibliographic Records 1998). The explicit linking of metadata purpose to user needs is important. It suggests that a consideration of

OAI-PMH-based services should begin with an examination of the needs of digital library users. What is the nature and range of tasks that digital library users undertake?

The FRBR study itself suggested four basic user tasks that might be addressed by metadata records: *find, identify, select*, and *obtain*. Other researchers, writing both before and after the publication of the FRBR report, have elaborated on these four basic tasks and/or suggested other metadata-mediated tasks. In her book *The Intellectual Foundation of Information Organization* (Svenonius 2000), Elaine Svenonius provides additional historical perspective on the changing role of bibliographic records over time and adds *navigate* to the four user tasks proposed by the FRBR report. The navigate task is reliant on an understanding of how resources correlate one to another (that is, how they order, are organized into collections, and/or otherwise can be grouped or clustered) and requires that such relationships and organizational arrangements be expressed in a form that can be understood and acted on by computer applications. Other researchers have suggested that relationship and contextual metadata also can help support *interpret* as a metadata-mediated user task. "Once potentially useful material has been extracted from sources ... work begins in earnest. It is at that point necessary to develop an intuition for the retrieved information, to 'make sense of it' " (Paepcke 1996). Interpret focuses on comprehending retrieved results considered in aggregate. Still others (for example, Coyle 2004) have proposed models for the ways metadata support institutional functions and tasks (as distinct from end-user tasks). Functions such as information resource *preservation* and *promotion* are concrete examples of institutional tasks supported by metadata.

Clearly, the tasks and library functions enumerated here overlap, and distinctions between them blur in practice. Metadata and metadata-mediated services may simultaneously support multiple functions or tasks. The point of reviewing research on the functions of metadata and on the tasks that metadata can enable or facilitate is to appreciate the relationship between tasks and services. A task-oriented model of services can help drive and define service objectives and is useful to have in mind when developing or analyzing digital library services.

Search and discovery, or finding in the nomenclature of the FRBR report, was the primary user task supported by the initial generation of OAI service providers. In introducing a set of early, influential OAI service provider projects funded by the Andrew W. Mellon Foundation, Don Waters, program officer for the foundation's scholarly communications grant program, expressed their shared purpose this way: " ... these seven projects will explore the requirements for developing scholarly-oriented portal services based on the use of a variety of Internet technologies, including the new Metadata Harvesting Protocol to make the contents of library catalogs and other elements of the 'deep' Web more easily accessible" (Waters 2001). In 2001, the focus of OAI service provider implementations was on making digital scholarly information more visible to larger, physically dispersed audiences. Priority was given in these early projects to debugging harvesting workflow and performing rudimentary normalization and indexing of harvested metadata. Presentation was basic. These service providers harvested widely—mostly in unqualified DC metadata format—and provided keyword searching and some normalized field-specific searching. The objective was to help users discover the existence of resources. Other end-user tasks and library functions remained the purview of content providers.

While finding was then and remained in 2006 a high-priority user task, experience of early projects highlighted the need for additional work to extend the role of OAI-PMH beyond just basic search and discovery (for example, Cole et al. 2002; Halbert, Kaczmarek, and Hagedorn 2003). Scholar feedback and usability studies of early OAI service provider implementations supported this assessment (for example, Hagedorn 2003; Shreeves and Kirkham 2004). The evolution of OAI-PMH-based services during the first six years since the protocol's public release has led to implementations of services that encompass user tasks beyond finding. Second-generation OAI service providers focused on details such as context for harvested metadata records, metadata enrichment, and the discovery of useful new relationships between and among harvested metadata records. It was during this phase that OAI-PMH-based projects began enhancing and adding services especially designed to address user tasks such as identify, select, interpret, and navigate.

Identify is the task of differentiating one resource from another and of confirming that a retrieved metadata record describes a specific resource sought—for example, as in the context of "known-item" searching, a scenario in which the end user has prior knowledge of a particular resource and is simply trying to find it again. The select task, which is closely related, is the task of choosing the appropriate resource to meet an information need, not only in terms of content relevance, but also in terms of format, language, and suitability for intended use. For instance, when select is considered as an end-user task, it can be about which digital view of a sculpture (for example, in profile or straight on) is most appropriate. These tasks are informed by many of the same metadata elements used to support finding—in DC semantics, elements such as title, creator, subject, and description. However, additional metadata elements also can support identify and select tasks—elements such as identifier, format, type, and language. Normalizing and enriching metadata to facilitate user-mediated identification and selection of relevant resources are different from normalizing and enriching metadata for machine indexing. Also, non-textual information not normally found in harvested records (for example, thumbnail representations of resources) can facilitate more efficient end-user identification and selection.

Interpret is the task of comprehending retrieved results. How does a set of search results considered in aggregate begin to answer the end user's information need and inform the use of individual resources? Services designed to facilitate interpretation may make use of some of the same item-level metadata elements used to support selection and identification; however, where the brief author-title-format record of a results-list display might suffice for basic identification or for a binary decision as to appropriate/not appropriate, really making sense of retrieved results, both individually and collectively, requires a more in-depth review of complete metadata records. Contextual information also becomes critical for interpretation. Item-collection relationships as well as item-item relationships can help an end user place a set of described resources in proper context one-to-another and thereby better comprehend where the resources collectively and individually fit relative to other content. Similarly, navigate, the task of moving through a listing of search results or between related metadata records, relies heavily on relationship metadata. Effective navigation can be facilitated by sorting, ranking, and clustering services and the normalization of metadata elements such as date, type, and subject that support the implementation of such services.

As OAI-PMH has evolved, OAI service providers have focused increasingly on interface and metadata processing approaches that support these tasks. The collaborative OAI-PMH-based metadata sharing project of the CIC (Committee on Institutional Cooperation) begun in 2003 (Foulonneau et al. 2006) provides an illustration of the way second-generation OAI service providers support the user tasks identify, select, interpret, navigate, and find. For the CIC project, post-harvest metadata processing services were implemented to normalize metadata values and structure and to add access points that would better support specific end-user tasks (Foulonneau and Cole 2005). From the primary CIC metadata portal,[2] users can sort search results on a variety of different metadata attributes, filter them by resource type, and otherwise navigate by resource type, owning institution, and collection membership. An alternative, experimental search service deployed during the CIC project exploited normalized spatial coverage metadata values to allow users to browse resources (that is, to navigate the metadata aggregation) using point-and-click maps. A third portal created and tested with end users exploited collection-item relationships added to harvested metadata during processing to enhance finding and to provide added context to facilitate the selection, navigation, and interpretation of both item-level and collection-level resources relevant to users' queries (Foulonneau et al. 2005). To facilitate end-user identification and selection of resources, the CIC project also implemented a service that automatically generated (from URLs embedded in metadata records) image resource thumbnails and Web page "thumbshots" (that is, thumbnail-sized representations of a Web page) suitable for display on CIC portal search-results pages. Images generated were posted to a Web-accessible directory, and URLs pointing to generated thumbnails and thumbshots were embedded in corresponding metadata records during post-harvest processing (Foulonneau, Habing, and Cole 2006).

As OAI service providers implement increasingly sophisticated services, access to minimal descriptive metadata alone (for example, unqualified DC) is proving insufficient. Sophisticated services require access to richer, more extensive metadata and in some cases to instantiations or views of complete digital resources. For instance, the thumbnail-generating service implemented by the CIC project required Web-accessible views of the resources described by harvested metadata records. Thumbnails could not be generated for resources that were not Web accessible (or for which only restricted access was allowed, for example, password-protected resources). Metadata records describing resources for which no thumbnails were available were disadvantaged when presented in CIC portal search-results lists.

Resource-clustering services are another example of a class of OAI-PMH-based services that benefit from access to richer metadata and/or access to full content. These services mine harvested metadata records and/or the full text of complete resources described by harvested metadata to reveal relationships between resources. Results can be used to sort resources anew, to enhance ranking algorithms, or to discover and identify new virtual clusters of related resources. The output of such services then can be applied to facilitate end-user selection, navigation (browse), and/or interpretation tasks. An example of one such service was built by Emory University as part of the OAI-PMH-based MetaCombine project (Krowne and Halbert 2005).

Ultimately, digital libraries are about information resources. Obtain is the task of retrieving for use a version or view of an information resource. Preservation as a function presumes an available information resource, as does the promotion function. As OAI service providers look to address such tasks and functions, the need for more complex metadata and for more complete models of full-content resources takes on added urgency. Especially necessary are information resource data models that can do more to facilitate resource reuse and repository interoperability at the level of full-content digital objects (Bekaert and Van de Sompel 2006).

A number of issues can hamper cross-repository services designed to support the obtain, preserve, and promote functions. Different repositories may disseminate digital resources of a given type in differing formats. For instance, digital text resources may be disseminated in HTML, XML, PDF (Adobe's Portable Document Format, multiple versions extent), DjVu (a PDF-alternative format supported by Lizard Tech, Inc.[3]), or individually scanned page images. Image- and multimedia-type digital resources have even longer lists of potential dissemination formats. Some repositories will disseminate multiple instantiations or views of a single intellectual resource, with some views potentially less complete or having a lower fidelity or resolution than other views, and each view potentially with its own conditions of use and intellectual property rights. Reuse of resources implies the potential to create additional views or variants of intellectual resources, further dispersed and having distinct attributes, relationships, and conditions of use.

In considering the evolution in both the scope and sophistication of OAI-PMH-based digital library services, the challenge going forward is to move beyond a foundation of services based largely on minimal descriptive metadata (for example, unqualified DC) to services that can exploit richer forms of metadata supporting robust and reliable access to multiple views of full content. This is akin to undertaking a transition from a metadata-based economy to a resource-based economy. In the latter model, metadata is understood as simply a surrogate or specialized view of a resource—just as a thumbnail can be thought of as a surrogate for an image resource. While OAI-PMH will continue to be important in such an environment, this transition will drive further extensions and iterations of metadata formats and likely lead to additional protocols and community agreements supporting more robust repository interoperability at the level of full-content digital resources (Van de Sompel et al. 2006).

Several OAI-PMH-based proof-of-concept experiments have anticipated this challenge and are helping to scope the additional work needed to implement functions such as obtain and preserve. The aDORe repository architecture developed by the Los Alamos National Library (Bekaert, Liu, and Van de Sompel 2005) relies on OAI-PMH and another interoperability standard called OpenURL.[4] (OpenURL has been approved by the American National Standard Institute and the National Information Standards Organization under the rubric Z39.88.) The aDORe experimental architecture has been used successfully at Los Alamos to construct a large-scale, modular digital object repository (including scientific journal article literature) supporting scientific research. Of particular interest with this implementation was the use of OAI-PMH to facilitate the dissemination of instantiations of full-content resources and the accommodation of the Open Archival Information System (OAIS) reference model.[5] The focus of OAIS, approved in 2003 by the International Organization for Standardization (ISO) as ISO 14721, is the preservation of digital information resources.

The Aquifer Asset Actions experiment (Chavez et al. 2006) prototyped another OAI-PMH-based approach that considered multiple dimensions of the obtain task in a digital context. This work was carried out by the Aquifer Initiative[6] Technology Architecture Working Group under the auspices of the Digital Library Federation.[7] As the authors of this work reported, many metadata records harvested using OAI-PMH provide only a single URL pointing back to the resource described. The specific view pointed to by the supplied URL (or URLs when multiple are present) is up to the OAI data provider and is often not labeled (this issue is discussed in more detail later in the chapter). The Aquifer Asset Actions experiment postulated that more sophisticated cross-repository digital library services could be supported if metadata records shared using OAI-PMH always included multiple, typed URLs providing predictable access to specific views of the resources described. "Asset action" sets are XML nodes containing labeled URLs that point at agreed-to, predefined views of a resource. The specific views are a function of the type of resource. For instance, in this model, metadata describing basic digital image resources would always include individual URLs pointing to (at least) a thumbnail view, a view of the image presented in context on the data provider's Web site, a medium-resolution view, and a high-resolution view.

As a proof of concept, a prototype OAI service provider portal was developed at the University of Illinois at Urbana-Champaign (UIUC) to aggregate digital image resource metadata records containing asset action sets. Metadata with asset action sets were provided by Tufts University, Indiana University, Northwestern University, and the Chicago Historical Society. The portal demonstrated advanced service features including thumbnail-based search result displays, an image annotation service, and an image "book bag" that could be used to e-mail metadata and thumbnails of selected images or to generate PDF or Rich Text Format (RTF) documents containing metadata and medium-resolution views of selected images. Additional navigation and selection features also were implemented to facilitate quicker user access to views of resources needed. A digital object collector tool, *Collectus*, originally developed by the University of Virginia for local use on University of Virginia collections, also was integrated into the experimental portal. This tool, deployed as a Java Web Start application using the Java Network Launching Protocol (JNLP),[8] provided client-side image manipulation functions (for example, image zooming, rotating, contrast, and brightness) and allowed users to save metadata about user-defined image collections to a local workstation XML file. The successful integration of Collectus into a portal providing cross-repository access to distributed resources from other universities demonstrated the utility of the asset action experiment approach.

The Los Alamos aDORe project and the Digital Library Federation's Aquifer Asset Action work highlight the potential of OAI-PMH-based services, but also suggest a need for additional interoperability protocols and community technical agreements. This will be discussed further in chapter 9. The rest of this chapter discusses additional practical issues to consider when implementing digital library services over metadata aggregations.

HETEROGENEITY OF CROSS-COLLECTION METADATA AGGREGATIONS

Impact on Aggregation Collection Identity

Cataloging procedures change over time. Cataloging rules and policies and the metadata formats used when describing digital resources differ from institution to institution and sometimes within the same institution. Descriptive practices vary by domain (for example, libraries, museums, and archives). As described in chapter 6, not only is there variability in metadata formats used, there is additional variability in how individual metadata formats are used by different practitioners. These factors all tend to make aggregated metadata heterogeneous.

Centralizing metadata rather than centralizing full-content resources has additional implications. A collection developed using OAI-PMH contains only harvested metadata, but for the purposes of some services, the service provider aggregation is seen by users as virtually including resources that physically remain on dispersed data provider servers. For the OAI service provider, this compounds the collection-development process. Full-content resources are not actually included (meaning that wholly resource-based collection-development policies cannot be used), but they bear on the aggregation identity. From the perspective of the OAI service provider, resource type, format, and granularity are less controlled. The collection identity of a cross-repository metadata aggregation is always partly in the hands of the data providers.

The heterogeneity of OAI-PMH-based metadata aggregations has multiple consequences. Consider an OAI-PMH-based Web portal providing access to resources about the "American West" in the nineteenth century. Constituent collections represented in the metadata aggregation will grow at different rates according to differences in the aggressiveness of the collection-selection policies implemented. While differential growth can be tracked by the OAI service provider, it cannot be controlled for directly. (Table 8-1 illustrates how much one or two data providers can dominate a multi-repository metadata aggregation in terms of numbers of records contributed.) Definitions of what constitutes the American West may vary by data provider, as may policy on the authority of resources to include. These factors are more difficult to track by monitoring metadata alone. Descriptive metadata contributed by one OAI data provider may be better suited than those from a different data provider for searching by the audience of the service provider's portal, resulting in differential retrieval that favors one collection over another. All of these factors will influence the effective identity of the metadata aggregation in ways that the OAI service provider cannot fully control and in some instances in ways that may not be easy for the service provider to discern. This in turn has implications for the coherence of services that can be built over metadata aggregations.

This circumstance necessitates that the OAI service provider approach collection development of the metadata aggregation as a collaborative enterprise. Service providers cannot define the collection identity of a metadata aggregation unilaterally. Good communication with data providers is essential. Data providers should provide clear, complete documentation of local

TABLE 8-1 Distribution of a metadata collection aggregated using OAI-PMH; the composition of the CIC metadata portal collection as of January 2006.

Institution	Metadata included in the CIC metadata portal aggregation[a]	
	Number of records	Percent of aggregation
Indiana University	38,623	7.06
Michigan State University	13,154	2.40
Ohio State University	10,896	1.99
Pennsylvania State University	4,300	0.79
University of Chicago	15,243	2.79
University of Illinois at Chicago	1,807	0.33
University of Illinois at Urbana-Champaign	124,713	22.79
University of Iowa	7,949	1.45
University of Michigan	266,934	48.79
University of Minnesota	31,561	5.77
University of Wisconsin	31,982	5.85

[a] Values shown were as of January 2006. Records from Purdue University and Northwestern University were added to the aggregation later in 2006.

collection-development policies and objectives and should share details of local collection-selection practices. Information about resource authority, accrual policies, and conditions of use criteria used in the selection process is essential. Data providers should consider modifications in OAI set structures to facilitate service provider collection development. As described in chapter 7, service providers may need to filter out unwanted records during post-harvest processing.

Finding and Creating Common Access Points to Heterogeneous Content

Experience with OAI-PMH has confirmed in practice the anticipated heterogeneity of metadata aggregations (Shreeves, Kaczmarek, and Cole 2003; Stvilia et al. 2004; Shreeves et al. 2005). An impact of heterogeneity is readily visible in the frequency of use of basic metadata elements. As described above, this stems from a variety of sources. Table 8-2 illustrates the variation in the use of DC subject and description fields according to type of institution providing the metadata (in this instance, academic libraries, museums, and collaborative, multi-institutional digital libraries).

As described in chapter 7, OAI data providers can address this problem in some measure through post-harvesting normalization of metadata values and semantics. Such normalization should be informed by a thorough analysis of the metadata harvested and by anticipating the indexing and access-point requirements of planned services. Services implemented by data providers may differ from data provider to data provider and will differ from those implemented by service providers who harvest data provider metadata. These differences are visible in the character of harvested metadata. A major challenge for the service provider is to identify concepts common across all harvested records that represent potential index and access points for services that the service provider wants to implement.

OAI service providers must look for compromises that best suit both the needs of the services they seek to implement and the metadata available for harvesting. Services reliant on fine-grained semantics included in some metadata formats (for example semantics that distinguish among contributors,

TABLE 8-2 Variations in Dublin Core element usage for harvested metadata describing digital cultural heritage resources by type of institution providing metadata.

	Percent of harvested records containing element	
	Subject	Description
Digital libraries	78	36
Museums and historical societies	93	93
Academic libraries	15	13

Source: Shreeves, Kaczmarek, and Cole 2003.

creators, authors, artists, and other agents responsible for or involved in the creation of a work) cannot always be implemented given the different ways that such concepts are treated or sometimes not treated in various metadata formats. The inconsistency with which such elements may be used across a large aggregation of harvested metadata can be problematic. Semantic trans- formations and normalization should be undertaken to match service objec- tives. For instance, through appropriate mapping of metadata values, records structured to support fielded keyword searching—for example, unqualified DC records designed to support fielded keyword searching by title words, subject heading terms, etc.—can be transformed to support retrieval of resources according to facets such as *who*, *where*, *what*, *when*, and *why*. Faceted retrieval of resources relies on the organization of resources into orthogonal categories according to specific aspects or features of the resource or its con- text. A facet used to organize cultural heritage resources might be themes (that is, what)—a painting has to do with religion, politics, or war. Another facet might have to do with locale (that is, where)—a photographic image is set in Rome, Venice, or London. Some researchers have suggested that the retrieval of resources by such facets is well received, especially by users seeking digital cultural heritage information resources (Van Kasteren 2003; Yee et al. 2003).

Distinctions in metadata values useful in a data provider context may not be useful for the service provider. For example, an analysis of cultural heri- tage metadata records harvested by the UIUC from a dozen OAI data pro- viders yielded more than 1,400 distinct metadata values for the resource-type element (Cole et al. 2002). Some data providers used only a handful of unique values to express the resource type for all resources held; at the other extreme, one used 886 unique resource-type values. The fine-grained dis- tinctions in resource type used by the latter data provider could not be main- tained in the context of the UIUC aggregation, and in any event was not useful for implementing the desired browse-by-resource-type service wanted. Resource-type values had to be normalized (in this instance to the DC-type vocabulary).

As described in chapter 7, OAI service providers also can augment meta- data records during post-harvest metadata processing. Again, this should be done with service objectives in mind. For instance, provenance details may be added to metadata records to provide a context useful for interpreting search result sets and navigating by institution and collection.

Issues with Controlled Vocabularies

Normalizing or enriching records in order to implement controlled vocabula- ries across a heterogeneous metadata aggregation can be difficult and expensive to implement. Before undertaking any such effort, the trade-off between the likely benefits of controlled cross-collection access should be considered in the context of the specific services planned. Such an analysis should consider how the controlled vocabulary would be used and the relevance of the terminology

selected for the anticipated audience. In the case of cultural heritage repositories, popular access points are geographic locations and names. If a focus of
planned service is to facilitate clustering and browsing of resources by spatial
coverage values, the effort to standardize the way in which geographic locations
are encoded across a metadata aggregation may be warranted.

Terminology issues also can be especially relevant for aggregations containing multilingual content. A service built over such an aggregation may need to
handle metadata records in multiple different languages and/or may send users
to resources in multiple different languages. Here it is important that both the
language of the resource and the language of the metadata value strings are
clearly delineated and machine understandable. The language of the resource
itself should be specified within an element of the metadata record itself, but
values may need to be normalized (for example, to a standard code as described
in chapter 7). For an OAI metadata record, the language of the metadata values
themselves may appear in the <about> section of the record. Alternatively,
for each XML element of the metadata format used, the language of that value
can be defined by using the xml:lang attribute (for example, <subject
lang="eng">). If complete language information is not included in the
record as harvested, the OAI service provider should add it.

Conversely, some researchers suggest that implementation of subject-
controlled vocabularies across an aggregation in the context of a search
service aimed at a general audience might be less worthwhile. This was the
conclusion offered in a report prepared for the European Commission
Directorate-General for the Information Society. "The controlled vocabularies
in use today target the highly specialized and knowledgeable academic community, with the effect, that—if offered online—indexes are rarely used. As
Sandy Buchanan, resource manager at SCRAN [the Scottish Cultural Resources Access Network], knows from experience: '80 percent of our users use text
searches, and only 20 percent make use of structured searches such as indexes.
What we need are tools that are comfortable for people. It is not about
adapting the users to the Internet, but the other way around' " (Geser and
Mulrenin 2002, p. 199). For providing context helpful for interpretation, non-
normalized subject and spatial coverage information may be adequate. Implementing formal subject terminologies may make more sense for a tightly
focused portal aimed at a scholarly audience. Thesauri also can be useful generally to facilitate search query expansion; however, positive benefits can be
achieved from such search query expansions even without normalizing all
metadata records in an aggregation to a common controlled vocabulary.

A viable option for the OAI service provider is to take a hybrid approach to
the use of controlled vocabularies. Normalize only those few metadata element structures and values that are critical to the services you wish to implement, and do so only to the fidelity necessary to support the services
delivered. It can be easier to normalize a modest number of collection records
rather than all of the item-level records in an aggregation, so exploit collection-
item relationships when possible. There are a number of options available
when implementing controlled vocabularies across a heterogeneous metadata

aggregation. For instance, the following are possible strategies for the use of subject vocabularies across an OAI-PMH harvested aggregation:

- Normalize all item-level (and/or collection-level) subject headings encountered
  to a single vocabulary optimized for the service(s) being implemented.
- If most harvested records include subject headings from recognized controlled
  vocabularies, define mappings between vocabularies in use so that the service
  can apply equivalences dynamically across vocabularies as necessary to support
  services.
- If service will limit users to free-text searching, it may be useful when encoun-
  tering subject terms from hierarchical-controlled vocabularies to augment
  records with broader terms—for example, the subject heading `Nicaragua
  History—Filibuster War, 1855-1860 Campaigns` could be added to
  records already having either of the following headings: `Rivas, Battle of,
  Rivas, Nicaragua, 1856` or `Santa Rosa, Battle of, Costa Rica,
  1856`. This sacrifices some precision but enhances recall, especially in the con-
  text of a free-text search service.
- Use data mining and machine-learning techniques to classify automatically harvested records according to a preferred subject classification scheme (Krowne
  and Halbert 2005).

Regardless of the approach, care must be taken to not confuse end users.
Normalized or augmented headings should be visible to users (usually in
addition to the original heading) so that they can understand why a particular
record was returned in response to a particular query.

FROM METADATA TO RESOURCES

OAI service providers create collections of metadata records; however, the
collection of interest to end users is the aggregate of resources described by
those records. Metadata are used only as a way to organize, manage, retrieve,
identify, and describe resources. Resources described by the metadata aggregation comprise the virtual distributed collection of the service provider.
OAI-PMH is meant to be invisible to the end user. Users may recognize the
distributed and dispersed nature of an OAI-PMH-based collection, but they
still assign some responsibility for the resources to the OAI service provider
(Shreeves and Kirkham 2004). The way a service provider links to resources
can be a key indicator of the quality of the service provided. Dead links, out-
dated content, and difficult-to-obtain resources can reflect poorly on the
service provider.

In presenting their services to end users, OAI service providers describe
not the metadata they aggregate, but the virtual collection of full-content
resources over which their services operate. As discussed above, the identity
of this virtual collection is a shared responsibility of the data provider and the
service provider. The collaboration extends beyond just collection development issues. The PictureAustralia project, an early adopter of OAI-PMH,
defines and describes facets of the data provider-service provider collaboration in its online *Guide to the PictureAustralia Service*,[9] noting (for example)

FIGURE 8-1   Illustration of a direct link from a harvested metadata record to a complete resource.

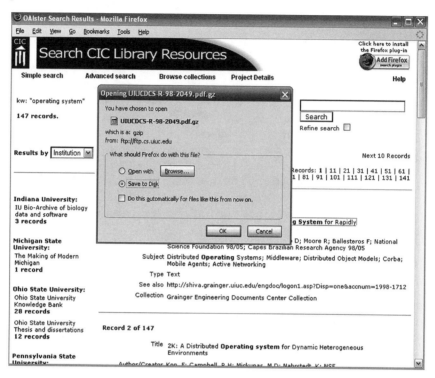

that users of the central service will contact them with questions specific to individual resources held by individual data providers. (As necessary, Picture-Australia forwards these e-mails to the appropriate data provider.)

The responsibility of the OAI service provider to understand the nature of and confirm the proper working of metadata-embedded links back to full-content resources cannot be overstated. In some circumstances, it may be a reasonable subject for negotiation between the data provider and the service provider. The PictureAustralia's service guide advises participating data providers that, "It is also necessary to give some thought to the links provided to the user when they reach the image provider's site. The links should provide access where available to: copyright conditions; an ordering capability; [and] the local image service, for further searching, and reference assistance."[10]

Figures 8-1 through 8-4 illustrate the diversity of links encountered in harvested metadata records, even across scholarly resources made available by a single institution (in this case, the UIUC). Figure 8-1 illustrates the result a user would see when clicking on a link from a harvested metadata record designed to take the user directly to the scholarly resource described (in this case a compressed PDF document) without further intermediation or contextual information provided by the data provider. The disseminated metadata record and the OAI service provider's presentation of that record is assumed adequate to support end-user identification and selection of the resource as appropriate to his or her information need.

FIGURE 8-2   Illustration of a link from a harvested metadata record to a view on the data provider's site of a resource surrogate in context; additional links to a view or views of the complete resource provided by the data provider.

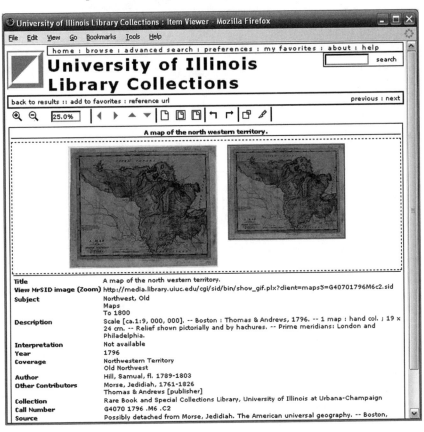

Other data providers prefer to provide links in disseminated metadata records that take users to a surrogate view of a resource in context on the data provider's Web site. This approach, illustrated in Figure 8-2, allows the data provider to further orient the user and provides tools and views that facilitate the manipulation and use of the resource. This approach can require the user to make more mouse clicks to view the resource and is not as amenable to machine processing of resources (for example, automated data mining) as the approach illustrated in Figure 8-1, but it allows for more flexibility in resource delivery and ensures that the user has access to more context than might be provided on the OAI service provider's site.

For complexly structured resources, the additional delivery flexibility and context can be essential. Figure 8-3 illustrates the destination of a harvested metadata link that serves as an entry to a book resource. Although not immediately evident on the view shown, both book-level and page-level metadata are provided on the data provider's site. Users can access digitized views of specific pages as well as contextual information helpful in interpreting and using the resource. Simply providing direct access to an individual, unlinked

FIGURE 8-3   Illustration of a link from a harvested metadata record to the entry page for a complex, structured digital resource, in this case a book of emblematica.

scanned page image without any additional context beyond a bare-bones OAI DC (`oai_dc`) metadata record describing the individual page in isolation would not be as effective for many users in this instance.

Finally, Figure 8-4 illustrates a link from an OAI metadata record to an online finding aid resource. In this case, the destination, rather than a digital article, digital book, or digital image, is the finding aid itself. The finding aid provides a further, more detailed description of archival content held in paper format (that is, non-digital) in the University of Illinois archives. This is useful information for a scholar wanting to know more about specific archive holdings, but can be frustrating for users expecting to link from the OAI service provider site directly to complete online resources (Shreeves and Kirkham 2004).

The heterogeneity and diversity of data provider Web sites do not necessarily lead to problems. The service provider, however, should analyze the functionality of data provider Web sites both from the perspective of the central service being implemented and from the user's point of view. This should be done systematically, comprehensively, and iteratively over time. The following questions illustrate how such a systematic analysis may be undertaken. For this illustration, it is assumed that the service being implemented will be built over an OAI-PMH aggregation of descriptive metadata and support end-user search and discovery of and access to distributed digital resources. Questions are grouped as having to do with *resource access, services,* and *context; resource interaction* and *customization features;* and *navigation functions.* The specific questions listed below were developed with a particular service

FIGURE 8-4   Illustration of a link from a harvested metadata record to a finding aid resource describing non-digital archival content.

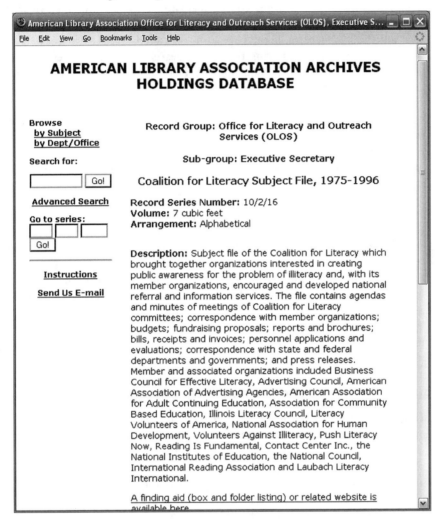

implementation in mind, but the general approach illustrated is relevant for other kinds of metadata-mediated services.

Resource Access, Services, and Context

- *Are there broken links?* This can be tested by automated means. Links should be tested periodically to validate the data provider's performance over time.
- *Does the metadata-embedded link point to a surrogate or "use" copy of the resource?* If so, is the full resource available and is it clear how to get to it?
- *Is the resource available in multiple formats?* The data provider's Web site might offer the resource in multiple formats. A text may be available in PDF, HTML, and XML, for example. The metadata-embedded URL might point to a single format view or to an intermediate page listing delivery options and allowing the user to select the most useful instance.

- *How many clicks are required to access a resource starting with the URL provided for the resource in the harvested metadata record?* Data providers frequently embed URLs pointing to intermediate pages—for example, their local version of a metadata record, a Web page introducing and providing more context for the resource, a login page (for restricted-access resources), a local search interface page (requiring the user to search again for the resource), or a collection-level entry page (requiring the user to browse within the collection site for the desired resource).
- *Does the data provider allow saving of metadata?* The metadata may be of some interest to the user, for instance, as a citation source. The data provider may allow downloading of the metadata in formats compatible with popular citation-tracking software.
- *Does the data provider allow ordering a copy of the resource or ancillary materials?* The resource itself, ancillary materials, or perhaps higher-resolution views of a resource may be available for purchase.
- *What context is provided for the resource?* Does the metadata-embedded URL point directly to the complete resource on its own, directly to a useful view of the resource, but with links to a resource description and/or related resources (that is, context), or to a surrogate (for example, a thumbnail) alongside a metadata description providing context. Views providing context can be desirable for end users. On the other hand, linking directly to the full-content resource on its own supports the implementation of services targeted for automated applications such as data mining tools (see also illustrations in Figures 8-1 through 8-4).

Resource Interaction and Customization Features

- *What can the user do with the resource and what additional services or features are provided to facilitate interaction (user or application) with the resource?* In addition to providing access to resources, the data provider's Web site might also offer functions tailored to its specific collection(s). Several image Web sites allow users to zoom in and out or otherwise manipulate images within a Web browser window. For textual resources, the Web site may enable users to access a table of contents, to search internal pages, to view the resource by book chapter in the case of a book, or to display a print-optimized view of the resource.
- *What are the conditions of use?* Does the metadata-embedded URL point to a page containing a clear statement of conditions of use (or at least to a page having a link to such a statement)?
- *What is the copyright status of resources?* Same question for copyright status of metadata.
- *Can the resource (or a pointer to the resource) be added to a user's personal, persistent portfolio?* (For example, can it be stored either locally on the user's desktop computer, or remotely on the data provider's site?) Such a feature may be targeted toward teachers or instructors interested in creating a virtual collection of resources relevant to a certain class.
- *Can a pointer to a resource be added to a session-duration book bag?* The ubiquitous "add to book bag" feature allows a user to accumulate links to a number of resources during a Web session. He or she may then purchase or download full-content resources or metadata and URLs en mass.

- *Can the resource be bookmarked easily?* This is another way of asking if resource URLs are persistent. An "add-to-favorites" feature allows users to retain links to automatically include a direct link to specific resources in the "Favorites" or "Bookmarks" list of their preferred Web browser.

Navigation Functions

- *Do metadata-embedded URLs take users to pages that clearly indicate where they have "landed" and provide ways to navigate the data provider's Web site?* Good Web site design should guarantee that a user will never be "lost" in a Web site (Minerva Working Group 5 2005). It is important to make sure the user recognizes the transition, especially when leaving the service provider's Web site for a data provider's Web site. Placing users on a page with obvious links to data provider browsing facilities gives the user a better sense of the data provider's resource. This improves the user's understanding of resource context and can encourage him or her to explore further the data provider site.
- *Are search functions available?* As above.
- *Does the data provider give the user a means to provide input and feedback?* The data provider's Web site might invite users to provide comments, suggestions, or simply ask questions to a librarian about the resources he has found. This is interactivity with users, at a granularity that cannot easily be mimicked by the service provider.

In systematically analyzing the URLs behind harvested metadata records, the service provider should give feedback to data providers. Comparing interfaces across data provider Web sites gives the service provider a unique vantage point. Feedback of this kind from service provider to data provider is a less-obvious benefit of OAI-PMH for data providers. Such interactions can help improve the quality and usability of digital library services offered by the data provider, ultimately enhancing end-user access to information resources.

QUESTIONS AND TOPICS FOR DISCUSSION

1. Several library user tasks were discussed in this chapter. What are some other library user tasks not mentioned above? What digital library services are suggested by these additional user tasks?
2. What specific services and resources, either online or in person, are offered by your institution's library to help users perform the tasks of find, identify, select, and obtain (that is, the four user tasks proposed by the FRBR report)? Can you think of additional new services that might be offered to help support these user tasks?
3. What are the prerequisites in terms of metadata aggregation collection policy and in terms of metadata semantics and value encodings necessary to support implementation of an image annotation service? Implementation of another digital library service of your choice?
4. What digital library services would be enabled or facilitated by the adoption of a single, aggregation-wide, normalized resource-type vocabulary? Or by the adoption of a single, aggregation-wide, normalized subject classification scheme?

5. Assume you are a data provider supplying metadata describing the resources contained in a Web-based collection of historical images. You have available high-resolution, medium-resolution, and thumbnail views of all images, and for each image you have a Web page giving information about the image. If you could only include one link per OAI metadata record, which would it be? Why? How would your decision impact on services that could be implemented by the OAI service provider who harvested your metadata?

SUGGESTIONS FOR EXERCISES

1. What services, both online and in person, are offered by your institution's library? Identify some of the user tasks or needs answered by each of these services. For each online library service offered, identify the discrete, component functions (for example, user authentication or query transformation or expansion) that are used as building blocks to construct the service. Which of these components are also used (or could be used) to support other services?
2. Assume you are a service provider who wants to create a Google-like service for finding digitized images from selected library special collections in your region of the country. Develop a list of metadata guidelines for your data providers, prescribing which metadata fields to use and providing rules for how to populate those fields. Now assume your objective was to implement a service for undergraduate instructors who want to select and gather images from this same corpus for use in teaching art history courses. How might your data provider guidelines change?
3. Perform a topical search on your favorite Web search engine. Visit at least a dozen of the resources found. Classify the character of the links you visited—for example, how many took you directly to a useful view of the resource, how many took you to an intermediate Web page requiring an additional click to get to the view of interest, how many were broken, how many were to image resources, how many to textual resources, how many were duplicative, etc.

NOTES

1. http://www.oaister.org/.
2. http://cicharvest.grainger.uiuc.edu/.
3. http://www.djvuzone.org/.
4. http://www.niso.org/standards/standard_detail.cfm?std_id=783.
5. http://nost.gsfc.nasa.gov/wwwclassic/documents/pdf/CCSDS-650.0-B-1.pdf.
6. http://www.diglib.org/aquifer/.
7. http://www.diglib.org/.
8. http://java.sun.com/products/javawebstart/index.jsp.
9. http://www.pictureaustralia.org/guide.html.
10. Ibid.

REFERENCES

Bekaert, Jeroen, Xiaoming Liu, and Herbert Van de Sompel. 2005. aDORe, a Modular and Standards-Based Digital Object Repository at the Los Alamos National Laboratory. *Digital Libraries: Cyberinfrastructure for Research and Education.*

Proceedings of the Fifth ACM/IEEE-CS Joint Conference on Digital Libraries [Denver, June 7–11], 367. New York: Association for Computing Machinery.

Bekaert, Jeroen, and Herbert Van de Sompel. 2006. *Augmenting Interoperability across Scholarly Repositories: [Final Report from] a Meeting Sponsored and Supported by Microsoft, the Andrew W. Mellon Foundation, the Coalition for Networked Information, the Digital Library Federation, and the Joint Information Systems Committee.* New York: Andrew W. Mellon Foundation, http://msc.mellon.org/Meetings/ Interop/FinalReport.

Chavez, Robert, Timothy W. Cole, Jon Dunn, Muriel Foulonneau, Thomas G. Habing, William Parod, and Thorton Staples. 2006. DLF-Aquifer Asset Actions Experiment: Demonstrating Value of Actionable URLs. *D-Lib Magazine* 12 (10), doi: 10.1045/october2006-cole, http://www.dlib.org/dlib/october06/cole/10cole. html.

Cole, Timothy W., Joanne Kaczmarek, Paul F. Marty, Christopher J. Prom, Beth Sandore, and Sarah Shreeves. 2002. Now That We've Found the 'Hidden Web,' What Can We Do with It? The Illinois Open Archives Initiative Metadata Harvesting Experience. *Museums and the Web 2002: Selected Papers from an International Conference*, eds. David Bearman and Jennifer Trant, 63–72. Pittsburgh, PA: Archives & Museum Informatics, http://www.archimuse.com/mw2002/papers/ cole/cole.html.

Coyle, Karen. 2004. Future Considerations: The Functional Library Systems Record. *Library Hi Tech* 22 (2): 166–174.

Foulonneau, Muriel, and Timothy W. Cole. 2005. Strategies for Reprocessing Aggregated Metadata. *Research and Advanced Technology for Digital Libraries, Proceedings of the 9th European Conference, ECDL 2005, Vienna, Austria, September 18–23.* A. Rauber, S. Christodoulakis, and A. M. Tjoa, eds. Lecture Notes in Computer Science 3652. Berlin: Springer-Verlag.

Foulonneau, Muriel, Timothy W. Cole, Charles Blair, Peter C. Gorman, Kat Hagedorn, and Jenn Riley. 2006. The CIC Metadata Portal: A Collaborative Effort in the Area of Digital Libraries. *Science & Technology Libraries* 26 (3/4): 111–135.

Foulonneau, Muriel, Timothy W. Cole, Thomas G. Habing, and Sarah L. Shreeves. 2005. Using Collection Descriptions to Enhance an Aggregation of Harvested Item-Level Metadata. *Digital Libraries: Cyberinfrastructure for Research and Education. Proceedings of the Fifth ACM/IEEE-CS Joint Conference on Digital Libraries [Denver, June 7–11]*, 32–41. New York: Association for Computing Machinery.

Foulonneau, Muriel, Thomas G. Habing, and Timothy W. Cole. 2006. Automated Capture of Thumbnails and Thumbshots for Use by Metadata Aggregation Services. *D-Lib Magazine* 12 (1), doi: 10.1045/january2006-foulonneau, http:// www.dlib.org/dlib/january06/foulonneau/01foulonneau.html.

Geser, Guntram, and Andrea Mulrenin. 2002. *The DigiCULT Report: Technological Landscapes for Tomorrow's Cultural Economy, Unlocking the Value of Cultural Heritage (Full Report).* Luxembourg: European Commission Directorate-General for the Information Society/Office for Official Publications of the European Communities, http://digicult.salzburgresearch.at/downloads/dc_fullreport_30602_screen. pdf.

Hagedorn, Kat. 2003. OAIster: A "No Dead Ends" OAI Service Provider. *Library Hi Tech* 21 (2): 170–181.

Halbert, Martin, Joanne Kaczmarek, and Kat Hagedorn. 2003. Findings from the Mellon Metadata Harvesting Initiative. *Research and Advanced Technology for*

Digital Libraries, Proceedings of the 7th European Conference, ECDL 2003, Trond-heim, Norway, August 17–22, ed. T. Koch and I. T. Sølvberg. Lecture Notes in Computer Science 2769. Berlin: Springer-Verlag: Berlin.

IFLA Study Group on the Functional Requirements for Bibliographic Records. 1998. *Functional Requirements for Bibliographic Records.* Munich: K. G. Saur, http://www.ifla.org/VII/s13/frbr/frbr.pdf.

Krowne, Aaron, and Martin Halbert. 2005. An Initial Evaluation of Automated Organization for Digital Library Browsing. *Digital Libraries: Cyberinfrastructure for Research and Education. Proceedings of the Fifth ACM/IEEE-CS Joint Conference on Digital Libraries [Denver, June 7–11],* 246–255. New York: Association for Computing Machinery.

Lavoie, Brian, Geneva Henry, and Lorcan Dempsey. 2006. A Service Framework for Libraries. *D-Lib Magazine* 12 (7/8), doi: 10.1045/july2006-lavoie, http://www.dlib.org/dlib/july06/lavoie/07lavoie.html.

Minerva Working Group 5, ed. 2005. *Quality Principles for Cultural Websites: A Handbook.* Rome: The Minerva Project, http://www.minervaeurope.org/publications/qualitycommentary/qualitycommentary050314final.pdf.

Paepcke, Andreas. 1996. Digital Libraries: Searching is Not Enough—What We Learned On-Site. D-Lib Magazine 2 (5), http://www.dlib.org/dlib/may96/stanford/05paepcke.html.

Shreeves, Sarah L., Joanne S. Kaczmarek, and Timothy W. Cole. 2003. Harvesting Cultural Heritage Using the OAI Protocol. *Library Hi Tech* 21 (2): 159–169.

Shreeves, Sarah L., and Christine M. Kirkham. 2004. Experiences of Educators Using a Portal of Aggregated Metadata. *Journal of Digital Information* 5(3), *Article No. 290, 2004-09-09, http://jodi.ecs.soton.ac.uk/Articles/v05/i03/Shreeves/.*

Shreeves, Sarah L., Ellen M. Knutson, Besiki Stvilia, Carole L. Palmer, Michael B. Twidale, and Timothy W. Cole. 2005. Is "Quality" Metadata "Shareable" Metadata? The Implications of Local Metadata Practices for Federated Collections. *Proceedings of the Twelfth National Conference of the Association of College and Research Libraries, April 7–10, Minneapolis, MN,* ed. H. A. Thompson, 223237. Chicago: Association of College and Research Libraries.

Stvilia, Besiki, Les Gasser, Michael Twidale, Sarah L. Shreeves, and Timothy W. Cole. 2004. Metadata Quality for Federated Collections. *Proceedings of ICIQ04—9th International Conference on Information Quality,* ed. Shobha Chengalur-Smith, Jennifer Long, Louiqa Raschid, and Craig Seko, 111–125. Cambridge, MA: Massachusetts Institute of Technology, http://www.iqconference.org/ICIQ/iqpapers.aspx?iciqyear=2004.

Svenonius, Elaine. 2000. *The Intellectual Foundation of Information Organization.* Cambridge, MA: MIT Press.

Van de Sompel, Herbert, Carl Lagoze, Jeroen Bekaert, Xiaoming Liu, Sandy Payette, and Simeon Warner. 2006. An Interoperable Fabric for Scholarly Value Chains. *D-Lib Magazine* 12 (10), doi: 10.1045/october2006-vandesompel, http://www.dlib.org/dlib/october06/vandesompel/10vandesompel.html.

Van de Sompel, Herbert, Michael L. Nelson, Carl Lagoze, and S. Warner. 2004. Resource Harvesting within the OAI-PMH Framework. *D-Lib Magazine* 10 (12), doi: 10.1045/december2004-vandesompel, http://www.dlib.org/dlib/december04/vandesompel/12vandesompel.html.

Van Kasteren, Joost. 2003. Development of the Semantic Web Must Begin at the Grass Roots Level—An Interview with Janneke van Kersen, Dutch Digital

Heritage Association. *Towards a Semantic Web for Digital Resources*, 12–13. Digicult Thematic Issue 3. Salzburg, Austria: DigiCULT, http://www.digicult.info/downloads/thematic_issue_3_low.pdf.

Waters, Donald J. 2001. The Metadata Harvesting Initiative of the Mellon Foundation. *ARL Bimonthly Report 217* (August): 10–11, http://www.arl.org/newsltr/217/waters.html.

Yee, Ka-Ping, Kirsten Swearingen, Kevin Li, and Marti. Hearst, 2003. Faceted Metadata for Image Search and Browsing. *Proceedings of the SIGCHI Conference on Human Factors in Computing Systems [Ft. Lauderdale, Florida, April 5–10, 2003]*, 401–408. New York: ACM Press.

CHAPTER 9

Concluding Thoughts

Developing the technical infrastructure for a large-scale digital library composed of disparate, independently managed, and physically dispersed component collections and content is a bit like reverse engineering an onion from the inside out with only a hazy vision of what the finished vegetable will look like. We understand that the technical infrastructure desired will be multilayered, with each layer simultaneously dependent on interior layers and a prerequisite for outer layers. We have an idea, albeit an imperfect one, of the skin of services that will overlie the multiple layers of technical infrastructure, but we are not at the outset in a good position to name or even count all the layers of essential infrastructure individually. The truth is that *a priori* we do not know all the layers we will need or all the resources—that is, in terms of money, human effort, and expertise—we will require to implement the desired final system. As we design and add each new layer of technical protocols, best practices, and standards, we keep thinking (or hoping) that we will be ready next for the outermost skin of robust and innovative digital library services, only to discover that there is more work needed to enable the full suite of services and functions we want. Each new layer tends to be larger and more complex. Each new layer once completed suggests the need for additional layers of protocol and community consensus.

Early work with OAI-PMH has served to whet the appetite. As a protocol and a model for sharing digital information resource descriptions, OAI-PMH has proven effective; however, end-user services based on aggregated metadata are proving challenging to do well. (One should have expected no less.) The ancillary infrastructure, human capital, and expertise required to use OAI-PMH effectively and to achieve desired results are not trivial and have proven greater in magnitude and scope than some originally anticipated. There are two main reasons.

First, it was anticipated that OAI-PMH would enable a largely automated, low-human-effort approach to the process of aggregating metadata. However, facilitating the transport of metadata is not the same as facilitating the generation and use of metadata end to end in a digital library context.

Metadata creation and use remain in large part a human-mediated process, and human factors affect the success of the process. As noted by Carl Lagoze and his coauthors in a paper presented at the 2006 Joint Conference on Digital Libraries, OAI-PMH does not obviate the need for human expertise and effort. " ... [M]ore problematic was the reality that the personnel requirements to share metadata were deceptively high due to what can be characterized as a 'knowledge gap' " (Lagoze et al. 2006). In the context of the National Science Digital Library (NSDL), Lagoze and his coauthors discovered that data provider domain expertise, metadata expertise, and technical expertise were all factors critical to the success of their strategy to implement a highly automated OAI-PMH-based metadata aggregation process. Too often in their experience building NSDL, data provider expertise was lacking in one or more of these areas. As discussed in chapter 5, "technically low-barrier" is a relative term, a fact especially evident to projects aggregating a large number of small data providers. For NSDL, inadequacies in data provider domain, metadata, and/or technical expertise has meant that the process of using OAI-PMH to aggregate metadata for the NSDL could not be automated to the degree originally anticipated. This has led to a revision of their original architecture. While such considerations have more to do with the magnitude of benefits potentially achievable using OAI-PMH than with the technical details of the protocol itself, they cannot be neglected when implementing OAI service providers. Problems with metadata consistency and quality especially are ongoing matters of concern for OAI service providers (Shreeves et al. 2005; Tennant 2004).

Second, OAI-PMH is a metadata-centric protocol, not a resource-centric protocol. Many of the descriptive metadata formats discussed in chapter 6 have inadequate semantics for providing multiple, well-labeled (that is, well-differentiated), actionable links to variant views or instantiations of resources described. As mentioned in chapter 8, in certain kinds of digital library contexts, this lack can limit the ability of OAI service providers to implement services that address primary end-user and institutional needs and requirements. Work done around the OpenURL standard[1] and experiments such as the Aquifer Asset Action experiment (Chavez et al. 2006) illustrates the kinds of services that can be enabled by well-defined and clearly labeled actionable links to specific views of content resources. Clearly more attention is needed regarding the use and reuse of distributed digital information resources and to the expression of actionable URLs in metadata records. Again, this is not primarily a limitation of the protocol itself. The importance and complexity (in the context of distributed digital library applications) of bridging the gap between descriptive metadata records and the content resources they describe was not fully anticipated when OAI-PMH was introduced.

Therefore, OAI-PMH can be said to provide an essential layer of technical protocol and standardization, but on its own it is not enough. Additional layers of best practices and community agreement on issues critical to the shared use and reuse of harvested metadata records and the resources described by harvested metadata are also required. OAI-PMH serves as a layer of digital library technical infrastructure somewhere midway between the innermost and outermost layers—enveloping and reliant on core digitization technologies, metadata standards, collection building and management policies, and Web-based resource transport, presentation, and use protocols. OAI-PMH is clearly a useful step in the right direction; also, obviously, it is not the final step. It is difficult to visualize the complete vegetable when all you have in hand are the innermost layers of the flesh, but this is exactly what is needed to succeed.

The preceding chapters of this book detail experiences with OAI-PMH in digital library settings over the course of six years, beginning with alpha-phase testing of the protocol in the fall of 2000. Digital libraries have evolved over this time, and while the protocol itself has stayed relatively fixed since its formal introduction in January 2001, the ways in which OAI-PMH is used have evolved in response to digital library developments and as practitioners have gained experience in the use of the protocol. This chapter collocates and highlights a few of the most important lessons learned from this body of experience. There is still much more that needs to be understood about how best to exploit OAI-PMH, share metadata, and construct useful services over aggregated metadata. Three of these needs are discussed in the middle section of this chapter. OAI-PMH has proven a useful tool for digital library projects. Clearly, OAI-PMH has been and will continue to be an important component of the technical infrastructure supporting the development of digital libraries and the delivery of digital library services. However, just as clear is the need for additional protocols and community agreements that can complement and extend OAI-PMH. This chapter closes with a discussion and some informed speculation about what will come next to build on, extend, and possibly in some specific details supplant what OAI-PMH has so far enabled. This anticipated work comprises the next layer of the onion.

A SUMMARY OF ESSENTIAL LESSONS LEARNED

Our collective understanding of what a digital library is and our approach to the scope and design of digital libraries is constantly changing and evolving. It is not possible to fully anticipate all the ways in which digital libraries will be used in the future, and all the functions digital libraries will fulfill. As a result, there is no one right way to implement OAI-PMH. By design, OAI-PMH can be used with a variety of different metadata formats and to transport descriptive information about a variety of different kinds of resources. Over time, OAI-PMH has been used in different ways and to fulfill different functions in support of digital libraries. Nonetheless, there are several clear lessons of general applicability that can be drawn from early experiences with OAI-PMH.

Rich, high-quality metadata from data providers enables the implementation of richer, higher-quality services. OAI-PMH has proven a satisfactory way to create large heterogeneous metadata aggregations that never existed before. The success of PictureAustralia[2] and the University of Michigan's OAIster service[3] illustrates the general utility for discovery of OAI-PMH-based systems reliant on minimal metadata—unqualified DC in the case of OAIster, and a minimal variant of unqualified DC in the case of PictureAustralia (two elements were added to unqualified DC to accommodate image thumbnail references). However, there is only so far OAI service providers can go relying on unqualified DC metadata. Even more problematic for OAI service providers is poor-quality metadata or metadata not suitable for sharing (Dushay and Hillmann 2003; Shreeves et al. 2005). The situation is exacerbated by the diverse spectrum of descriptive traditions and practices found, especially in the cultural heritage domain. Until about 2004, OAI data provider implementations were characterized by a minimal implementation strategy: being technically compliant with the protocol with the least investment. Early on, realistic approaches to metadata sharing were uncommon; a number of OAI data providers were sharing metadata with little if any thought about how they actually wanted the OAI service providers to represent their resources.

As discussed in chapters 6 through 8, feedback from OAI service providers and others (for example, Tennant 2004; Shreeves, Riley, and Milewicz 2006) has encouraged a general improvement in OAI data provider metadata quality and raised awareness of the importance of dissemination metadata well suited for sharing. In collaboration with the Aquifer Initiative of the Digital Library Federation (DLF) and supported in part by funding from the Institute of Museum and Library Services (IMLS), OAIster has implemented a more robust version of their general purpose OAI-PMH-based portal using MODS metadata.[4] As part of the same DLF project and in collaboration with the NSDL, sharable metadata best practices have emerged,[5] and a DLF-Aquifer-specific MODS application profile suitable for use with OAI-PMH has been published online.[6] OAI service provider projects using at least qualified DC have become more visible,[7] and experiments illustrating the potential benefits of richer formats are ongoing (for example, Chavez et al. 2006).

As described in chapters 6 and 7, richer metadata more suitable for inclusion in metadata aggregations are best achieved through the proactive collaborations of OAI data providers and OAI service providers. OAI data providers have an obligation to select metadata formats and application profiles appropriate to content. OAI service providers must take the time and effort to adapt and exploit the full richness of available metadata. Evolution on both fronts is taking place in parallel. As OAI data providers enhance and enrich the metadata they provide, OAI service providers are beginning to take advantage. As OAI service providers exploit richer metadata to implement more useful services, OAI data providers are encouraged to enrich their metadata. The process is iterative and requires resources be expended by both data providers and service providers. As service providers become more adept at automated metadata normalization—for example, the date normalization tool implemented by the California Digital Library (Landis, Toub, and Loy 2006) and the thumbnail-grabbing tool implemented by the University of Illinois at Urbana-Champaign (Foulonneau, Habing, and Cole 2006)—the division of labor between service provider and data provider becomes more clear. In order to encourage data providers to provide richer and more structured metadata, OAI service providers must focus on developing innovative new services. Wider implementation of more sophisticated services based on richer metadata will spur the creation of richer metadata and vice versa.

OAI service providers need well-thought-out collection-development policies, too. Early on, some OAI service providers were opportunistic in harvesting metadata. They did not give much thought to the dependency of service identity, quality, and cohesiveness on the identity, quality, and cohesiveness of the underlying metadata aggregation. As a result, intended service goals sometimes were obscure. A critical mass of relevant metadata is necessary to implement services useful to a particular audience. Service providers must take this into account.

OAI-PMH has not proven as technically lightweight for some segments of the digital library community as was originally hoped. As discussed in chapter 5 and alluded to again in the introduction to this chapter, human effort, some basic computing infrastructure, and expertise in relevant XML and Web technologies are prerequisites for the implementation of an OAI data provider. The last especially has proven a difficult challenge for some content providers, especially smaller cultural-heritage institutions (for example, small libraries, archives, and museums). A range of technical solutions has emerged to ameliorate the problem. As mentioned in chapter 5, several turnkey content-management systems have implemented at least rudimentary support for OAI-PMH (for example, CONTENTdm[8]). The OAI has released implementation guidelines for OAI static repositories.[9] Implementers have made available special solutions for other specific situations, for example, the University of Illinois at Urbana-Champaign's FileMaker to OAI gateway service[10] and the Museums and the Online Archive of California (MOAC) Community Toolbox.[11]

Users are looking for resources, not metadata. As discussed in chapter 8, the earliest examples of OAI service providers implemented analogs of online library union catalogs rather than full-fledged, integrated digital library systems designed not only to facilitate discovery of resources but also to help users more effectively use and navigate digital information resources. Subsequent attempts to build more sophisticated services revealed a host of difficulties in linking from discovered descriptive metadata records to useable instantiations of resources. An analysis of metadata records harvested by the collaborative OAI-PMH-based metadata sharing project of the Committee on Institutional Cooperation (Foulonneau, Cole, et al. 2006) discovered that almost a third of the harvested metadata records linked to elsewhere than to the exact resource described (for example, to intermediate jump-off pages or collection-level pages requiring additional clicks to get to the specific resource of interest). There remains confusion between metadata item identifiers and resource object identifiers. Accommodating full-content resources within a service can bring additional complications relating to intellectual property rights, multiple views of a single resource, and individually addressable parts of compound objects. While work in 2006 (for example, Bekaert, Liu, and Van de Sompel 2006, Chavez et al. 2006; see also chapter 8) has suggested new approaches, much remains to be done. Some of this work may fall outside the immediate scope of OAI-PMH (see below); however, issues to do with optimally relating metadata records to the resources they describe are still highly relevant to OAI service providers and the services they implement.

OAI-PMH does not do everything. One of the strengths of OAI-PMH has been its adaptability over time. The protocol has been used in ways that could not have been envisioned when it was written. Researchers at Old Dominion University and Los Alamos National Lab collaborated in experiments that used OAI-PMH to harvest complete resources (Van de Sompel et al. 2004). Other researchers demonstrated ways that OAI-PMH could be used to underpin an identifier resolution service—that is, the Extensible Repository Resource Locators (ERRoLs) service—and to facilitate access to and use of the Guidelines on Subject Access to Individual Works of Fiction and Drama (GSAFD) controlled vocabulary (Van de Sompel, Young, and Hickey 2003; Shreeves et al. 2004). These and similar efforts have extended the reach of OAI-PMH. At the same time, such work also has suggested and highlighted the utility of ancillary technologies and protocols that operate alongside OAI-PMH (and the need for the development of more such technologies and protocols).

Even with regard to discovery of digital information resources, technologies other than metadata harvesting can be useful, and different approaches can be more optimal in certain situations. OAI-PMH should be one of an arsenal of tools and technologies at the digital library architect's disposal. As discussed in chapter 1, metasearch technologies can coexist with and complement OAI-PMH-based solutions. OAI-PMH does not obviate the need for digital library registries to discover services and define metadata and resource formats, etc. The usefulness of OAI-PMH is dependent on a host of other digital library technologies, best practices, and community agreements. There is no single, canonical OAI-PMH project as such; there are projects that use OAI-PMH, usually as one of several supporting technologies. As described in chapters 7 and 8, digital library service implementations based on distributed collections must define content guidelines, application profiles, service objectives, and so on at the outset. Appropriate technologies and protocols, including but not limited to OAI-PMH, are then selected for use as the most appropriate to fit service objectives.

NEEDS GOING FORWARD

While lessons learned during the first six years since the introduction of OAI-PMH have been enlightening and have encouraged significant improvements in digital library services based on large aggregations of heterogeneous metadata, further research is necessary on a number of fronts. Entering 2007, three needs in particular stand out.

1. *The need to more clearly define information resource granularity, to understand collection identity, and to appreciate the relationship between a collection and its constituent items.* In 2002, IMLS posted a Request for Proposals (RFP)

for a project to create a collection registry and an OAI-PMH based item-level metadata repository encompassing digital collections and content created or developed under the auspices of the IMLS National Leadership Grant (NLG) program. In late 2002, a grant for this work was awarded to the University of Illinois at Urbana-Champaign, and the project was initiated under the rubric *IMLS Digital Collections and Content Project.*[12] The decision of IMLS to couple together both a collection registry and an item-level metadata repository was prescient in that it has encouraged consideration of issues of collection identity and descriptive granularity as part of this project. Earlier work done at Illinois under funding from the Andrew W. Mellon Foundation, which included a focus on how EAD might be used in conjunction with OAI-PMH (Prom and Habing 2002), and concurrent work being done at Illinois in collaboration with other members of the Committee on Institutional Cooperation (Foulonneau, Cole, et al. 2006) also have encouraged the study of these issues. Results so far make clear (not surprisingly) that users do not always query indexes or use resources at a single level of granularity. Multi-word queries frequently contain keywords found at different levels of descriptive granularity (Foulonneau et al. 2005). End-user information needs are best met by a range of resources, described at different levels of granularity, for example, by collections, by items, or by combinations of both. Data gathered from NLG grantees by the IMLS Digital Collections and Content project team confirm that questions of collection definition represent not just a theoretical problem but one that is being contemplated by practitioners and both actively and passively responded to in the daily work of digital library development (Palmer et al. in press).

Going forward, OAI data providers and service providers need to understand and learn more about how collection identity is transferred, transformed, and created in the process of metadata aggregation, how item granularity and interrelationships can best be handled in the development of new digital library projects, and how agreements on these issues can be exploited to provide enhanced services to end users. Put another way, digital library designers need to address issues of aggregation and disaggregation—that is, how to treat and model clusters, collections, and other groupings of related resources, whether predefined or discovered during the act of metadata or resource aggregation, and how to treat and model componentization of information resources. The latter action, componentization (a term borrowed from software engineering), involves the segmentation of information resources into smaller, independently reusable components of content—for instance, making independently addressable the components of a scholarly journal article such as sections, bibliographic references, figures, graphs, and data tables.

2. ***The need to understand archetypical behaviors (views) of specific classes of resource objects and to agree on means to obtain standard views of content.*** The initial focus of OAI-PMH has been on descriptive metadata, but recent work demonstrates that the protocol also has the potential to facilitate the sharing of complete resources (Bekaert, Liu, and Van de Sompel 2006). The demand and utility of specific views of resources for use in specialized analytical tools and to facilitate specific digital library functions and services is high. As of 2006, techniques to crawl or spider information resources directly from Web servers tended to be crude, and the objects gathered by such means were not always in the form or fidelity needed for the desired purpose (Foulonneau,

Habing, and Cole 2006). To effectively exploit OAI-PMH to harvest complete resources, we need better and more explicit agreements on the ways resources are modeled and disseminated. Consider a complex textual resource made up of ordered page images and associated text created by applying optical character recognition (OCR) software to page images. For some purposes, an end user (or a digital library tool) might require individual page images. For other purposes, an end user might require the text created by the OCR process, or, for other purposes, multiple page images suitably packaged for page-turner software. There needs to be community agreement on how disseminations of resources (and other potentially useful views of content class members) are modeled, labeled, requested, and distributed.

3. *The need to define expectations.* Chapter 8 discussed models and definitions of digital library services based on assessments of user tasks and objectives. While considerable groundwork has been laid in identifying and defining use cases and models of end-user needs, this research has not been fully synthesized. As of 2006, functional definitions of digital libraries were inconsistent and varied significantly from domain to domain. Relationships between digital libraries and applications such as institutional repositories, learning-management systems, meta-search utilities, and traditional online public access catalogs (OPACs) remain hazy. There is not yet broad, clear, and explicit consensus on the essential functions and services that define a generic digital library. One can argue that this is because no complete exemplar yet exists, but nonetheless it behooves the community to seek better, more explicit agreement on the nature of digital libraries, digital library services, and the expectations of digital library users. To realize essential technical infrastructure we need to understand how object properties and attributes relate to delivered functions and services. Given that many metadata elements can support multiple functions, we need especially to understand how normalization and enrichment done to support one function effects metadata usability for other functions.

WHAT NEXT?

As digital libraries mature, there is a growing interest in creating digital library services that go beyond simple search and discovery. A number of practitioners (for example, Miller 2005) have labeled the next generation of digital libraries *Library 2.0* or otherwise made analogies to the *Web 2.0* view of software and Web application evolution. Web 2.0 as a term dates from 2004 and was popularized by Tim O'Reilly and others (O'Reilly 2005). The Library 2.0 model, which postulates a parallel movement toward more robust, flexible, and componentized library applications and services in the Web 2.0 era, has led to an emerging appreciation of the critical need for multiple layers of complementary technology (for example, service, format, and vocabulary registries), protocols (for example, OAI-PMH and SRU), and community agreements (for example, resource object data models, taxonomies of resource types, and resource views).

The underlying principles embodied in OAI-PMH are entirely consistent with the Library 2.0 worldview. OAI-PMH encourages a modular, componentized approach to digital library architecture. For example, practical experience with OAI-PMH has confirmed the general utility of dividing the digital library universe into content providers and service providers. Such a bimodal view of the digital library universe is simplistic, but just as the client-server model remains useful in some contexts as a view of intrinsically complex network interactions, so too is the OAI content provider-service provider paradigm useful as a model for designing digital library architectures. Such a model encourages the creation of architectures that facilitate a componentized view of digital library services and attribute different roles and responsibilities to each participating partner. In such a model, content providers can assert a measure of control over their resources and strive for a clearer, more explicit understanding of their obligations as content providers and of the expectations they should have of service providers. Service providers can focus on the shared, cross-repository services they want to build and leave the content creation and primary resource management responsibilities to content providers.

While OAI-PMH anticipated and is well positioned to be a part of the Library 2.0 evolution, efforts to redesign digital library architectures are highlighting the need for additional community-based agreements, protocols, and standards that complement OAI-PMH. The problem is less any deficiency inherent in OAI-PMH than it is the lack of community agreement and consensus on metadata standards, architecturally useful models of digital content objects, metadata crosswalks, thesauri, name and term authority, and practices for the normalization and enrichment of harvested metadata (the list goes on). The widespread implementation of OAI-PMH has encouraged the re-examination of the objectives of digital libraries and the services they are designed to deliver. Results from projects using OAI-PMH are helping to stimulate and guide the development of the additional community consensus and technical architecture agreements essential to support robust, high-quality, innovative digital library tools and services. Use models are being re-examined anew to better understand what more is needed. Two examples from the realm of scholarly communications serve to illustrate trends in digital library architecture.

Institutional repositories (see also the discussion in chapter 3) have long been touted as a cornerstone of scholarly communications evolution. At some institutions, libraries play a lead role in the creation and implementation of institutional repositories. However, definitions of institutional repositories are evolving. Originally envisioned primarily as archives for static scholarly output—essentially digital storehouses for online analogs of traditional print journal articles—the institutional repository is now being looked upon as a dynamic element of an academic institution's *information fabric*. Tyler Walters of the Georgia Institute of Technology suggests, for example, that institutional repositories might host conference proceedings and other less-formal forms of scholarly conference output, support production processes for open access e-journals, host multimedia capture of scholarly symposia and other events, and serve as a home for blogs, wikis, and discussion group forums used in scholarly collaborations (Walters 2006). These functions presage a more dynamic and expansive view of institutional repositories and suggest a need for models of institutional repository content which can support reuse and componentization of information resources at a finer granularity than has been common in the scholarly communication realm to date.

Other researchers are looking at ways to reconceptualize fundamental facets of the scholarly communication process. For example, Marko Rodriguez and his coauthors have proposed a new model for selecting scholarly peer reviewers based on networks of coauthorship (and potentially citation) deduced from automated analyses of metadata harvested from ePrint repositories (Rodriguez, Bollen, and Van de Sompel 2005). OAI-PMH is embedded in the model proposed by Rodriguez, Bollen, and Van de Sompel; however, further extension of the proposed implementation as discussed in their article would require additional modeling of full-text resources described by harvested metadata records (for example, in order to discover citation patterns which are not always visible by inspection of metadata records alone). Such extended implementations would require additional agreements and machine-actionable protocols to enable automatic retrieval of full-text. Rodriguez, Bollen, and Van de Sompel also propose that the OAI service provider managing the peer-reviewer recommendation service would create additional new metadata property values for examined scholarly resources which (ideally at least) should then be reintegrated into the metadata items held by the OAI data providers originally harvested. This also would require additional protocols to be used in concert with OAI-PMH.

These two examples and many more like them simultaneously reinforce the utility of OAI-PMH and suggest the need for additional, complementary protocols. As a layer of a robust, multi-layered infrastructure underpinning a digital library, OAI-PMH has its own intrinsic value. However, OAI-PMH is most effective when implemented with quality content and metadata held in well-managed and well-maintained content provider repositories. Less obviously, the full utility of OAI-PMH is most likely to be realized when used in the context of community agreements on a host of additional matters—for example, metadata semantics and structure, collection identity, descriptive granularity, common conventions for dissemination of full content, resource data models, and the shared understanding of targeted digital library functions and services. Agreements, consensus, and technical conventions on a wide range of issues affecting digital libraries are essential to create an adequately robust technical infrastructure on which to build the next generation of useful digital library systems.

In late 2006, with new funding from the Andrew W. Mellon Foundation, the Open Archives Initiative undertook development of a new protocol focused on Object Reuse and Exchange (OAI-ORE). It is anticipated that this new OAI-ORE protocol will complement and enhance OAI-PMH and will enable the implementation of digital library services that exploit deeper and more granular access to content resources beyond the level of descriptive metadata. OAI-ORE likely will build on research conducted in 2005 and 2006 by Carl Lagoze (in connection with NSDL), Herbert Van de Sompel (in connection with the aDORE project mentioned in chapter 8), and others. Descriptions of this preliminary research, referenced in part under the rubric *Pathways Core Framework*, have been published (Van de Sompel et al. 2006, Warner et al. 2006). The Pathways Core Framework proposes a tri-part functional model—*Harvest*, *Get*, and *Put*—intended to be applied to full content rather than just metadata. The Pathways Core Framework also proposes a content resource surrogate object model and serialization that could associate (in a highly structured way) multiple, well-defined views or instantiations of content resources. The latter aspect of the Pathways Core Framework is more prescriptive (potentially representing a higher technical barrier) than anything embedded in OAI-PMH. This more prescriptive approach is complementary to the low-technical barrier approach of OAI-PMH and is expected to enable implementation of different, complementary digital library services. The Pathways Core Framework also calls for implementation of service, format, and semantic registries, and the adoption of robust and reliable identifier schemes independent of both OAI-PMH and OAI-ORE. Development and initial testing of this protocol is anticipated to take two years. As of this writing, the exact shape and impact of this new OAI protocol is uncertain, nor is it clear whether there will be explicit dependencies between the two OAI protocols. Regardless, it is likely that OAI-ORE will provide another, crucial layer of digital library infrastructure complementary to that already provided by OAI-PMH.

QUESTIONS AND TOPICS FOR DISCUSSION

1. Develop several real or potential lead-user scenarios for OAI-PMH, that is, challenging, forward-looking usage scenarios that were not necessarily anticipated by the authors of the protocol when OAI-PMH was written. Below are a few examples of such scenarios. For each scenario, discuss service objectives and the technical or content-related issues that might arise if using OAI-PMH to implement. Would OAI-PMH on its own be sufficient? If not, what extensions and/or additional protocols or community agreements would be required for successful implementation? Sample lead-user scenarios—use an OAI-PMH-based architecture to:

   • Replicate and/or synchronize two coequal metadata repositories (as opposed to creating a conventional unidirectional OAI data provider to data harvester relationship).
   • Disseminate and share digital objects together with or instead of metadata.
   • Disseminate and share non-descriptive metadata (for example, administrative, preservation, and/or technical metadata).
   • Disseminate and share controlled vocabularies, name authority lists, or other forms of authoritative terminologies.

2. Identify, describe, and discuss new digital library services and digital library functions that could be implemented in the future on top of aggregated metadata and distributed content resources. Try to think of services or functions that:

- Take advantage of descriptive metadata.
- Exploit multiple levels of descriptive granularity, for example, collection-level descriptions and/or componentization of digital information resources (that is, descriptions of parts of digital objects).
- Are customized for discrete, widely dispersed, and relatively granular user communities (for example, as encouraged by the Library 2.0 view of digital library services).
- Take advantage of controlled (and well-defined and well-labeled) and reliable links to digital information resources. Consider how such services might work and the ways in which content would need to be transferred to enable those services. Would content need to be centrally replicated and maintained, or could content be transferred in real time as needed? Would content ever need to be transferred to or through a central service provider, or could it just be made available on demand to individual clients as needed?

3. When an institution implements an OAI-PMH data provider service for a repository of information resources, it shares its content through metadata surrogates. Is that always a good idea? When might an institution not want to share all or part of the metadata it has created? Describe two contrasting scenarios, one for which implementation of OAI-PMH would be a good idea and one where implementation of OAI-PMH would be less desirable, or at least require significant modification of metadata workflow and/or resource definition.

4. Identify three or four other protocols related to or possibly overlapping OAI-PMH (for example, metasearch, Web spidering, semantic Web, or persistent identifier schemes). Describe and discuss how each protocol relates to OAI-PMH in scope, intent, and/or design. How is each protocol complementary to or competitive with OAI-PMH? How might each protocol be used in conjunction with OAI-PMH?

5. Put yourself in the role of a working librarian, archivist, or museum curator. Identify hypothetical scenarios or projects for which you would favor the use of OAI-PMH. What two or three arguments would you lead with to persuade your institution's administration it was worthwhile to implement OAI-PMH for your project?

NOTES

1. http://www.niso.org/standards/standard_detail.cfm?std_id=783.
2. http://www.pictureaustralia.org/.
3. http://www.oaister.org/.
4. http://www.hti.umich.edu/m/mods/.
5. http://oai-best.comm.nsdl.org/cgi-bin/wiki.pl?OAI_Best_Practices.
6. http://www.diglib.org/aquifer/
   dlfmodsimplementationguidelines_finalnov2006.pdf.
7. http://cicharvest.grainger.uiuc.edu/.
8. http://www.oclc.org/contentdm/.
9. http://www.openarchives.org/OAI/2.0/guidelines-static-repository.htm.
10. http://www.diglib.org/architectures/oai/imls2004/training/index.htm, also available as a PowerPoint presentation at http://www.diglib.org/architectures/ oai/imls2004/training/oaitools.ppt.

11. http://www.bampfa.berkeley.edu/moac/community_toolbox.html.
12. http://imlsdcc.grainger.uiuc.edu/.

REFERENCES

Bekaert, Jeroen, Xiaoming Liu, and Herbert Van de Sompel. 2006. aDORe, a Modular and Standards-Based Digital Object Repository at the Los Alamos National Laboratory. *Digital Libraries: Cyberinfrastructure for Research and Education.* Proceedings of the Fifth ACM/IEEE-CS Joint Conference on Digital Libraries [Denver, June 7–11], 367. New York: Association for Computing Machinery.

Chavez, Robert, Timothy W. Cole, Jon Dunn, Muriel Foulonneau, Thomas G. Habing, William Parod, and Thorton Staples. 2006. DLF-Aquifer Asset Actions Experiment: Demonstrating Value of Actionable URLs. *D-Lib Magazine* 12 (10), doi: 10.1045/october2006-cole, http://www.dlib.org/dlib/october06/cole/10cole.html.

Dushay, Naomi, and Diane I. Hillmann. 2003. Analyzing Metadata for Effective Use and Re-use. *2003 Dublin Core Conference: Supporting Communities of Discourse and Practice—Metadata Research & Applications.* September 28–October 2, 2003, Seattle, Washington. S. Sutton, J. Greenberg, and J. Tennis, eds. Syracuse, NY: Information Institute of Syracuse, http://dc2003.ischool.washington.edu/Archive-03/03dushay.pdf.

Foulonneau, Muriel, Timothy W. Cole, Charles Blair, Peter C. Gorman, Kat Hagedorn, and Jenn Riley. 2006. The CIC Metadata Portal: A Collaborative Effort in the Area of Digital Libraries. *Science & Technology Libraries* 26 (3/4): 111–135.

Foulonneau, Muriel, Timothy W. Cole, Thomas G. Habing, and Sarah L. Shreeves. 2005. Using Collection Descriptions to Enhance an Aggregation of Harvested Item-Level Metadata. *Digital Libraries: Cyberinfrastructure for Research and Education. Proceedings of the Fifth ACM/IEEE-CS Joint Conference on Digital Libraries [Denver, June 7–11], 32–41.* New York: Association for Computing Machinery.

Foulonneau, Muriel, Thomas G. Habing, and Timothy W. Cole. 2006. Automated Capture of Thumbnails and Thumbshots for Use by Metadata Aggregation Services. *D-Lib Magazine* 12 (1), doi: 10.1045/january2006-foulonneau, http://www.dlib.org/dlib/january06/foulonneau/01foulonneau.html.

Lagoze, Carl, Dean Krafft, Tim Cornwell, Naomi Dushay, Dean Eckstrom, and John Saylor. 2006. Metadata aggregation and "automated digital libraries": A retrospective on the NSDL experience. *Opening Information Horizons. Proceedings of the 6th ACM/IEEE-CS Joint Conference on Digital Libraries [Chapel Hill, June 11–15], 230–239.* New York: Association for Computing Machinery. Preprint available at http://www.arxiv.org/abs/cs.DL/0601125.

Landis, Bill, Steve Toub, and Dave Loy. 2006. California Digital Library Date Normalization Tools. Presented at Metadata Enhancement and OAI Workshop [Atlanta, GA, July 24–25]. Atlanta: Emory University Library, http://www.metascholar.org/events/2006/meow/viewabstract.php?id=8.

Miller, Paul. 2005. Web 2.0: Building the New Library. *Ariadne* 45 (October 2005), http://www.ariadne.ac.uk/issue45/miller/.

O'Reilly, Tim. 2005. *What Is Web 2.0: Design Patterns and Business Models for the Next Generation of Software.* Sebastopol, CA: O'Reilly Media Inc., http://www.oreilly.com/go/web2.

Palmer, Carole, Ellen Knutson, Michael Twidale, and Oksana Zavalina. In press. Collection Definition in Federated Digital Resource Development. *Proceedings of the 69th Annual Meeting of the American Society for Information Science and Technology.* Medford, NJ: American Society for Information Science and Technology.

Prom, Christopher J., and Thomas G. Habing. 2002. Using the Open Archives Initiatives Protocols with EAD. *Proceedings of the 2nd ACM/IEEE-CS Joint Conference on Digital Libraries,* 171–180. New York: Association for Computing Machinery.

Rodriguez, Marko A., Johan Bollen, and Herbert Van de Sompel. 2006. The Convergence of Digital Libraries and the Peer-Review Process. *Journal of Information Science* 32 (2): 149–159. Preprint available at http://www.arxiv.org/abs/cs.DL/ 0504084.

Shreeves, Sarah L., Thomas G. Habing, Kat Hagedorn, and Jeffrey A. Young. 2004. Current Developments and Future Trends for the OAI Protocol for Metadata Harvesting. *Library Trends* 53(4): 576–589.

Shreeves, Sarah L., Ellen M. Knutson, Besiki Stvilia, Carole L. Palmer, Michael B. Twidale, and Timothy W. Cole. 2005. Is "Quality" Metadata "Shareable" Metadata? The Implications of Local Metadata Practices for Federated Collections. *Proceedings of the Twelfth National Conference of the Association of College and Research Libraries, April 7–10, Minneapolis, MN,* ed. H. A. Thompson, 223–237. Chicago: Association of College and Research Libraries.

Shreeves, Sarah L., Jenn Riley, and Liz Milewicz. 2006. Moving towards Shareable Metadata. *First Monday* 11 (8), http://www.firstmonday.org/issues/issue11_8/ shreeves/.

Tennant, Roy. 2004. Metadata's Bitter Harvest. *Library Journal* 129 (12): 32, http:// www.libraryjournal.com/article/CA434443.html.

Van de Sompel, Herbert, Carl Lagoze, Jeroen Bekaert, Xiaoming Liu, Sandy Payette, and Simeon Warner. 2006. An Interoperable Fabric for Scholarly Value Chains. *D-Lib Magazine* 12 (10), doi: 10.1045/october2006-vandesompel, http:// www.dlib.org/dlib/october06/vandesompel/10vandesompel.html.

Van de Sompel, Herbert, M. L. Nelson, Carl Lagoze, and Simeon Warner. 2004. Resource Harvesting within the OAI-PMH Framework. *D-Lib Magazine* 10 (12), doi: 10.1045/december2004-vandesompel, http://www.dlib.org/dlib/december04/vandesompel/12vandesompel.html.

Van de Sompel, Herbert, Jeffrey A. Young, and Thomas B. Hickey. 2003. Using the OAI-PMH … Differently. *D-Lib Magazine* 9 (7/8), doi: 10.1045/july2003-young, http://www.dlib.org/dlib/july03/young/07young.html.

Walters, Tyler O. 2006. Strategies and Frameworks for Institutional Repositories and the New Support Infrastructure for Scholarly Communications. *D-Lib Magazine* 12 (10), doi: 10.1045/october2006-walters, http://www.dlib.org/dlib/october06/ walters/10walters.html.

Warner, Simeon, Jeroen Bekaert, Carl Lagoze, Xiaoming Liu, Sandy Payette, and Herbert Van de Sompel. Pathways: Augmenting interoperability across scholarly repositories. *International Journal on Digital Libraries.* Preprint available at http:// arxiv.org/abs/cs.DL/0610031.

Index

AACR2 (Anglo-American Cataloging Rules), 122–23, 130–31, 147

\<about> node, 38, 76, 90, 91, 149

Academic Research in the Netherlands Online (ARNO), 59

aDORe repository, 167, 168

American National Standard Institute, 167

Andrew W. Mellon Foundation, 12, 163, 191, 194

Anglo-American Cataloging Rules (AACR2), 122–23, 130–31, 147

Apache, 87

application profile, 121, 147, 188

Aquifer Asset Actions, 167, 168, 186

Aquifer Initiative, 167, 188

ARL (Association of Research Libraries), 48, 52–53

arXiv, 8–9, 43, 45

ASCII, 103

asset action sets, 167

Association of Research Libraries (ARL), 48, 52–53

baseURL, 7, 75, 102, 149

Berlin Declaration, 54–55

Bethesda Statement, 54

bibliographic records, 162, 163

BioMed Central, 45, 51

Bollen, Johan, 194

Boolean search criteria, 38

broadcast search, 15–17

Brogan, Martha, 21

Bruce, Thomas, 131, 132

Buchanan, Sandy, 172

Budapest Open Access Initiative (BOAI), 44, 53–54

C++, 58

California Digital Library, 147, 188

camelCase, 75

CAN/MARC, 122

Cataloging Cultural Objects (CCO), 124, 147

Categories for the Description of Works of Art (CDWA), 124

CDS Invenio, 58

CDWA-Lite, 124, 129

CERN, 58

character case, 28, 75, 92

Chemistry Central, 51

Chicago Historical Society, 167–68

CiteBase, 45

client-server, 6, 21, 23–24

Coalition for Networked Information (CNI), 46

Cogprints, 45

collection identity, 168–70, 190–91

Collectus, 168

Committee on Institutional Cooperation (CIC), 169t; analysis of links by, 189–90; collection-development policy of, 139; on descriptive granularity, 191; filtered searches by, 156; on item-collection relationship, 151; on normalization, 142, 147; Web-accesible views by, 165–66

Common Gateway Interface (CGI), 87–88

complex hierarchies, 5

CONTENTdm, 88, 189

About the Authors

Timothy W. Cole is mathematics librarian, interim head of library digital services and development, professor of library administration, and adjunct professor of library and information science at the University of Illinois at Urbana-Champaign. A member of the library faculty at Illinois since 1989, he has held prior appointments as systems librarian for digital projects and assistant engineering librarian for information services. He is principal investigator for an Institute of Museum and Library Services (IMLS) National Leadership Grant exploiting OAI-PMH to build a collection registry and metadata repository for digital content developed under the auspices of IMLS grant programs. He is past chair of the National Science Digital Library (NSDL) Technology Standing Committee and a former member of the OAI Technical Committee. He has published widely on OAI-PMH, metadata, and the use of XML and SGML for encoding science and mathematical scholarly communication, and has spoken about these topics at multiple venues, including the IMLS Web-Wise Conference, the American Library Association's annual meeting, the American Society for Information Science and Technology's annual meeting, the American Association of Law Libraries' annual meeting, the NSDL's annual meeting, the Joint Conference on Digital Libraries, the CERN workshop on Innovations in Scholarly Communication (OAI4), and the Open Archives Forum. As an adjunct in the University of Illinois' Graduate School of Library and Information Science, he has taught and lectured on OAI-PMH, metadata, digital library systems, and the implementation of distributed information systems.

Muriel Foulonneau is a specialist in metadata and distributed digital library systems. She is particularly interested in information organization and the creation and usage of collections in digital environments. She works at the Centre de la Communication Scientifique Directe of the French Centre National de la Recherche Scientifique (National Center for Scientific Research). She helps standardize open access and institutional repositories in Europe within the scope of the Digital Repository Infrastructure Vision for European Research (DRIVER) project (Networking European Scientific

Repositories). She was the project coordinator at the University of Illinois at Urbana-Champaign for the CIC-OAI metadata harvesting project, an initiative for developing common best practices for sharing metadata among the CIC group of research universities in the United States. She is part of the Digital Library Federation and NSDL best-practices expert group on the Open Archives Initiative and sharable metadata and is a co-chair of the DCMI Collection Description Application Profile Task Group. She previously worked as an information technology advisor for the French Ministry of Culture and Communication. She was a participant in the Minerva Project, a collaboration among European ministries of culture on the digitization of cultural heritage resources. She has also served as an expert for the European Commission for research projects related to digital heritage.